M
Mul

Mirjana Radovic-Markovic
Muhammed Ayinla Omolaja

Management Dynamics

In The New Economy

VDM Verlag Dr. Müller

Impressum/Imprint (nur für Deutschland/ only for Germany)

Bibliografische Information der Deutschen Nationalbibliothek: Die Deutsche Nationalbibliothek verzeichnet diese Publikation in der Deutschen Nationalbibliografie; detaillierte bibliografische Daten sind im Internet über http://dnb.d-nb.de abrufbar.

Alle in diesem Buch genannten Marken und Produktnamen unterliegen warenzeichen-, marken- oder patentrechtlichem Schutz bzw. sind Warenzeichen oder eingetragene Warenzeichen der jeweiligen Inhaber. Die Wiedergabe von Marken, Produktnamen, Gebrauchsnamen, Handelsnamen, Warenbezeichnungen u.s.w. in diesem Werk berechtigt auch ohne besondere Kennzeichnung nicht zu der Annahme, dass solche Namen im Sinne der Warenzeichen- und Markenschutzgesetzgebung als frei zu betrachten wären und daher von jedermann benutzt werden dürften.

Coverbild: www.ingimage.com

Verlag: VDM Verlag Dr. Müller GmbH & Co. KG
Dudweiler Landstr. 99, 66123 Saarbrücken, Deutschland
Telefon +49 681 9100-698, Telefax +49 681 9100-988
Email: info@vdm-verlag.de

Herstellung in Deutschland:
Schaltungsdienst Lange o.H.G., Berlin
Books on Demand GmbH, Norderstedt
Reha GmbH, Saarbrücken
Amazon Distribution GmbH, Leipzig
ISBN: 978-3-639-37237-3

Imprint (only for USA, GB)

Bibliographic information published by the Deutsche Nationalbibliothek: The Deutsche Nationalbibliothek lists this publication in the Deutsche Nationalbibliografie; detailed bibliographic data are available in the Internet at http://dnb.d-nb.de.

Any brand names and product names mentioned in this book are subject to trademark, brand or patent protection and are trademarks or registered trademarks of their respective holders. The use of brand names, product names, common names, trade names, product descriptions etc. even without a particular marking in this works is in no way to be construed to mean that such names may be regarded as unrestricted in respect of trademark and brand protection legislation and could thus be used by anyone.

Cover image: www.ingimage.com

Publisher: VDM Verlag Dr. Müller GmbH & Co. KG
Dudweiler Landstr. 99, 66123 Saarbrücken, Germany
Phone +49 681 9100-698, Fax +49 681 9100-988
Email: info@vdm-publishing.com

Printed in the U.S.A.
Printed in the U.K. by (see last page)
ISBN: 978-3-639-37237-3

MANAGEMENT DYNAMICS IN THE NEW ECONOMY

Professor Muhammed Omolaja,Ph.D

Professor Mirjana Radovic-MarkovicmPh.D

2011

© MANAGEMENT DYNAMICS IN THE NEW
ECONOMY

The book reviwers:

Prof. Dr. Brenda Nelson-Porter, North Central University and CEO of
Brigette's Technology Consulting and Research Firm, USA

Prof. Dr Raghu Bir Bista , Tribhuvan University, Nepal

Publisher:

VDM Verlag Dr. Müller, Saarbrücken
Germany

Forward

Managers within each service sector are challenged to transform their organization using available talent. Two longitudinal mini-studies conducted by Brigette's Technology Consulting and Research Firm (2004-2005) revealed that management and leadership are interlinking processes that need to be understood to achieve maximum performance and satisfaction. Several male managers acknowledged that managing is more difficult than leading junior personnel. Difficulties concerning managerial practices resulted from various issues: junior personnel's primary motivation that involved seeking employment stability; personality conflicts; and the lack of people and communication skills, education, specialty, and human capital. Dimensions of challenges faced in leadership practices involve the lack of understanding on how junior personnel function in the workplace and the need to eliminate micromanaging.

In the second study, several female junior personnel viewed managing as more essential than leading in certain work environments. Leading by means of mentorship was not viewed as a high priority. Managers were not asked to serve as mentors for a multitude of reasons: no personal relationship was desired, managers did not possess the necessary experience or leadership style, advancement opportunities were scarce, and self motivation stimulated by observation has been key to job satisfaction. One junior personnel revealed that the mentoring process involves micromanaging.

Management dynamics in the new economy assists in processing several great models, theories, and techniques that managers can employ to improve managerial experiences and enhance manager-employee relations. The mentioning of *Maslow's* categorization of needs gave the perception that this monograph will:

- inspire managers to achieve growth goals
- help managers understand workplace behaviors and the needs of employees
- teach managers the importance of working in groups, setting the example, being attentive, and practicing stewardship

3

As managers journey through *Management dynamics in the new economy*, a sense of the dynamics of many enterprises and cultures, models used to formulate policies and make decisions, and natural qualities and responsibilities of managers will be conceptualized. Readers will learn how to effective communicate using techniques designed in planning phases. Readers will discover that managing is not routine, and through deploying the 4Ms--multi-tasking, mastering, mentoring, and motivating--managers will gain the respect of a leader. Peter Block wrote, "No one should be able to make a living simply planning, watching, controlling, or evaluating the actions of others."

Prof. B. L. Nelson-Porter, CEO and Founder
www.brigettes.com

ACKNOWLEDGEMENTS

This major undertaking has received the whole-hearted supports of many individuals and groups. We are grateful to the book Reviewers: Prof. Dr Raghu Bir Bista of Tribhuvan University, Nepal and Dr. Brenda Nelson-Porter, Assistant Professor at North Central University and CEO of Brigette's Technology Consulting and Research Firm, USA for their professional advice and experience sharing. Special appreciation must however go to Dr. Brenda Nelson-Porter who after a though perusal of the manuscript offered to write its foreword. Also, we are grateful to Prof. M. Manfred and Prof. N. Shirley of Pebble Hills University as well as Dr. D. Gottshalk of South Asia University, UK and Prof. Dejan Eric of Institute of Economic Sciences, Belgrade ,Serbia for the parts they played in our academic life.

To Prof. J. O. Abioye, Prof. D. A. Alabi, Prof. K. A. Balogun, Prof. R. I. Akintoye, Prof. Alaba. Adenuga, Prof. David B. Ekpeyong and Prof. S. A. Tella: all of Olabisi Onabanjo University as well as Prof. J. O. Obikoya of Tai Solarin University of Education we say thank you for your encouragement. Finally, our thanks are due to our families and institutions where we are employed. No book would be possible without the combined supports of all sides.

M. A. Omolaja
M. Radovic-Markovic

PREFACE

This book is response to, the clarion calls by students, lecturers and practitioners for a monograph on *Management dynamics in the new economy* which would stand the test of time in satisfying the needs of the academic and professional students, managers and administrators, and at the same time, meeting the yearnings of other consultants in small, medium and complex organizations. This volume adequately takes care of these requirements as it covers the principles and practice of modern management in the contemporary industrial and even governmental settings with a great deal of details.

In writing the book, we enjoyed the applications of our long time academic and professional experience as lecturers of Principles and Practice of Management, Corporate Administration as well as Corporate Policy and Strategic Management. Our practical experience for years as Management Consultants also offered significant input into this book. Throughout the text, our purpose had always been to continuously provide the readers with an understanding of the roles which a sound knowledge of modern management techniques and tools plays in organizations, irrespective of their scope or size, orientation, purpose and even sector in which they operate.

Written with the needs of the layman in mind, the volume is written in simple and plain language and this would help in the process of understanding for beginners in the domineer of managerial studies and likewise for other users. Furthermore, at the end of every chapter, a list of revision questions is provided and at the end of the book is a list of past examination questions. Most of these questions were taken from past examination papers for undergraduate, postgraduate and professional students of General

Management especially Corporate Policy and Strategic Management.

Consequently, the book is of great relevance to the doctoral, masters and undergraduate students of Management Studies, Small Business Management, Entrepreneurship, Business Administration, Public Administration, Accountancy, Economics, Banking and Finance, Psychology, Sociology, Education and allied disciplines. For the Professionals and Consultants, this text will serve as a reference source, an interpreter of the arcane and translator of the specialized terminologies in various aspects of modern management practices and research.

M.A. Omolaja
M. Radovic- Markovic

TABLE OF CONTENTS

CHAPTER TWO: MANAGEMENT FUNCTIONS

**CHAPTER THREE: ORGANIZATION IN MODERN
                   MANAGEMENT**

CHAPTER FOUR: SPECIALIZED MANAGEMENT TECHNIQUES

CHAPTER FIVE: CONTROL IN MODERN MANAGEMENT

CHAPTER TEN: MANAGING EMPLOYEES AT WORK

CHAPTER ONE

NATURE OF MANAGEMENT

Things to Consider:
* Definition of Management
* Managers and Management
* Managers and Entrepreneurs
* Qualities of a Good Manager
* Managerial Skills
* Manager's Job and Responsibilities
* Manager's Orientation toward Change
* Levels of Management
* Managerial Structure
* Managerial Problems
* Management and Leadership Styles
* Common Management Styles
* Management and Leadership

1.1 DEFINITION OF MANAGEMENT

Management has been defined by various scholars; academics and professionals alike. Hence, there are many perspectives by which the concept of management may be considered. For instance, management may be taken as an activity, as a process, as an academic discipline, as a profession, as a science, as an art, and as a group of people.

As a process, management is the process of achieving objectives through efficient use of resources. It is the process of planning, organizing, coordinating, directing and controlling the activities of people. It is the sum total of all activities involved in organizing men, money, materials, machines, methods and time, and also maintaining, directing, coordinating, supervising and controlling them to produce or provide, for a profit, the goods and services for the benefits of the members of the society

In this definition, management is being considered as an activity or task to be performed. Hence, if we are in doubt about a person's ability to perform a task in any way, we ask *"Can he or she manage?"* If the answer is in affirmative, then we are sure that the person can do the work. Otherwise, he or she is unable to do it. Managing in this case implies *coping with a situation* while management in the same context implies the ability *of someone to do something.*

Also, *Mary Packer Follet*, an industrial sociologist, defined management as an *act* when she said that "Management is the act of getting things done through other people". Looking at this *Follet's* definition, the modern management philosophers have found an inadequacy in it because the definition tends to see the "other people" as mere "working tools" rather than as "working colleagues or collaborators". Hence, the more popular opinion is that *"Management is the act of getting things done through, and with, other people.* This is a more acceptable definition of management, making use of Mary Parker Follet's words, but in a more explanatory manner. Another school of thought comprising *Fredrick Winslow Taylor* and his colleagues in the *scientific management school* has defined management as the process of organizing, motivating, forecasting, communicating, controlling, directing and leading, human and material resources towards accomplishment of a predetermined goal in an organization. This is another way of defining management as a *process.*

However, considering management as an academic discipline, *Oyedijo (1995, P.1)* was of the opinion that *management is "the systematic study of formal modern organizations and the way they Organize and coordinate their functions, how they formulate and implement policies, plans and decisions, the way they allocate human, material and financial resources, how they produce, distribute and sell goods and services, how they relate to other organizations and the government, etc".* Hence, this is what people studied when they are awarded Bachelor of Science (B.Sc.), Master of Science (M.Sc.), Doctor of Philosophy (Ph.D. or D.Phil.) and Doctor of Science (D.Sc.) Degrees in Management.

Such academic pursuits are normally undertaken in the Universities, Polytechnics and Colleges. Meanwhile management as a professional practice is achieved partly by professional courses and training on the one hand, and partly through practical experience on the job on the other. Both of these, however, would lead to management development.

Management may also be considered as a group of people. That is, the group of people that is charged with the responsibilities of carrying out of the affairs of an enterprise is also known as management. In this case, the Board of Directors in every organization, consisting of functional managers in the enterprise, represents the management of the organization. As a science, management process employs the use of scientific procedures, principles, philosophy and methodology in solving managerial problems. This implies that managerial process is orderly, systematic and controlled in a scientific manner.

The various methodologies of management scientists such as observation, survey, experimentation, quantitative and qualitative analysis make management a scientific endeavor. Finally, the philosophies and methodologies of realism, positivism, empiricism and postmodernism which are all prominent in the modern management thinking further justify the inclusion of management within the scientific disciplines especially due to the nature of the contemporary management environment that is becoming more dynamic, turbulent, complex, interconnected or interlocking than ever before! This current trend in response to the Behavior of the global management environment requires management practice to be more of a science than of an art when compared to what obtains in the past.

From these perspectives of management, one would observe that management means different things to different people at different times and places depending on the person defining it as well as the time and place of the definition. Therefore, there is no single generally-agreed upon definition of management. In fact, there are as many definitions of management as there are management experts such as philosophers, analysts, consultants, professionals or practitioners.

1.2 MANAGERS AND MANAGEMENT

There are many types of managers with different titles or designations. For instance, in a small business "*the manager*" may be the owner of the business or a person appointed by the owners. In a larger business, there may be a number of different managers such as a "Sales Manager", who may himself be under the control of a "General Manager". There may also be more "junior" managers such as "Assistant Managers", "Supervisors" and "Foremen". However, no matter what their designations may be, managers are people who organize, lead and control the activities of other people so that a common goal is achieve. The goal may be the manufacture of an article or the running of a shop so that it successfully sells to customers, etc.

However, the work of any manager can be divided into two parts. First there is the *technical* side, which differs from managers to managers. This requires a thorough knowledge of the work being performed by the business, or section of the business, in which he is employed or which he controls. A sales manager, for example, must know everything about the goods being sold by his business, who buys the goods, how to distribute the goods to them, and so on. On the other hand, a "Works" or "Production" Manger must know everything about the articles being made, the materials from which they are made, the machines which are used to make them, the various manufacturing processes involved in making them and so on.

The second side is common to all managers, and is the one with which we are mainly concerned at this stage in the book. It is the *human* aspect, and it involves dealing with men and women at work; teaching them, guiding them, supervising and controlling them and, above all, leading them so that they work together as a team to perform as efficiently as possible the duties for which they are employed and paid.

Management, in this case, is the work performed by a person or a group of people; it is the art of managing others. The term "the Management" is often used to refer to a group of people in senior positions in an enterprise, but we are concerned with the work done by these people. Every organization, other than that of a "sole trader" who is in business on his own, consists of a number of people who work together to achieve a stated purpose.

All members of the organization are collectively a "team" in exactly the same way as eleven men on a football field are. However, in the case of a football team, there will be a team captain and, in many cases, a team manager, who stays off the field but who gives advice, guidance and instructions to the members of the team. The manager and the captain organize the players into a playing unit; a group who are *together* determined to beat their opponents and not just eleven individuals all playing separate games with the same ball. This is tantamount to control of the team by directing the energies of the players towards a common aim; which in this case is to score goals against their opponents to beat them.

Taking the same example a stage further, we can think of each team in the Football Association or Club as a department of a business, each having its own supervisors (the captain and members), and the Council of the Association as the Board of Directors which lays down the policy to be followed. This is the way in which many large enterprises are organized. You can see that the larger the number of people employed in an enterprise, the greater the efforts required to control them. In every organization, there must be someone who decides what is to be done, how it is to be done, when it is to be done and who is to do it. In smaller businesses, this will all be done by the owner or the person appointed the manager. In larger enterprises, however, especially the very large ones, there may be many people who share the ownership of the organization; they have each bought a number of "shares" in the enterprise, and therefore they are called *shareholders*.

It would be very difficult and time consuming to have to consult with each shareholder every time a decision had to be made, especially as many of them may not work in the business or know anything about its operations. They are mainly interested in what *profit* the business makes from its activities, as they all share this profit according to how many shares they own. These shareholders, therefore, elect a group of people to attend to, or direct, the affairs of the business for and on behalf of, the shareholders. The people so elected are called *Directors* and the group of them is called the *Board of Directors*.

There are a number of words used to describe a group of people, both managers and employees, who are working together to make a profit from their activities. These include business, firm, concern, undertaking, organization, company and corporation. In general use, they have similar meanings, although some of them may have more specialized meanings when used in a certain way. However, for simplicity, we shall use the words interchangeably in this book.

All different types of business activities which together make up the modern Business world can be divided roughly into three sections as follows:

(a) *Industrial Concern:* Some, like mines, extract raw materials such as coal, iron, copper, and so on. Others manufacture or process the raw materials so that their original form is changed and converted into a more useful form; factories are typical examples.

(b) *Commercial Concerns:* These buy and sell raw materials and the articles manufactured by the Industrial Concerns. There is a very wide range of businesses in this section, buying and selling a huge variety of different items; there are small shops and stores as well as large supermarkets and department stores.

(c) *Service Concerns:* These provide various services, like transport, banking, insurance, etc., for the industrial and commercial concerns and for other service concerns

All the three forms of business are quite dependent on one another for success. The reason for this is easy to understand. Before any business can start to operate, it must have money with which to buy materials or goods and machinery, and to pay for the rent or purchases of buildings or premises, to pay salaries to workers, etc. In many cases, banks will safe-guard the money of these businesses, or lend them money.

Factories, offices and shops use electricity for lighting, heating or cooling, and for power to run the machines they need in order to be able to operate efficiently. Both banks and electricity companies are service concerns, and without industrial and commercial concerns, they would have few customers to make articles for sale to the community as a whole, and the commercial concerns actually sell the articles to the consumers; that is, the people who will use them. Without industrial and commercial concerns, there would be no way for the industrial concerns to get their products to the people who want to buy them to use.

However, every type of business, whether it is industrial, commercial or service, must be run and controlled efficiently if it is to succeed in its aim of making profit from its activities. This is the function of management. Before any business can begin to operate, a broad *policy* must be laid down by the owner or shareholders or Board of Directors. The policy must first lay down what type of business is to be started, and what work the business is to do. Is it going to be an industrial concern? If so, what articles is it going to manufacture? Or is it going to be a commercial concern and, if so, what is it going to buy and sell? Or is it going to be a service concern, and what service or services is it going to provide? Once the main factors have been decided upon, the policy can go into greater detail. For example, in a commercial concern, it will have to be decided what type of shop or store will be run, what size it will be, and the type of customers for which it will cater, where the business will be located, and so on.

Next, *plans* have to be drawn up to show how the policy will be put into operation. This is where the manager first comes in as he is likely to be consulted by the owner or Board of Directors on the practical details, the costs of buying or producing the goods, what staff will be needed, the size of premise needed, and what is available, and so on. Once all these facts have been made available, it is possible to lay down the plans stating what work will be done, how it will be done, by whom it will be done and when it will be done. The next stage is the *coordination* of efforts, which is one of the functions of management. It is tantamount to building the team and making it into one complete unit.

Coordination is far more than simply directing a number of people to start work. Each person must know what he or she is to do, how to do it, and so on. There must be no wastage or duplication of efforts. It also ensures that the right people are put in the right place at the right time with the right goods to be sold or the right materials from which articles are to be made; that the right machinery, office equipment or furniture is available in the right places and at the right times. One of the most difficult tasks of management is concerned with people and it is called *motivation*. To a large extent, motivation is "leadership", as it implies getting the whole team to work willingly and well in the interests of the business. *Motivation is the injection of morale and loyalty into the working team so that they will carry out their duties properly and effectively with maximum economy, and in a willing manner without disputes and discrepancies.*

Once operations are under way, there must be managerial *control* of them. All staff must be supervised and checked to ensure that they are working in the most efficient manner. In the same way, all operations, whether selling or manufacturing, must be checked to ensure that they are running smoothly, machine must be checked and their performance recorded. Control also includes the maintenance of records of performance, in sale or production, as this record will serve as a guide to planning future levels of activities or operations.

Let us now summarize what we have so far discussed about the functions of management as follows:

(i)   *Planning:* This is the way in which the policy laid done is carried out,

(ii)   *Coordination:* this is the bringing together of all efforts to achieve the desired goal in the most efficient way,

(iii) *Motivation:* This is the creation of a high morale or working spirit amongst all those employed by the business, and

(iv)   *Control:* This is the supervision of the work performed by all staff and machines, and the maintenance of records of performance.

Here is a simple example to demonstrate to you further how all the aforementioned four functions work together in practice. Suppose a motor car is taken to a garage for servicing and a mechanic is given instructions on what to do with the motor car (the General Plan). Before he starts working on the car, he must see exactly what needs to be done, and he must decide how he is going to do it (Planning). He will then tell his assistant or apprentice what he must do, and he will ensure that any spare parts, oils, greases, etc, are available (Motivation and Co-ordination).

He will then check that his assistant does the work properly and when the job is complete, he will write on the job card what has been done, what spare parts and oils, etc, have been used, and how long the job took (Control). This is management in its simplest form, but you can see that all the four functions are involved, and that the managerial side is quite separate from the technical side of the job.

1.3   MANAGERS AND ENTREPRENEURS

The questions many people usually asked is *"Are managers and entrepreneurs born or made?"* As some experts say, managers are born, not made. This claim does not seem very encouraging for those who do not share this opinion. There are some other opinions beside this, which consider other characteristics, which also play an important role in managers profiling. As the matter of fact, if psychologist point out that personality is of great importance and that maybe it is a prevailing factor in achieving success, it does not mean that it cannot be corrected; precisely, it can be corrected through our behavior. In addition, one's personality may change and develop through process of education and permanent training. Accordingly, we may say that personal attributes influence complete personality shaping through an interaction with other characteristics.

In some studies, managers are analyzed through all their characteristics, while in others only business reports and results are analyzed. All kinds of managers are also studied –

production managers, sales managers, finance, marketing, tourism and project managers. In this program, we will focus on basic attributes, which differ among entrepreneurs and managers, as well as on differences in types of responsibilities, activities and the way in which they are conducted. We will stress the differences, having in mind that for a long time no difference was made between entrepreneurs and managers. The first true distinction was made in the early 20th century defining the manager as "a person responsible for other people's work", while the entrepreneurs were "persons who initiate new beginnings". Only since 1950, managers were defined as "persons who contribute to the company which employs them and indirectly to the whole society".

In contemporary scientists' opinion, a manager is a result manufacturer, an excellent governor and integrator of all company's functions. A manager initiates action systematically, integrating human resources for that purpose. He has an ability to continuously develop company's market, financial and human resources. A manager evaluates his work by how well the group he manages works, then by individual and group results of group members and by extent of achieved goals. He fears not the competition of capable and talented people, because a manager is of the same kind. A manager seeks results from work and has no monopoly on information nor uses them as a source of power. HE works hard and gives an example to other employees.

Unlike the manager who is a specialist in his work, an entrepreneur tends to be universal, because entrepreneurs include all aspects of company's activity. They have wider range of activities and greater responsibility comparing to managers. Accordingly, entrepreneurs work looking towards both the future and the present time. They lead new products and services creation and development, which result in numerous business opportunities, while managers manage projects, workers and companies thus keeping all the company's functions in balance (Drucker, 1994).

Beside these differences, managers and entrepreneurs do not compete with each other nor do their works. On the contrary, the best business results are made as results their activities synergy.

1.4   MANAGER'S TASKS AND MANAGER'S PERSONAL QUALITIES

One of the researches conducted in the USA, Canada, Sweden and Great Britain used as a basis both approaches; personal qualities and work results of managers, but also their business logs, which consisted of all their commitments. By keeping business logs, they compile important information from inner and outer environment, which they use in their business reports and business plans. When making business plans, they do it implicitly in daily actions context and rarely do they develop those for certain time period. It is indicative that their plans are only in their heads as flexible, but very precise thoughts. In other words, manager often responds under businesses pressure and does not look like planner the classics have described.

This research also showed that an average manager, in eight hours per day, change 583 different activities. Therefore, it means that he performs an activity every 48 seconds. Synthesis of this research gives an interesting image of managers, which is very different from Fayol's classical approach. It is also different from an image of manager's job. As a matter of fact, there are many prejudices regarding the range of jobs a manager should do, as well as regarding manager's business competencies and responsibilities. Accordingly, numerous myths that have little in common with job demands and expectations from a manager were created. Some of them concerning jobs that cannot be accepted without reserve and without special consideration, and these we shall analyze individually as follows:

Myth 1: Manager is a systematic planner

Myth 2: An efficient manager does not have usual duties that should be done

Myth 3: Older managers need more complete information than the younger managers, which are preferably provided through an informational system.

Myth 4: A manager is expected to spend the most of his time in planning and the least in contact with customers and other clients.

Despite this opinion, various researches have proved quite opposite facts; manager activities are not continual and are strictly oriented towards taking action. They are the first to come and the last to leave from work. Besides that, according to logs of more than 160 English managers, they work more than two days without a pause of thirty minutes. Around 93% of their daily activities, they spend in communication with the customers and other business associates. They use analytical approach in determination of customers' needs, supply expenses, market segmentation, competition, profitability and financial projections. Accordingly, manager is expected to make rational business decisions. Making rational decisions is generally based on good problem diagnostics, analyzing alternative solutions and their comparison and selection of these solutions as a basis for making business action. Most of the experts think that making rational business decisions is the most important and the most difficult manager's business activities. Managers prefer verbal media, phone conversation and business meetings. Lately, the most important information they get come through global network. They are equally necessary for all age groups of managers.

Having in mind that for every businessperson the ultimate goal is achieving success and making profit, we will point out the attributes, which determine design of successful managers' personality. At the same time, these are the same attributes the scientists point out as significantly related to the achievement of business results. Consequently, if he is to make a success in his chosen career, a manager must possess, or acquire, the following personal qualities:

(a)   Thinking Clearly,
(b)   Using Initiative,
(c)   Following Policy,
(d)   Adaptability,
(e)   Organizing Ability,
(f)   Motivation and Encouragement,
(g)   Setting Good Examples,
(h)   Communication,
(i)   Listening Ability,
(j)   Business Abilities,
(k)   Ability to Increase Profit,
(l)   Culture of Behaviors,
(m)   Training, and
(n)   Delegate of Authority and Assign Responsibilities.

We shall consider these qualities one after the others in the following subsections

1.4.1   Thinking Clearly

A manager must train himself to approach any problem in a clear frame of mind. He must not make *snap* decisions, but must consider each problem carefully before reaching his decisions. He must be able to think clearly in an orderly manner, arranging all the facts and considering all the information available to him. In short, he must be able to think logically. This does not mean that he must take a long time before reaching his decisions, as in some cases, a decision must be reached very quickly. With practice and experience, a manager should be able to *marshal* or synchronize all the facts logically in his mind, and reach a sensible decision in a short possible time. Of course, more complex or unusual problems may need longer consideration and investigation, but the manager must not be hesitant in reaching his decision.

1.4.2   Using Initiative

In a properly organized enterprise or establishment, each member of the organization will know exactly what his responsibilities are and how much authority he has. Within the limit of those powers, the manager is expected to use his initiative; he must not expect his superiors to tell him exactly how every little task should be performed. He is in a position of responsibility and must, at times, make decisions on problems which are outside his normal range of responsibilities. At such times, he must consider what the policy of the business is over such matters, decide what has to be done and then do it. This implies using his knowledge of the business. Naturally, as soon as possible, he will make a report stating what the circumstances were, what action he took and his opportunity of assessing his subordinates' ability and also gives them the chance to alter his instructions if it becomes necessary.

1.4.3   Following Policy

In many cases, a manager will be given a statement of the policy which his business is to follow: he must therefore follow such policy or guidelines correctly and jealously. The manager himself may not necessarily think that this policy is correct but *he must follow it just the same way as he see that his staffs follow it.* Changes in policy frequently mean changes within the areas of responsibility of the managers and the work of their staffs. Consequently, the managers must be able to cope with these changes.

1.4.4 Adaptability

This follows on from the above sections but it is wider in scope because, apart from policy changes, advances in machinery in the factory, shop or office can involve major changes in methods and requirements. The manager must, therefore, be flexible in his mind and attitude in order to deal with such changes and the effects that they may have on his staff. The day-today running of a department also calls for adaptability as many problems of a wide nature vary from dealing with one type of problem to another.

1.4.5 Organizing Ability

One of the main duties of a manager is the organization of people and things. However, first he must be able to Organize himself and his own duties. This involves classifying each problem which arises and assessing its importance so that urgent matters are attended to before routine matters. He must also arrange his work so that he makes the fullest possible use of his working days.

A manager must be an understanding man, able to impose his will upon his staff and also able to obtain a little other information about them from relevant sources to be able to speak to an employee by name; a manager who remembers that an employee supports a certain football team, or has a sick child, makes that an employee feel that the manager is interested in him as a person rather than as a mere production unit. Indeed, the good manager is interested in him and will find time to discuss his problems with him if it becomes necessary.

Such a manager will earn the respect and loyalty of his staff if he is sincere, and this brings with it a measure of self-discipline so that the staffs are unlikely to act in a manner which will upset the manager. Much of this, of course, comes from the example set by the manager, which we shall discuss later in this book. However, it must be understood that a manager should not hesitate to take disciplinary action if it becomes necessary. Nothing is worse than a week, ineffective manager!

1.4.6   Motivation and Encouragement

While a manager must maintain a high degree of discipline, he should also be able to recognize when his staffs are working especially well and to give praise when it is due. This, in itself, is a form of encouragement. A manager whose department is working under great pressure is not encouraging his staff if at the end of the normal working day he goes home to his dinner leaving his staff working hard on overtime. This does not mean that because one section of the enterprise is working late, the Managing Director should also stay, but the section head, at least, should encourage his staff by remaining with them until the job is done. A good manager cannot be a *clock catcher*.

Motivation is considered to be something that drives people to behave the way they do. Numerous factors influence this acquired attribute of manager. The most important are:

- Manager's capability; that is, individual intelligence and knowledge;

- Job perception; that is, everything a managers wants or thinks is necessary to be done;

- Other peoples influence, that is, the pressure of other employees towards an individual, the pressure of the family and the social groups he belongs;

- Type of job; that is, extend to which the job is giving the possibility of advancing, responsibility, and satisfaction.

1.   Motivational process analysis suggests several ways and techniques, which should be applied in order to improve performance. These are:

2. - Trying to understand associates' needs by using *Maslow's* categorization of needs - security, self-fulfillment, and respect;

3. - Discovering not only what is important for associates, but also what they want. Therefore, manager has to modify his approach according to that information;

4. - The use of money reward is very important as a basic motivational factor. Money is important because it satisfies great range of needs, improves life standard, enables self-fulfillment and people can demonstrate their own success;

5. - It is important to understand that money is not the only reward people want. They have to be motivated to achieve something special in their jobs or to take greater responsibility. This kind of reward can be more important than money reward;

6. - The reward will be more effective if people know in advance, what they can expect from the hard work. Therefore, the relation between success and reward should be defined precisely, that is, every company has to have an adequate rewarding system;

7. - Identification of human needs is important in order to enable the satisfaction of those needs through rewarding system;

8. - Increasing individual responsibilities can also be a technique for increasing motivation;

9. - Individuals get support in their efforts for contribution in work planning and new motivational techniques innovating.

10. - Finally, one should consider McGregor's opinion that it is the most important "*to create circumstances that will motivate individuals to give their maximum in accomplishing business tasks thus accomplishing company's success*".

1.4.7   Setting Good Examples

As the manager does, so do the staff. The manager who always arrives at his office 10 minutes late, who is not properly shaven, who is untidily dressed or who leaves absolutely on time every day, does not set a good example to his staffs. He cannot therefore complain when his staffs copy his bad habits. If a manager wishes to obtain the best from his staffs, he must be prepared to set them a good example, even to the point of proving that he has a fair knowledge of every job in his own department. Again, no one expects the managing director to be able to perform skilled operations such as turning metal on a lathe, but he *must,* at least, know what is involved in the operations and be able to discuss it intelligently.

1.4.8   Communication

Managers must have ability to establish good communication with the customers, suppliers, employees and financiers can be more successful in business than the others which lack communication skills. Therefore, every manager has to prepare for communication depending on the group of people he is referring to and be very enthusiastic when entering this relationship. He also has to know the ultimate goal of communication, he has to estimate the cost of different communication types (customer conferences, catalogs, trading presentations, advertising, exhibitions, phone calls, etc.), as well as which type will give the best results. Besides that, a manager who wants to establish good communication has to know the company's organization well, to know how to anticipate customers' demands and to make permanent effort for maintaining and upgrading his own communication skills.

In small companies, communication is conducted directly through appropriate channels to the recipient who should decode the message. In order to complete the process, the recipient has to provide reply to the sender. In this way, misunderstanding of the message can be corrected, which enables clear communication among employees, customers and other clients. Therefore, it can be rightfully said that communication skill is condition *sine qua non* of business success.

1.4.9   Listening Ability

Few managers are good listeners, although this ability is of great importance. A person capable of careful listening is not only able to collect more information important for the business, but also to make better communication with its environment. There are a number of reasons why people cannot listen carefully. First, they may not be able to focus on any reason. Second, they may be preoccupied with themselves or their own problems, Third they may be focusing too much on what they should say next. And they may not be interested to listen and to comprehend what they are hearing.

In order to gain qualities of a careful listener, a manager must primarily focus not only on words, but also on speaker's facial expressions because it also bears a special message. It is also necessary to make short memos of every conversation and to accent main conversation points. It is desirable not to interrupt the speaker and to show him signs of approval by his gestures.

1.4.10 Business Abilities

Business abilities are important in adopting changes process. For instance, all of those who can see that changes will contribute to improvement of their personal position will accept changes. However, those who have long standing working experience on certain positions may see those changes as a negative impact on their positions and working experience and therefore be completely resistant to changes.

11.   Managers find it much harder to adopt changes than any other team member does. Above all, this is because managers always face additional problems compared to other team members. Besides that, team members can ask for help from managers, while managers are not expected to do so.

12.   Specific problems that managers face may include the following:

13.   - They often face numerous objections from their associates;

14.   - Changes can decrease their salaries or status;

15.   - Changes can bring many new assignments;

16.   - They carry out all the responsibilities for introduction and application of changes.

17. As showed above, managers get greater responsibilities than other working team members do. They can easily handle that pressure if they can quickly react, change and give maximum efforts in all the domains of their responsibilities.

1.4.11 Ability to Increase Profit

18. It is very important to be popular, primarily because popularity increases self-esteem and moral. Therefore, many managers use different techniques to increase their popularity and some of these are:

- Discover what your bosses love – Before you start to work for a company, try to make a contact with your future bosses. Notice their look, behavior, are they married or divorced, what are their hobbies, etc. In addition, when you meet important people for the first time, it is important to pay attention to their office, in other words, whether it is tidy or not. All of these will help you determining your bosses' personality and to develop your own attitude in relation with them.

- Try looking the way they look – meaning your dressing style should be appropriate to your bosses wishes and demands.

- Listen actively – If you can listen carefully to your bosses and associates and to be supportive, you become more interesting. In addition, if they use "body technique", you have to learn to use it, too. It is considered that eye contact is often used in everyday communication, especially in business meetings. Besides that, one should pay attention to where and how one is sitting on business meetings. If we are too close to our bosses and other associates, it can be a sign of improper behavior or extreme desire to be intimate with them. In many Western European countries and in the USA there are strictly defined rules for how and where we should sit on business meetings, in other words what is the proper distance? Businesspeople from Southern Europe are more tolerant, while the least tolerant are the Japanese.

- Show your diversity – Try to show your knowledge, education and capabilities in the best possible way.

- Quickly respond to your bosses' demands.

- Do not bother your bosses too much with your own problems.

- Provide you bosses support when necessary, in other words be loyal.

- Win your reward – Everyone likes to be rewarded. There is a belief that a reward improves work and job devotion for 87.5%. In lack of reward, motivation and devotion drop to 65.1%. Therefore, one should work hard to deserve a reward. It does not only mean to achieve top results in business, but also to improve own behavior, develop business cooperation and to gain trust among bosses and associates.

1.4.12 Culture of Behaviors

In his study *"How to be an ever better manager"*, *Michael Armstrong* had pointed out that profit is a result, not goal of successful management. Therefore, in his opinion, profit is not a measure of success. CEO of *"International Harvester"* once pointed out that everything one needs to do in business is to make a good team of managers and to sell goods at higher prices than they were bought. Hence, three key factors for increasing profit exist and these are:

(a)   Decreasing expenses: In order to make maximum profit possible, manager should use inputs only up to the level enabling the profit margin (i.e. marginal product value) to exceed the marginal costs (the price of input unit on the reproduction commodities market). This important manager's behavior rule influences the demand for reproduction commodities.

(b)   Increase in sales: The sale is also of great importance for increasing profit. Maximizing the sales depends on marketing. There are two marketing approaches. The first is the analysis of desires and buying models according to possible future needs. The second is the creation of desires that are not present now, but are developed with supply of new product and services.

A company can maximize its breakthrough on the market by discovering new markets for its products or by improving them. It can also offer new products to new or existing markets. Good marketing means that company presents its product to customers by advertising, public relations and all other ways that will increase sales. Besides the fact that sales depend on good marketing, they also depend on well-trained, motivated and controlled sales units, as well as the distribution. Namely, sales will not be successful if customers wait for a long time for delivery of goods or if wrong distribution channels are used.

(c) Efficiency: This is also important for profit increase. It should be achieved in the domains of productivity (higher profits per fewer employees), finances and procurement.

However, in order to estimate appropriate company's profit-making ability, it is necessary to conduct competitive analysis, prepare strategic plans, carry out production analysis, productivity analysis, market analysis, sales analysis, customer analysis (procurement analysis), distribution analysis and expenses analysis.

19.   Apart from sales and efficiency increase and expenses decrease, profit maximization can be achieved through prices increase. Although the best way for profit increase is to decrease expenses, the greatest effect on profit increase in long term is sales increase. William Hall had analyzed 64 companies in his study, in order to see which companies make the highest profits. His analysis showed that the most successful companies are those whose goods are at the lowest prices and those whose product are of the top-quality.

1.4.13 Training

It is not the job of everyone in a managerial post to be responsible for training as a whole. However, every manager is responsible for training of his subordinates to a limited extent. He must, for instance, make sure that new staffs are trained in their jobs. This will probably be done by people who are actually doing the jobs already but the manager must supervise the training. In   addition,   the manager must also train the men immediately below him so that they can do his jobs as well as their own. *In the contemporary business world, there are thousands of men who have climbed a certain way up the ladder and have then stuck at a certain point. Opportunities for promotion came along but somehow such people are never the ones chosen although they may be excellent at their jobs. The reason for this unfortunate situation is that such people are so valuable in their present jobs that the company cannot afford to promote them unless there are trained people to take over their work!.*

These men have never trained anyone for their post and have thereby completely jeopardized their own progress. In the other direction, of course, a manager must try to learn as much as he can about the work of his immediate superiors because he may have to do their jobs in times of sickness or absence on leave, and also because this fits him for promotion.

1.4.14 Delegate of Authority and Assign Responsibilities

There is little point in training a man to do a job if he is not allowed to practice his skills so acquired. One of the new trends found amongst the amateur managers in practice is a reluctance to assign responsibility and delegate authority. Many otherwise capable managers are guilty of this fault. The principle behind all management is dealing with people, organizing them so that the work they have to do is done properly, at the right time and with no wastage either of time or materials; that is, coordination and motivation.

Many managers are excellent in this respect and can keep their departments absolutely *on the top line* except for one thing; that is, this type of manger spends so much of his working day actually supervising others that he has no time to carry out the rest of his tasks. He is the man who takes a full brief-case home every evening and spends a large part of his leisure-time doing work which he should have done in the office or factory. This is not management; it is a mere supervision. The manager who is doing his job fully and properly gives to every one of his younger officers the full amount of responsibility which they can successfully cope with is a good one. The first batches are their responsibilities, a little more is added and so on, until the officers are carrying all that can be expected of them! The senior man can still exercise his supervisory powers by calling for regular reports from his subordinates and by making inspections from time to time but he must leave the responsibility where it belongs.

Very few, if any, people are born with all the personal qualities that we have listed above. However, these qualities can be acquired with practice and patience. The first step is to take a hard, long look at yourself and to decides, honestly, which of the qualities listed you do not possess. When you have done so, you can start to take action about the qualities you lack. For example, if you are not a punctual person. You may buy yourself a wrist watch and (or) an alarm clock so that you will get up a few minutes earlier in the morning. Then make a special effort to Organize yourself (you cannot expect to be able to Organize others if you are not Organized yourself) so that you will arrive at work on time and, better still, a few minutes before the time. You can, with care, train yourself to acquire all the 10 qualities which after a while will come naturally to you.

1.5   MANAGERIAL SKILLS

In addition to acquiring the 14 qualities stated in the above section, there are other areas of knowledge which the manager must acquire if he is to be successful: that is, *knowledge of the business, human knowledge, diagnosis and economics.* The knowledge of the business which is tantamount to *technical knowledge* required by a manager will depend upon the type of work on which he is engaged. If he is involved in production, or in one of the service concerns, he will need a degree of technical knowledge (skill). He must have a sound understanding of his machines and equipment in terms of accuracy, possible speeds of output, etc. He must understand his materials, strengths and weaknesses, and so on.

If he is involved in a commercial concern, he must have some knowledge of standard commercial practice such as bookkeeping, maintenance of records and some knowledge of the product with which he deals, as well as its distribution, either retail or wholesale. He needs not be skilled in all aspects of the work under his control, but he must understand the basic principles of all techniques involved.

Again, a good manager must understand people. All production is obtained through people, and a manager must feel and appreciate the needs and outlooks of people. This knowledge is essential to a manager, and in his dealings with disputes, he *must* appreciate opposing views to be able to deal with a problem in the best possible manner. A manager may have to deal with people in many different positions.

For instance; there are personnel on his staff, such as assistants, office staffs, factory workers and even cleaners, He will have to maintain contact with his superiors, the general manager, the managing director, and the board of directors and their chairman and perhaps influential shareholders invited to special meetings and functions, He will almost certainly need to meet suppliers of goods and also customers of the business. In all these contacts, he must know how to act in the best interests of his business, when to be firm and determined and when to be conciliatory and even subservient. In short, he must be very understanding of the psychology, Behavior and reactions of variety of people in different walks of life and in many different circumstances.

The *diagnosis skill* of a manager is also known as conceptual or administrative skill. This is the knowledge, acumen or know-how which a manager or administrator requires to make decisions that will improve and promote the welfare of the entire organization rather than the performance of a particular division within it. The skill also relates to the ability of a manager to think in terms of the total perspective of the enterprise, to relate a divisional performance to the working and functioning of other units and departments as well as the entire organization, to perceive the organization as a whole when planning and performing.

This implies that a manager must be able to network his enterprise with the larger society within which it operates and perceive the organization where he works as having a harmonious relationship with the larger business, social, economic, political, technological and ecological environment. It is actually this skill that will allow the manager to plan and execute plans with due regards to organizational policies, strategies and culture. Finally, an understanding of basic economics is essential to a manager who wishes to be successful. Likewise, finance is important in business as all work rotates around money or financial structure of the business. Hence, a manager must have at least a fair knowledge of financial analysis and management.

Some points can be made clear in respect of the mix of the skills required of a modern manager. The first is that as managers move higher along the hierarchy of their organizations, the technical skills that helped them obtain their first jobs become less important while their ability to use their conceptual skill and knowledge to set goals for the whole enterprise and their human skill to direct others become much more valuable. This difference in the skills required by managers stems from the diversity of the functions they perform. While junior managers deal with day-to-day, tactical or operational problems of the firm, senior managers are concerned with setting total direction for the firm; that is, they become more and more concerned with the strategic and long-range problems as well as with broad policies, plans, and objectives all of which require the ability to think of the enterprise as a whole total system concept and in terms of external parameters.

The second point is that the mix of skills of modern managers differs for different stages of organizational growth and development. Early in the life of an organization, technical and human skills are probably more essential. As an organization grows, develops and becomes more complex, administrative skills are likely to become more critically important for organizational survival and success. During a period of transition, transformation and rapid change, upper level managers have to draw more heavily on their technical and conceptual skills. The third point is that managers sometimes possess less than the adequate amount of skills required of them. While a precise skill definition is very difficult, the above general skill classifications can be used as a base point from which to form staff training and development plans.

Another way of looking at essential skills and knowledge of managers is by considering their education and training in terms of intellectual capital.

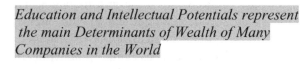

Education and Intellectual Potentials represent the main Determinants of Wealth of Many Companies in the World

One of the scientists who stressed the importance of knowledge for business success is *Thomas Stewart*, the author of "*Intellectual Capital: The New Wealth of Organization*", which point out to intellectual capital as the main determinant of wealth of many companies in the world. It is important to say that Stewart makes a clear distinction between three types of intellectual capital; that is, human, structural, and relational.

Human capital consists of individuals with high education and high intellectual potentials, structural capital consists of patents, inventions, databases and similar, while relational capital means good contacts with suppliers and customers. When intellectual capital is analyzed like this and when potential entrepreneur makes an introspective of own capabilities and knowledge, then determination of personal entrepreneurial skills should be added which often include capabilities of adapting to market demands, self-confidence, etc. By identification of this kind and by knowing one's own intellectual and other potentials for entrepreneurial and managerial jobs, it is not hard to anticipate what can be expected from future business thus determining one's own place on the road to success.

Apart from the above, we intend to turn attention of new business owners to that although they rightfully expect success; it does not mean that it is 100% certain. Namely, for a business success it is important to fulfill many other conditions, as well as to eliminate many common starting mistakes. Also, it is important to carefully choose business idea and to determine whether it fulfils al the criteria in your case in order to transform it to business with positive results. Accordingly, many scientists and consultants lately say that one should bet on good ideas, because only good ideas can make profit. However, considering this, we should have in mind that ideas cannot be practically realized without managerial skills and knowledge.

Professor Katz pointed out the difference between technical and practical knowledge, which every manager must have. For gaining technical knowledge formal education is needed, while practical knowledge require only informal education, i.e. learning through experience in practice. It is interesting to mention that many business owners think that they do not need manager knowledge and experience because most of them prefer micro businesses that do not require complex organizational management. However, many experts state that due to the lack of knowledge of organizational management their businesses remain small and do not expand. (*Ronstadt, 1984*) In other words, for a company to grow fast and to advance, knowledge and business experience is essential. This is confirmed by the latest researches that prove that knowledge united with experience is a winning combination when choosing teams, business control and expansion of business opportunity.

Having in mind that due to fast changes in technique and technology especially in the last decade of 20th century, new kinds of business and jobs appeared, the need for new knowledge became very clear. Accordingly, everywhere in the world the existing education system is being redefined and educational programs that have to closely relate to practice are being improved. For that sake, "new schools for entrepreneurs and managers" are founded, which are based on modern programs and courses meant for various groups of businesspeople.

For instance, some of the courses are meant for entrepreneurs for gaining basic knowledge of business and the goals is to help them test their ideas in practice (Manpower Service Commission in London, Manchester, and Glasgow). Educational Centers are also being established, which are especially for women and men between 17 and 24, who do not have enough academic qualification, but who wish to start their own business. Also, in Great Britain for some years there is training Centers intended for black people who wish to involve in entrepreneurial activities (*New World Business Consultancy, London*).

Apart from mentioned above, there are many agencies that specialize different kinds of consulting services. They have their own internet web sites through which one can make a direct contact and get an advice, essential literature, etc. More popular are virtual faculties which are founded all around the world and which enable connection between businesspeople and business students with lecturers from all around the world, no matter where they actually might be. Participating in courses and testing over internet essentially change previous way of gaining knowledge in classical classrooms and enable fast information exchange, more access to the newest knowledge and experiences in this domain and saving the time and money.

Thus, scientists' anticipation from many decades ago that in this millennium the classic way of education will be slowly substituted with some other forms of education, in which learning from homes and offices with the help of computers, and network connection with educational Centers, were true. Interactive education should provide a completely new dimension of gaining knowledge and to make it easier for those who attend certain courses to learn faster and easier.

Beside modern ways of gaining knowledge, practical experience is combined with formal education more and more. Increasing knowledge level, skill level and qualifications of employees is the key factor in market competition. Therefore, permanent training is considered to be protection for both the employer and the employee in the non-stop marketing competition. Education and training are continuous processes and, as it was said before, are conducted in many ways – in companies and outside them. Programs developed for domestic managers and entrepreneurs of both sexes, should be planned in such way to stress entrepreneurial activities and their development.

Accordingly, some courses should uncover the secrets of managerial and entrepreneurial Behavior, others to uncover the secrets of business plans, some to show them business strategies, etc. This form of permanent training should encourage creativity, providing good background to businesspeople. Cumulatively, it must contribute to tendency to innovate production processes, products, or corporative strategies. In order to achieve this, all training programs should be preceded by a preparation in form of answering at least few questions: To whom this training is intended? How long will it take to complete? What are the results that are expected? Who will lead the conduct of the training depends on various answers whether scientists, businesspeople or both. Also, it should be known in advance whether the training will be during working hours, how the results will be evaluated, whether the skills presented can be applied in common practical work, what are the costs of training, etc.

1.6   MANAGER'S JOB AND RESPONSIBILITIES

Manager's job has many responsibilities, including the ceremonial activities. Besides that, the earlier mentioned research showed that managers in small companies are highly engaged in routine jobs, because smaller companies cannot form a group of specialists for certain jobs. Their job is also collecting important information for business. A great deal of essential information is available to them because of their status, which they forward to their associates. Together with their associates, managers compose business strategy, company's policy and practically carry it out. At the same time, business strategy and plans serve as a road map for making a choice between numerous business opportunities in order to achieve the desired goal.

In addition, one of their basic duties is the environment analysis. It has to be analyzed both from internal and external aspect. During the internal analysis, they have to be able to test organizational advantages and weaknesses. This analysis usually covers the following areas:

- Quality of product,
- Expenses structure,
- Business market share,
- Management,
- Organization,
- human resources,
- Interpersonal relationship among employees,

- Financial reserves,

- Innovative capabilities, and

- Customers' loyalty.

When analyzing externally, a manager has to be able to analyze environment where the company does its business, to test market trends, economic and political circumstances. Famous scientist *Peter Drucker* (1994) added two more assignments to manager's responsibilities. The first assignment is like the one that conductor of symphonic orchestra has and thanks to whose efforts vision and leadership an appropriate music sensation is achieved. However, a conductor has his partite ready and he is only an interpreter. Having that in mind, a manager is expected to keep in balance all company's functions. He is also expected to constantly monitor company's results. Therefore, in comparison, an orchestra conductor's job is the best example of manager's assignments.

Busting the myth of managers' role and assignments in leading the business and definition of his work assignments and responsibilities has the stand in better understanding of this prestige profession regarding which only ten or more years people are educated for in our country. Better understanding of managers' role, ways and range of work allows setting more realistic goals and expectations. In that manner, compromising of professional ethics is avoided and also his assignment under various jobs does not justify the name and competencies, and often compromise its reputation.

1.7 MANAGER'S ORIENTATION TOWARD CHANGE

Huge number of variables can determine manager's personal capabilities for accepting changes. these include social characteristics, manager's personality, personal goals and business capabilities. The most important social characteristics in this regard are manager's age, his social and economic status and his education.

It is logical to expect that older managers will find it harder to accept changes, because most of them do not realize that changes are an important part of their lives. Social and economic status is more often analyzed as different lifestyles than like belonging to corresponding class. The ones that have resistance to changes are more likely to come from higher classes than vice versa. Finally, people that are more educated are readier to accept changes than those with lower education, although it should not be generalized. Again, important personal attributes of managers that usually affect his adjustment to changes include level of self-confidence. People who have little or no self-confidence have lower capabilities for adjusting to change. A manager's developed value system of importance for individuals may also affect his resistance to change.

Personal goals are also important, whether they contribute to satisfying manager's needs inside or outside the organization. Therefore, they are important in the process of manager's adjustment to change. Lastly, business capabilities of managers are also very important in adapting to changes process. For instance, all of those who can see that changes will contribute to improvement of their personal position will accept changes. However, those who have long standing working experience on certain positions may see those changes as a negative impact on their positions and working experience and therefore completely resist to changes.

1.8   LEVELS OF MANAGEMENT

A pragmatic approach to the study of managerial level within an organization is to classify management duties, functions and responsibilities on the basis of *levels of authority and accountability within an organization.* In a contemporary industrial organization, for instance, three managerial levels may be identified. These are the *Institutional Zone* having institutional functions (Zone A), the *Executive Zone* where policies and programs are actually executed or implemented (Zone B) and the *Lower Management Zone* having operational functions (Zone C). The Institutional Zone may also be called the strategic or top management level while the executive zone may be referred to as the tactical level of management.

Using this analogy, management functions within the modern day organizations have been labeled *strategic functions, tactical functions* and *operational functions.* This approach or perspective takes the cognizance of the fact that there are levels of operations, duties and responsibilities within the contemporary undertakings in the modern industrial society.

Strategic functions are basically the responsibilities and duties carried out by senior or top management personnel like the Board of Directors of the UAC of Nigeria Limited or the Odu'a Group of Companies in the formulation of long-term policies, strategies, plans and programs of the organization. Strategic functions may involve improvement in the organization's responsibility or responsiveness to its environment as well as its duties pertaining to competitive positioning at the international market.

In essence, strategic functions are said to be planning oriented, long-term in nature, known and performed by just a few members of the organization, and because of the fact that the top management level is the institutional zone; strategic functions and responsibilities normally relate to the entire organizational corporate operations and responsiveness. This kind of operations is, however, unstructured and typical examples are market penetrating activities, projected manpower costs determination as well as expected new technological changes or development decisions making.

Tactical functions are performed by middle management personnel to decide how best to use the resources of the organization to meet the strategic objectives set by the senior management. Tactical operations are carried out over a shorter planning period, perhaps, a month or a quarter of a year. They may also be performed for medium-term planning purposes ranging from one to five years. Such activities pertain to all efforts directed at policy and strategy implementation as well as procedure formalization for corporate effectiveness and efficiency.

Operations of this kind may also include sales projections, cash flow forecasts and capital expenditure budgets. It also involves items such as production within a particular department as well as organization and control of departments which influence production and productivity improvement. In essence, such duties and functions are mostly executed by departmental heads like Marketing or

Sales Manager, Financial Controller and Personnel Manager in an Industrial Organization, Heads of Accounting, Business Administration, Political Science, etc, in an academic and research institutions like the Universities, Polytechnic and Colleges. They may also be performed even by the Director Generals in the State or Federal ministries.

Duties at this level are also carried out by members of the same department in an organization. Other things usually done by the personnel at this level are resources procurement in the department and operations rate monitoring and control in the department. Some of the operations at this level are structured while others are unstructured. *Operational responsibilities* allow supervisors, foremen, chief clerks or junior management to ensure that specific tasks are properly planned, performed and controlled. It is concerned with the day-to-day routine operations and running of the business or organization.

It consists of duties pertaining to individual workers in the organization; what a worker does? How efficient and how effective is the programs and procedures being implemented within the organization? All these are parts and parcel of operational responsibilities and functions. Such duties and functions are performed within a short period of time and they are very specific in nature, work oriented, repetitive in nature, highly structured, individual oriented and mostly carried out by people on the shop-floor for the purposes relating to outstanding responsibilities, machine maintenance and so on. The diagram in Fig. 1. illustrates further the managerial levels in modern organizations.

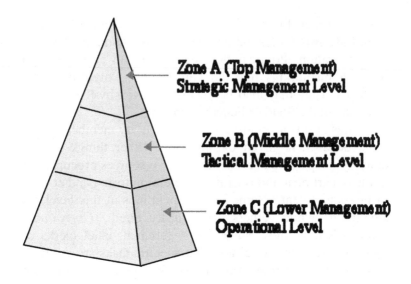

Zone A (Top Management)
Strategic Management Level

Zone B (Middle Management)
Tactical Management Level

Zone C (Lower Management)
Operational Level

Fig. 1. Levels of Management
t

In essence, the mechanism that is usually used to depict the managerial levels whether in its horizontal or vertical dimensions schematically is called organizational pyramid. It denotes the fact that organizations tend to take a pyramidal form. This is because as we moves successively to higher levels along the ladder of responsibilities, fewer persons are needed. This fewer persons, however, are managers and executives with increasing and heavy responsibilities. This is represented by the diagram that follows in Fig. 2.

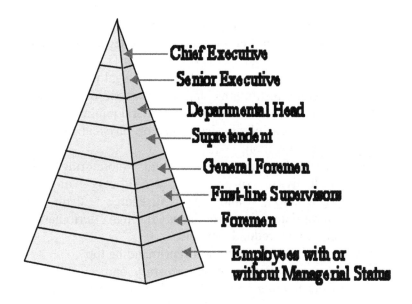

Fig. 2: Expanded Levels of Management

Meanwhile, the concept of managerial level is very important for a thorough understanding of the management functions being performed at each of the levels. These functions may be exemplified in the following ways:

(a) *Strategic Level*: This is also called institutional, top management or strategic zone in the organizational hierarchy, and the principal management functions that are usually performed at this level include;

   (i) Formulation of Broad based policy and corporate objectives for the organization, as well as determination of appropriate policies and programs to accomplish these corporate objectives,

   (ii) Development of appropriate strategies: determination of corporate plans, programs and paradigms, and mechanisms to achieve the corporate goals of the organization, (iii)Investigation, appraisal or evaluation, and approval of corporate or strategic decisions, plans and budget of the organization,

(iv) Liaison with outside consultants, legal practitioners, financial institutions and government departments, and local community and the general public

(v) Judicial use of physical and non-physical assets of the organization,

(vi)Searching for, employ and monitoring, the productivity of the key officers of the organization, and to discharge them at appropriate time perhaps through termination, retirement, redundancy, etc,

(vii) Appraisal, promotion or reprimanding top executive officers where necessary, and

(viii)Coordination and integration of the tasks or operations of the entire organization at the corporate level.

(b)   *Tactical Level*: At the tactical, middle management or administrative level, the principal managerial responsibilities of every manager or administrator include:

(i)Bringing up ideas, and making available information leading to policy formulation and strategy development at the top management level.

(ii) Translation of corporate policies and strategies into effect as appropriately as they relate to each department or division, that is, implementation and application of organizational policies and strategies   as may be appropriate or necessary.

(iii) Formulation of medium-term departmental or divisional policies, plans and objectives, and also ensuring their successful implementation application.

(iv) Coordination, integration and harmonization of the operations and control of extraneous performance of the various divisions, subdivisions and even employees individually and as groups towards the attainment of corporate goals of the enterprise. Formulation or development of appropriate managerial or organizational structure, and maintenance of orderliness and discipline to facilitate a smooth flow of operations in the enterprise.

(c) *Operational Level:* Since the responsibilities of the operatives involve the routine activities of the organization, management functions at this level would include:

(i) Effective supervision and monitoring of the day-to-day activities on the shop-floor. Included in these activities are tasks involving production, accounts, sales information processing material handlings, monitoring, and so on.

(ii) Supervision and monitoring of reports compilation.

(iii)Determination of good outputs and defective ones and guiding against unwanted performance on the shop-floor, and

(iv) Assisting in implementation of corporate and divisional policies, and strategies.

1.9 MANAGERIAL STRUCTURE

The concept of *managerial structure* is not new in management literature. However, the distinction between managerial structure and *organizational structure* is not so much clear that the two terms are often used synonymously. The major line of demarcation hinges on their orientations and applications. While managerial structure deals with human aspect of the enterprise, organization structure specifically relates to the *techno-structure* or technical aspect of the organization. Therefore, managerial structure is not so different from organization structure. It is just the structure by which management team members are related in their positions. It consists of managerial levels comprising the staff line managers, middle level managers and top managers.

Managerial structure is only a part of the entire organization. Other concepts related to organizational theory include organizational hierarchy. In the *traditional concepts* of *organizational hierarchy*, positions are arranged according to authority as can be observed in the diagrams in Fig. 3. The arrangement in structures so depicted however is a matter of semantics and interests. This is because an organization may desire a use in any of the two approaches. The position holder at the top of the organization in the business sector usually called the president or Managing .Director has the highest authority. The next level, usually contains the vice president or the Deputy Managing Director, has delegated to it positions of the president authority. Hence, his scope of authority is smaller but complete overall positions reporting to it. The next level is the departmental heads which have a still smaller scope of authority, down to the individual worker.

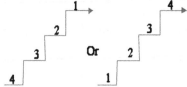

Fig. 3: Managerial Hierarchy in Diagram

Whatever the case, it must be made clear that a manager at any level in a hierarchy is responsible for the activities of all units or sub-units reporting to him. However, if this condition is to hold, the manager must:

(a)   Be strongly involved about what is taking place,

(b)   Be able to exercise complete control over everything under his jurisdiction

From these requirements follows a number of anticipated practices in modern organizations such as the:

(a)   That each person should have only one superior officer (unity of command) who ensures that activities are precisely coordinated to accomplish sub-visit goals,

(b)   That there should be clear channels of communication up to the manager providing him with adequate information to make necessary decisions, and

(c)   That following down from him will be a sense of orders which will be obeyed by all those in subordinate positions.

Characterized by this approach, therefore, is the fact that information, orders, instructions, directives, decisions, and acts of coordination and control are arranged in vertical or hierarchical manner. In reality, however, many events in the managerial structure naturally follow this ideology.

In this respect, managerial structure is the skeletal analogy which depicts the relationship between the various position holders within an organization in actually fact, managerial structure is the diagrammatic representation of the relationship among organizational members. It shows the arrangement of individuals and their responsibilities within the organization, the structure is however composed of staff line managers, middle level managers, top managers, functional and general managers and their subordinates.

Hence, when we think of large or complex organizations, we envisage a structure of managerial positions which shows departments or divisions, positions and their reporting relationships. That as, who reports to who and who is responsible for what duties in the organization. In the meantime, a typical managerial structure in modern complex organizations appears as follows in Fig. 4. Hence, the scope of authority is smaller but it is complete over all positions reporting to it. The next level or position perhaps called departmental or divisional heads have a still smaller scope of authority and so on down to the individual operative on the shop-floor. How then is the study of managerial structure contributing to the study of organizational Behavior and performance? The answer to this question may be provided simply by listing the major contributions of the concept of managerial structure as follows:

(a)   It facilitates the organizational control and coordination,

(b)   It assists resources acquisitions and maintenance,

(c)   It serves as an agent for organization,

(d)   It allows advice and services to be provided up and down the entire organization leading to effective down-to-earth and bottom-up management practices,

(e)   It makes easy division or allocation of works or staff activities to avoid unnecessary conflicts, friction and rivalry among the staff members,

(f)   It helps to establish clear line of authority which specifies orders, commands, instructions and directives which must be obeyed by subordinates for organizational stability and effectiveness,

(g)   It enables the employers to know who are responsible to them and to whom they are responsible at a given points in time (unity of command)

(h)   It emphasizes effective span of control in an organizational setting.

(i)   It provides for clear channel of communication for effectiveness through growing information, orders instructions and directives directly to the concerned individuals and groups in the organization, and

(j)   It facilitates arrangement of organizational activities in vertical or horizontal manner which results in organizational effectiveness if properly implemented.

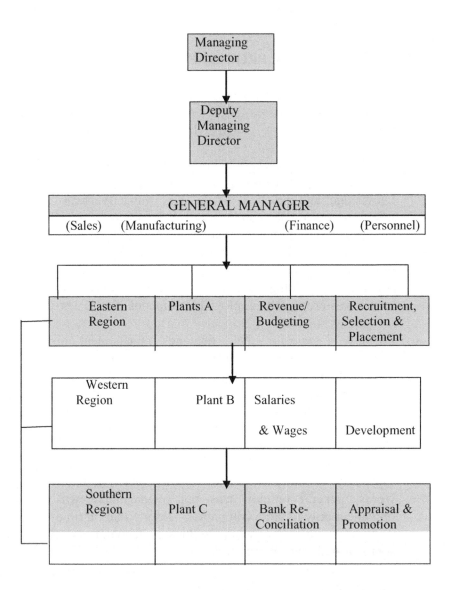

Fig. 4: Hypothetical Managerial Structure of a
Complex Organization

1.10 MANAGERIAL PROBLEMS

Problems of managerial nature are second by importance when businesses failures are in question. In this domain, problems arise usually from various reasons including the following:

(a) *Starting a Small Business;* This means the existence of desire to own a business, as well as owning appropriate knowledge and practical skills. Unfortunately, many new business owners underestimate the importance of entrepreneurial knowledge and skills. Without previous experience, education or training, new owner is weakly prepared to manage and run his new business. Logical solution for gaining practical knowledge is that new owner was previously employed at someone else's, who ran similar business.

(b) *Business Expansion*; This demands engagement of external expert people, for which a number of new owners aren't prepared at all, because they think that they can handle all work and to control everything by their own. Actually, in business practice, it was considered for a long time that small businesses shouldn't pay much attention to managers and management, which still reflects on many businesses, especially on those which are ran at home. In other words, general opinion was that management was immanent only to large companies. Despite that, in time it became clear that small businesses demand more sophisticated and more organized management even than large companies. Also, the true manager role wasn't clear in managing and conducting small businesses.

Thus, in some studies, managers are observed from an aspect of their personal qualities, knowledge and capabilities, while in other studies special attention is turn to their business results. Also, all types of managers are observed – production managers, sales managers, tourism, marketing, finances, project managers, and their contribution to every business success is evaluated. Lately, project managers become more important, who with their specific knowledge and skills should contribute to make an estimate, analysis and evaluation of a project easier, and to help to make certain corrections or complete goal changes in project on the run, if they become inappropriate.

Therefore, the risk is reduced and the possibility of making big mistakes is eliminated, which consequently reduces costs, influences on higher level of resources use and optimization of time use. One should have in mind that they, with the help of Microsoft Project 2003 tool, as one of the best software of that kind, must not only measure the results, not only evaluate activities. It is necessary to make a list of project priorities and to hierarchically set tasks and goals in order to follow up on activities and to control effects on project. Also, in order to make a realistic picture of a project, it is necessary to integrally review relevant financial indexes. This is of extreme importance because of the relevant valorization of financial and project investment profitability. This primarily includes determination of all useful information for making valid decisions related to financial position and successfulness of a project.

In order to achieve all this, it is necessary to train a manager. Training process should provide appropriate instruments and techniques for every management level. Every one of them should learn organizational process for project management. One of the best ways to conduct this is to providing project managers with appropriate instructions (manuals) in which is described to the detail how project managers are supposed to work. After training, every management level is included into business with new set of knowledge and skills for practical work on the project. Education should include not only project managers, but also all employees, so every one should gain enough knowledge necessary for the job. Then, it is rightfully expected that all team members will have appropriate knowledge and skills.

1.11   MANAGEMENT AND LEADERSHIP STYLES

Every business success is directly related to management quality, because business cannot develop and advance by itself. It means that basic work is done properly. Therefore, manager's task is to set work assignments and goals, to determine how they should be achieved and to make necessary business decisions. Good management is the key to every business' success and it starts with setting working tasks and goals. Working tasks and goals can be separated and specified for easier monitoring. It is recommended to set them for several, six months, a year and five years periods with precise deadlines.

Therefore, an action plan should be determined with priority lists, because it is not possible to simultaneously conduct several business activities. However, in micro businesses (one person employed), the owner is doing both managerial and entrepreneurial work. Only in developing phase, an entrepreneur tries to separate his owner's function from manager's function because he cannot do all the work alone. Regardless of whether at the beginning an owner manages business alone or hires a team of managers, it is necessary to include the following elements in successful business management:

(a)   *Long Term Planning;* Every entrepreneur starts the business with a vision and accordingly all tasks and business goals have to be in harmony with that vision. Business plan may help as a kind of a road map to show the next steps and where to go next and what business strategies one should use. So, it has to have financial projections, production plan, organization plan, sales plan and marketing plan.

(b) Realistic Budget; It is necessary to have a budget, which is suites anticipated costs, salaries and other expenses. The budget is always planned monthly.

(c)   *Job Description* – Having the clear list of tasks and responsibilities for employees is the basis of every business. This rule is applied even if only one person is employed. It is recommended that, if he cannot handle it, an entrepreneur should hire an expert for this domain.

(d)   *List of Priorities;* Every manager should have a clear picture of what should be done daily and how the tasks should be ranked by priority.

(e)   *Detailed Work Plan;* It is necessary for achieving specific work tasks and goals. For instance, when should the production start? How long should advertising take? How many external associates should be engaged and for what period? How much time individual business activities take? When a work task should be completed?

(f)   *Holding to Ethical Norms and Behavior Standards in Work;* It is necessary in order to gain trust among employees, but also among customers and all other associates and company's services users. However, moral principles in business are often ignored in order to achieve the ultimate goal of every business – profit. Fifteen years ago, a research was conducted in the USA, which should show how much managers are trusted, i.e. in what amount do they hold to moral code. The results were disastrous. More than 60% of managers make profit by selling products of suspicious quality or in account of company's employees' health

Management style and its philosophy will change as business grows. Accordingly, an entrepreneur; that is, a business founder needs people with abilities significantly different from those needed for creating and realization of business ideas. Besides, entrepreneur as the business founder, although has those abilities, is not able to control the business due to its expansion. An entrepreneur is then forced to form a team of managers who will expertly and competently manage, plan and organize company's business according to business plan. The head of this team is usually general manager with wide range of authorities and task, regarding the following areas:

(a) Help with problem solving,

(b) Creating stimulating business environment,

(c) Providing necessary information, and

(d) Completing those business tasks, which team, is not able to complete.

Owners of small businesses, especially of those smallest by the size and number of employees, usually hire agencies, consulting companies or experts that act as team of managers, which leads the business externally. They are in contact with the owner and suggest strategic and other changes, new solutions, corrections to business' weaknesses, influence its growth and increase success.

1.12   COMMON MANAGEMENT STYLES

Regarding the fact that management style depends on type of business, and on manager's personality, many managers are different in their style of management. We will explain some of the styles which are usually in use in managerial practice today:

(a) *Machiavelli Style:* This style is based on the famous phrase "Goal justifies means". For a long time, this was an inappropriate style. However, under modern business conditions there are a lot of its supporters which think that in certain cases Machiavelli style has its place, especially when it's about hard, fast and dirty business game between competitions. Despite this opinion, if this management style was widely adopted and used, it would lead to low moral and untrusting relationship on market.

(b) *Optimistic Style:* Although it is better to look on a problem optimistically, it is considered that this style gives almost as negative results as pessimistic style. Namely, a balance between both styles is necessary in order to be unbiased when looking at the problem and to anticipate where, when, and why things go wrong.

(c) *Superman Style:* This style is about macho guys who have a high opinion of themselves and of their intellectual, organizational and other capabilities. Managers who adopted this style are self-confident which is not always rewarding, in other words, they think of themselves as of supermen and believe only in themselves and their estimations, thus risking to make wrong decision and to make a mistake, which is hard to correct.

(d) *Style of a Star:* This style represents managers' permanent wish to be have everybody's attention. The glory is more important than managerial experience and knowledge. This way, his communication with other people is not always successful because he is oriented to himself. Style of a star may be immanent to show business, but not in other types of business.

(e) *Style of Complete Safety:* Managers who use this style think that they will be successful only if they give enough attention to all the signals and warnings from inner and outer environment. However, having in mind quick changes, it would mean that managers and other businesspeople should pay more attention to solving problems than to developing a business. In this manner, this style of management would have negative impact on business success, although one must always have in mind that a certain amount of caution regarding possible influences on a business is necessary.

(f) *Guru Style:* Managers who use guru style ask for a confirmation of their decision from number of associates. They are often inferior to those who have expert skills from different domains of business. Regarding their inferiority in knowledge, they are not always capable of selecting advices and can easily make a wrong decision.

As it can be seen from the classification above, there are many management styles some of which cannot be ethically justified. Despite that however, they are used because in numerous cases profit is above all other interests particularly business norms, which should be ethically and legally established. Accordingly, the popular opinion includes the fact that:

(a)   There has to be a connection between ethics and manager's behavior. Many people act unethically. If they have a good moral, they wouldn't do something against moral principles, even if they have reason for doing that, and

(b)   Many people have problems with moral and ethics regarding the world we live in. People are more occupied with personal and existential problems than with correct behavior. Therefore, for every business, establishment of ethical rules is of great importance. Unless these standards are established, employees will not have a base for making decisions for company's best interest and usually business will not be successful under those circumstances. It is also good to employ morally upright personnel because it can be expected that they will be morally inclined towards both the company and their jobs. As a matter of facts, modern managers should regulate moral standards in organizations in order to protect the interests of everyone involved.

1.13   MANAGEMENT AND LEADERSHIP

In management studies few decades ago, leadership was thought of as management and in fact these two terms were considered to be the same. Nevertheless, in mid-eighties in many bookstores, one could find a book that treats this matter in a way which clearly distinct the two terms. Professor Carter, while researching the basic differences between managers and leaders, has identified five different approaches and definitions of leadership as follows:

(a) Polarization of group members around one central person,

(b) A leader is a person capable to influence on a group in order to realize set goals,

(c) A leader is a person chosen to lead the group,

(d) A leader is a person capable of directing the group towards set goals,

(e) A leader is a person who determines the behavior of a group

The above definitions are directed to basic characteristics of a leader but at the same time they show the differences between leaders and managers. Therefore, in order to understand better the leaders' role in a company, it is necessary to clarify leadership specifications Hence, the main difference between leaders and managers is that leaders represent heroes that are distinguished by strong individuality which guide their companies through transition roads using various methods (usually unorthodox ones), while managers represent persons who work in often limiting circumstances and in far less dramatic manner using ordinary methods and techniques.

In addition, leaders are expected to have far more knowledge, skills and experience, as well as courage in achieving set goals and tasks. A leader is also a part of the group, but is distinguished by his strong personality. According to his abilities, he tends to help the group to achieve common tasks, but never loses his identity by doing so. Under normal circumstances, a manager is expected to plan work and to control it, to group–up business activities, to select and train work force and to build and develop motivational system.

Under these circumstances, he is not expected to act like a leader, because, with his authority, he is capable of leading subordinated groups of people to achieving their individual and mutual goals. Namely, subordinated persons are lead by desire to work and to earn. However, when motivation level drops, when the difference between set and achieved goals becomes big, or when manager's authority weakens, in that case it is necessary to hire a leader. It is desirable for managers to have leadership capabilities, but it is not necessary for leaders to be or to become managers.

Many scientists who followed the famous psychologist, Maslow, and his theory, thought that the basic leadership function consists of providing answers to the company's demands, while the basic task is to satisfy the needs of all the employees; namely, most of the reactions and feelings of employees (managers and everybody else), which grow from organizational structure of a company, will be determined by the possibility for satisfying the employees' needs. In this view, precisely defined role in the company has important influence on employees' reactions.

In other words, when an employee knows his commitments, then he can determine his status in the company and acquire an appropriate job motivation and a feeling of job security. Beside precisely defined role of company's employees, personal feelings about job depend on whether job corresponds to employees' capabilities. By planning human resources, organizations are trying to use optimally individuals' capabilities, but not to conflict capabilities with job demands, but to coordinate completely them instead.

Considering that every employee is only a part of the total organization work, the communication system must be created in such a way to provide necessary information for employees. Information has to be quick, accurate, and always available. Sociologists like Selznick, find different functions for leadership in organizations. They observe a special role of a leader in setting goals and tasks in creating organization. Selznick defined Leader's creative function in 1957. According to his definition, "creativity means changing character and shape of organization, adjusting it to employees' way of thinking, thus increasing realistic expectations that set tasks will be accomplished"

Beside the above-mentioned definition, a leader's function in a company is seen through his ability to sustain its integrity; namely, many companies' survival is closely related to maintenance of company's values and identity. As many think, managers are often not capable of maintaining their company's identity or change it according to demands from inner and outer environment. Therefore, one can see an irreplaceable of leaders' assignment for fast production changes, tax problems solving or to changing ownership form of a company in order to gain new market positions.

The fourth function of a leader is to direct internal conflicts in order to provide agreement among employees. At the end, one could say that these approaches to leadership definition have mainly psychological and sociological character. That is, leaders must motivate people to work in harmony with one another and according to the company's goals and tasks, because by satisfying the company's needs, at the same time they satisfy their own. It means that a leader must understand problems of individuals in the company and those of the company itself. In addition, leaders are engaged for putting business plans into actions and closely connecting managers with other employees.

In modern organizations, quality of service or products and leadership styles are the main factors that influence business success or performance. Leadership style is usually determined by the picture that leaders have about people and their work. In literature, one can find a large number of opinions when it is about pictures that leaders form about people. For instance, according to McGregor, there are assumptions about two extreme leaders' opinion on people. He named them theory X and theory Y. Common for those theories is that both are based on assumptions that leaders have distinctive opinions on people and about the essence of their work.

Theory X however relies on the assumptions that an average person has an inherited characteristic to dislike work and to try to avoid it as much as possible, that most of people must be under control because of this characteristic in order to complete their work correctly and that people like to be led and guided, therefore they want to avoid personal responsibility, have few personal ambitions and want security above all. Consequently, leaders who stick to theory X fall under group of autocratic leaders. They tend to maximize control of employees. Autocratic leadership usually has negative impact on employees, especially if they express the need for their own independence.

On the other hand, Theory Y relies on the assumptions that spending spiritual and physical energy is natural as fun or rest, that people use self-control in order to achieve work assignments and goals, that employees' commitment to achieve set goals is greatly determined by company's rewarding system, that an average person tends not only to take responsibility, but asks for increase in responsibility, that creativity is widely spread among people when accomplishing organizational tasks, and that under existing operating terms, which are characterized by high degree of use of science and technology, the use of human intellectual capabilities is maximized.

Leaders who follow theory Y accept democratic leadership style. Democratic leaders have positive attitudes toward employees, include them in decision making process and encouraging independence in their work. They also tend to build a valuating system in individual's organizational environment. In small companies, not only that democratic leader asks employees' opinion, but he also tries to maximize the use of working time.

In addition, they provide free information flow on all organizational levels – horizontal and vertical. Japanese management largely relies on principles of theory Y. In modern literature, one can find Theory "Z", also known as theory of chance. The base premise of this theory is related to the fact that there is no leadership style, which has general use and which is always brings good results. Instead, this theory supports use of autocratic or democratic leadership depending on a situation, i.e., depending on circumstances.

1.14   MODERN MANAGEMENT AND "NEW ECONOMY"

Companies which started to make losses and to fall behind with its development are facing the dilemma about what to do and what to correct in order to make "the wheel of unsuccessfulness" turn in opposite direction. It is not always an easy task, because radical cuts in business strategy are usually necessary. Despite that, it is necessary to exclude any kind of subjectivism and to develop a critical attitude towards company's management. This is also the first step to make in order to revitalize a certain business. Under normal conditions, a manager is expected to plan businesses and to control them, to select and train the work force and to build motivational system for employees.

Under those conditions, he is not expected to act like a leader, because with his authority, he is capable of leading subordinated groups of people to realization of their common goals. However, when motivation of employees drops and when the gap between set and accomplished tasks widens, it is necessary to hire a leader and to change team of managers. That is, it is necessary to select good team of leaders and managers. Accordingly, what is considered to be good choice of managers? Most often, successful managers are distinguished by their attributes, as "communicative", "result-oriented", "decisive", "person with good knowledge and skills", etc. Leaders are most often considered to be "heroes", characterized by strong individuality, which lead the companies through the roads of transitions by using unorthodox methods.

Many scientists, who followed the famous psychologist, Maslow, thought that the basic function of leader is providing answers to company's demands, whose basic task is to satisfy the needs of all employees. However, sociologists like Selznick, find different functions of leadership. They observe a special role of a leader in setting goals and tasks in creating organization. In the same vein, leadership function gives a character to organization for short and long terms. This leadership function is creative. "creativity means changing character and shape of organizations, adjusting them to employees' way of thinking, thus increasing realistic expectations that set tasks will be accomplished" (Selznick, 1957). Beside for the mentioned, leadership function in a company is seen through the leader's ability to sustain its integrity. Namely, many companies' survival is closely related to maintenance of company's values and identity.

As many think, managers are often not capable to maintain company's identity or to change it according to demands from inner and outer environments. Also, many managers are often engaged on several different jobs, and have a hard time doing many set tasks. It makes additional confusion and leads to inadequately accomplished job. Accordingly, leaders must also be engaged. Before leaders are engaged and the team of managers is changed, their past results are examined in order to anticipate their future achievements. Theory, but not always in practice, has shown that a person with good business references and good attributes can gain company's trust to lead and organize new businesses. However, our opinions is that these expectations are not necessarily true, because a manager or a leader could have accomplished good business results in the past not because of his abilities and other qualities, but because of some other circumstances that were favorable at the moment.

Therefore, globally the attention when making a choice of managers is turned not only to work experience and previous results, but also to education and qualifications for doing work in a specific business context. In other words, it is considered that good education and good management skills in a business context is crucial for the success. When a decision should be brought concerning changes in slow progressing companies, a question is asked about who will help to revitalize the company and to launch the new business? Whether it should be a talented manager who is already employed in the company, or somebody outside the company who has already proved himself in starting and leading successful companies?

Many companies' experience showed that any of these two choices may be a huge risk for success. For example, a candidate inside a company may have good knowledge about company's finances; having participated in closing important contracts, but may have no knowledge about starting new businesses and conducting them. On the other hand, a manager from outside the company may have experience and results in starting new business projects, but has neither knowledge nor experience related to company's corporative culture. Therefore, the best choice might be engaging managers or leaders who, based on previous experience, have developed skill to easily recognize and solve problems and to overcome them quickly in new businesses.

Here is an example of a company that showed big losses and failed at the start, showing the basic mistakes in the business strategy of its team of managers. The company was Pandesic, established in 1997 in the USA. Company's founders were two famous companies - Intel and SAP. The purpose of founding partnership company Pandesic was to develop software and to sell it over internet. Not long after founding, 100 people were employed and many branches were opened in America and Europe.

Particularly, attention was on the choice of the team manager who was the most successful in the business and with highest achieved results in previous work. Forty million USD were invested in the business, so there was solid ground for development of prosperous business. However, only few years later, the company had 100 million USD losses and was closed in 2001. Logically, one must ask a question how this company could fail, considering all the circumstances (human and material) under which the company started to work and to develop. After detailed analysis of the manager's teamwork, it was discovered that the main cause for failure was the lack of a good business strategy on which all employees would agree.

The basic lack of business strategy is the fact that the company has developed software and distributed it through its channels on market, not determining market structure before that. Not knowing customer business demands, they didn't adjust their software accordingly. This led to a gap between software supply and demand. Soon after, it reflected on the company's big losses and the company had to close. Although it employed 40 top managers, none of them had previous experience in opening new markets and in new products disposal. Finding managers and forming a team is only the first step in achieving a company's success. However, considering the fact that success is not always human resources function but all the other resources, it is necessary to consider other resources.

Three aspects of the so called new economy will have a significant impact on small and medium companies: globalization, deregulation and new technology. Will these aspects offer new opportunities or bring difficulties? The answer could be both. What is certain is that only the most creative will remain and advance. Thanks to new technologies, this will also contribute business world to overcome all barriers, which were imposed by distance and differences in business size and scope. Global market is more and more becoming an arena in which small companies must learn to play the game with big companies.

Thanks to the internet and web sites, offer of products and service has become available at any moment on the global market. However, it is not enough to have a good site, it is more important to find good distribution channels. Many consider that the advantages of internet will be the use of only those younger than 40, considering that older generation hasn't grown with computers. Of course, this is often a prejudice, as well as the fact that new economy is often associated with internet. In the opinion of Professor

Anthony Hermens' from Harvard Business School, new economy is characterized by the need to adjust the best international managerial experiences to contemporary business conditions.

In the world today five largest music publishers, but also one small, due to the Internet, doubled the sales. This is typical for new economy, where technological deregulation and globalization dominates. New technologies are especially challenging for small businesses. However, according to John Bailey, from Carlton Consulting Group, a gap appeared between companies which use new technologies and those which resist this change. The reason for this lies in a fact that many companies still lack knowledge which new economy demands. Also, many small business owners are not yet ready to hire new and young people which would bring freshness in their way of conducting business.

For instance, many business owners wish to remain where they were, resisting consciously or unconsciously to all innovations in business. In perspective, this attitude will lead to business stagnation. However, there are other examples where consulting company owners are partnering with others in the same business in order to introduce innovations in their work and to refresh their knowledge. This is similar to example of five washers in Melbourne which were competition to one another other. Despite that, they decided to meet once a month and to share their experience and knowledge and to look for solutions in order to help one another other.

As a result, they came up with an idea to send their representatives abroad once a year in order to get to know the newest technologies in their branch and to exchange experiences. According to this example, cooperation and competition are side by side. It wasn't the case before in the business world. However, now the situation has to change, which means that it is necessary to understand when companies should be strong competitors and when to be cooperative. They should understand the fact that sharing their knowledge and experience will improve their businesses.

It is also necessary to say that many companies spend a lot of time and efforts to accept new economic trends, while others adopt them easily. The fact is that smaller companies are adapting faster and easier. An example of this is a CD music store. This company was located outside the city centre and therefore was turned to local market which was very small. This company then decided to expand its market and made the first step by creating a web site.

Almost overnight, the company not only overrode marketing limits of its local environment, but also made its goods available throughout the world. In the first year it had 300 orders over internet, the next year 600 orders and in 2004 it had 1200 orders- In year 2005 they expected 3000 orders because according to their data, every individual order includes 4 or 5 CDs. Not only that company doubles the number of orders, but also its sales expanded to overseas countries, which wasn't the case only 4 years ago. According to this company's data, they sold CDs in about 170 countries. Actually, this company sales more products in America than in Australia, where they come from.

The interesting fact is that orders come even from company's local area. This proves the claim that more and more individuals prefer to purchase over the Internet and to have mail delivery. This type of sale has many other advantages. At any time an order can be made, regardless of whether it is day, night or a holiday. Also, the company now has almost 4000 email addresses and is able to contact customers in order to inform them about new products, which wasn't the case before they came personally and left no contact addresses.

This example is another confirmation that small businesses have to accept and adjust sophisticated modern management techniques which were largely applied in big businesses. According to Andrew Vorbach from the University of Technology in Sydney, many of the traditional advantages have now disappeared, so the advantages are connected to large companies due to their breakthrough on market and capability for satisfying demands from ever growing market segment. What is left to small businesses managers is the possibility and the need to examine competition and their business behaviour all around the world.

Besides, they have to accept the fact that management has to change and that all employees should become an integral part of successful business formula with which they will share ideas about how to satisfy market demand in optimal way, at the lowest price and by using modern management technology available. In many cases, one of the limiting factors for small businesses to grow into medium businesses is inability to physically service large markets. Small businesses can do everything good, but in small volume. Thanks to web technology, it is possible to cover much larger market. Therefore, small businesses managers are suggested to eliminate all barriers which stand in the way of the use of new technologies, because they are now facing the challenges which new economy brings and because they face a completely new and non-traditional competition on the market. In many experts' opinion, flexibility in distribution and delivery is a key to success.

Also, greater flexibility is expected in terms of product prices, which doesn't mean that prices should be enormously high, but to take into consideration all the elements which form a product's price. In other words, it is very important for a seller to know in advance what customer is willing to pay for. Besides that, considering that statistics show that smaller businesses are more ready for long term investing than larger businesses, this attribute of their will especially fully express in the new economy conditions.

However, new economy is very often erroneously related to internet concept. However, this economy relies on the need of good informing and applying the best international modern managerial experiences, so small businesses more and more apply sophisticated management techniques, which are widely used in large businesses. Therefore, small businesses managers now face permanent task to gain knowledge and continual examination of competition all around the world. Besides that, they have to accept the fact that employees, stuff and manager team together make business formula of success which should find market, meet customers' demands and offer products and services at the lowest prices possible.

Also, Professor Vorbach is of the opinion that in some cases, the basic limiting factor for transforming small businesses to large or medium is inability to serve large markets. In other words, they perform well, but in small volume. For small businesses, according to this and other experts, the use of modern technology is extremely important for these companies because they largely depend on them. Therefore, small businesses existence in new economy is directly related to modern management technologies. The challenge which new economy brings to small businesses managers is the use of new technologies and completely new and non-traditional competition on the market. Namely, new technologies enable larger competition which is on the global market. Therefore, a key to success in understanding customers' expectations in advance in terms of price and product quality, that is, what the customers are and what are not willing to pay for. Also, it is very important to be flexible in product delivery. Due to internet use in the last five years, delivery costs are significantly reduced as well as gathering all the necessary related information.

For example, only five or six years ago, information about recommendations for buying and selling certain products were send through post mail and they were waited for several days. Now they are sent either over cellular phones through SMS or over internet through emails messages which are delivered almost instantaneously. Small businesses managers' and entrepreneurs desire to share knowledge and to apply business concept widely accepted form all stakeholders in organization are of great importance. A strategic alliance is formed among entrepreneurs in order to find the best business model, often a technical analysis is conducted, different investment ideas are examined and all for the sake of maximizing profit or income, but to minimize losses at the same time. At the end it can be concluded that new economy sets new standards of success and opportunities for revitalization of small businesses which are related to forming strategic alliance, new technology use, experiences and knowledge exchange among entrepreneurs and similar. This is something that small businesses must not ignore.

REVISION QUESTIONS
1. What do you understand by the term "*Management*"? Vividly discuss the main duties and responsibilities of the modern managers to justify their employment in the contemporary industrial organizations in your country.
2. Who is a manager and what are the main qualities and characteristics which a person must possess for him to be addressed as a manager?
3 Write short, but self-explanatory note on each of the following:

(a) Management: a science or an art,

(b) Management as a profession,

(c) Management as a group of people,

(d) Management as a process, and

(e) Management as a set of activities.

4. Discuss the concept of managerial levels as it is commonly found in modern management literature. Is the concept applicable in the contemporary management practice in your country?

5. Explain the following concepts citing relevant examples and making use of relevant illustrations where necessary:

(a) Managerial structure,   (b) Span of control,

(c) Unity of command,   (d)   Ladder   of responsibility,

(e) Authority and responsibility, and (f) Delegation.

6. In your own opinion, in what ways do you think the study of managerial structure may contribute to the study of organizational Behavior and performance?

7. In your own opinion, what do you understand by the term "New Economy" as it is used in industrial settings? How does it related to management of organizations irrespective of their nature, scope or sectors.

CHAPTER TWO

MANAGEMENT FUNCTIONS

Things to Consider:
*   Nature of Managerial Functions,
*   Planning and Controlling,
*   Organizing,
*   Staffing,
*   Directing,
*   Reporting,
*   Budgeting,
*   Leading,
*   Forecasting,
*   Motivating, and
*   Communicating

2.1   NATURE OF MANAGERIAL FUNCTIONS

Having been introduced into the definitions and nature of management, the question we should now ask ourselves is "What are the chief functions of management?" The answer to this fundamental question is not farfetched.   This is because it could be arrived at by simply examining the various roles which contemporary managers and administrators play in their respective organizations. However, it should be made clear, at this juncture, that such organizations spread across private and public sectors; and they may relate to both good producing and service delivering work environments or establishments.

The primary functions of management (or simply managerial functions) have been coded *POSDCORB*. This acronym is used to denote respectively planning, organizing, staffing, directing, coordinating, reporting and budgeting. However, the scientific management school championed by

F. W. Taylor has added to this list leading, forecasting, motivating, communicating, controlling and decision making. Let us now consider these management functions one after the other as in the following sections

2.2   PLANNING AND CONTROLLING

Planning is the management function which involves determination of future departmental and corporate objectives of an organization, and the specification of the means, tactics, strategies or techniques of achieving those goals in consonance with predetermined *budgetary allocation* and time specification. *Planning process* tends to explore the past events, merge the result with the present circumstances and project for the future requirements and performance of the organization.

Planning implies analyzing a situation, determining the goals that will be pursued in the future, and deciding in advance the actions that will be taken to achieve these goals. Plans are developed for entire organization, for specific work units, and for individual managers and workers. These plans may cover long period of time (5, 10 or 20 years) or a short time horizon (days or weeks). They may be very general (e.g. to improve corporate profit through new product development) or very specific (e.g. to reduce product defects on the assembly line by 10 percent over the next month through a system of employee incentive).

In each case, managers are responsible for gathering and analyzing the information on which plans are based, setting the goals that will be achieved, and deciding what needs to be done. Planning as described here is not an informal or haphazard group of decisions made in response to a crisis; rather, it is a purposeful effort directed and controlled by managers but often drawing on the knowledge and experience of employees throughout the organization. Planning provides individuals and work units with a *map* to follow in their future activities, although this *map* may specify various routes and destinations based on individual circumstances and ever changing conditions.

The importance and frequency of formal planning within organizations have grown dramatically especially during the first half of the 20th Century in many world organizations. Hitherto, most planning was unstructured and fragmented and formal planning was restricted to a few large corporations. However, because planning is a decision process, the main steps followed during formal planning is similar to the basic decision-making steps.

Hence, planning makes use of scientific explanation, prediction and forecasting. As the contingency approach to modern management advocates, planning begins with a situational analysis. That is, within the time and resource constraints, planners should gather, interpret and summarize all information relevant to the planning issue in question. Although situational analysis studies past events, examines influences from the external and internal environment, the outcome of this step is the identification and diagnosis of planning assumptions, issues and problems. No matter how explicitly or implicitly conducted, a good planning process must involve certain systematic mechanism as can be seen in the following paragraphs.

The first phase in the planning and controlling process is situational analysis which implies analyzing all the circumstances surrounding the operations of the enterprise. A situational analysis carried out by major medical centers in the United Kingdom in 1985 gathered extensive information from external groups such as consumers, physicians, government and regulatory agencies, insurance companies and hospitals. The analysis also included information from all departments within the organizations. Historical trends in financial data and the use of various hospital services were examined and projection was developed based on assumptions about the future. The situational analysis took

10 months, and the information was summarized in a planning document of 250 pages long. This is to give you the idea of the importance of this phase of planning to the entire planning process, the remaining steps took only three months and the final set of goals and plans was only 50 pages long.

The next phase is the determination of the aims, objectives or goals to be achieved by the individuals, groups or organizations. Based on the situational analysis, the planning process should generate alternative goals that may be pursued in the future and the alternative plans that may be used to achieve those goals. This step in the process should stress creativity and encourage managers and employees to assume a broad perspective about their jobs. Evaluation of the merits of these alternative goals and plans should be delayed until a range of alternatives have been developed.

For this purpose, *goals* are the targets or ends which the manager wants to reach. The goals should therefore be specific, challenging and realistic. For instance, we can say that government's goal of making general electric first or at second in all market centers in a town is specific and challenging. When appropriate goals should be quantified and linked to time frame. They should be acceptable to the managers and employees charged with achieving them, and they should be consistent both within and among work units. *Plans* are the actions or means which the manager intends to use to achieve goals. At a minimum, this step should outline the alternative actions that may lead to the attainment of each goal, the resources required to reach the goal through this means, and the obstacles that may develop.

Again, decisions makers must evaluate the advantages, disadvantage and potential effects of each alternative goal and plan. The decision maker (as the entrepreneur) must prioritize those goals or even eliminate some from further consideration. At the same time, the manager needs to consider the implications of alternative plans designed to meet high-priority goals. In some organizations, special teams of managers with diverse backgrounds conduct this evaluation. Often, the different perspectives and ideas such groups generate lead to a more balanced and comprehensive review of company goals and plans. In fact, this approach often identifies new alternatives or refines existing ones.

The planner is now in a position to select the most appropriate and feasible goals and plans. The evaluation process should identify the priorities and tradeoffs among goals and plans and leave the final choice to the decisions maker. Experienced judgment always plays an important role in this dimension. However, relying on judgment alone may not be the best way to proceed. Typically, a formal planning process leads to a written set of goals and plan that are appropriate and feasible within a predicted set of circumstances.

In some organizations, the alternative evaluation and selection steps generate planning scenarios. A different contingency plan is attached to each scenario. The entrepreneur pursues the goals and implements the plans associated with the most likely scenario. However, the work unit is prepared to switch to another set of plans if the situational contingencies change and another scenario become relevant. This approach helps to avoid crises and allows greater flexibility and responsiveness.

Once managers have selected the goals and plans, they must implement the plans designed to achieve the goals. Remember that the best plans are useless unless they are implemented properly. Managers and employees must therefore understand the plans, have the resources necessary to implement them, and be motivated to do so. If both managers and employees participate in the planning process, the implementation phase probably will be more effective and efficient. Employees usually are better informed about, more committed to, the plans, and more highly motivated when a goal or plan is the one that they helped to develop.

Noteworthy, successful implementation requires that the plan be linked to other systems in the organization, particularly the budget and the reward systems. If the budget does not provide the manager with sufficient financial resources to execute the plan, the plan is probably doomed. Similarly, goal achievement is linked to the organizational reward system. Many organizations use incentive programs and mechanisms to encourage employees to achieve goals and to implement plans properly. Commissions, salaries, promotions, bonuses, and other rewards are based on successful performance.

Although it is sometimes ignored, the final step in the formal planning process, monitoring and control is essential. Because planning is an ongoing, repetitive process, managers must continually monitor the actual performance of their work units according to the unit's goal and plans. Also they must develop control systems that allow the organization to take corrective action when the plans are implemented improperly or when the situation changes. Irrespective of the type of control, the following steps are required in the control process. The next phase is to establish standards of performance. Managers need to establish verifiable standards of performance and clearly state, for example, in unit of production or sales volumes what exactly the concrete level of performance should be. Budgets are a useful vehicle for the expression of quantifiable results.

Again, like all aspects of control, this is an ongoing repetitive process, with the actual frequency which is dependent upon the type of activity being measured. This is followed by comparing actual results against the predestined standards of performance. Most organizations only require actions to be taken when the deviation against standards is significant. Otherwise, no action is required. This is sometimes called the *Management by Exception* (MBE) principle. Hence, corrective action is taken *if and only if* the situation goes out of control or allowable limit. For instance, this becomes necessary when performance falls short of standard. The corrective action may involve a change in the standards originally established. Unless managers see the control process through to its conclusion, they are merely monitoring performance rather than exerting control. The emphasis should always be on devising constructive ways to bring performance up to standard rather than merely identifying past failures.

From the presentation so far in this section, it can be observed that controlling is an important management function through which modern managers at whatever level perform their managerial duties or carry out their assigned responsibilities. Simply put control is the managerial activity or operations which measures performance standard, determines the disparity and trigger corrective remedial action. *Oyedijo (1995, P. 20)* shares the perspective that controlling is an integral part of a manager's job which is a corollary, and inevitable, to planning. *Louis Allen* also agreed that management controlling is the work which a manager performs to assess and regulate the work of his department in progress and it involves the measurement and correction of the performance of the subordinates to make sure the goals of the organization and the plans desired to attain them are achieved optimally.

In the mean time, the control function is exercised continuously and, although related to the functions of organizing and directing, it is more closely associated with the planning function. The corrective action of control almost invariably calls for a restatement of plans. As a result, many students of the management process consider the planning and control functions as part of a continuous cycle of planning-control-planning. The basic steps involved in the control function in any modern establishment could however be illustrated as follows in Fig.5. In particular, it must be stated here that management control is closely linked with performance evaluation. It poses two questions, "Who evaluates?" and "What criteria should be adopted?" For clarity;

(a) *Shareholders* will judge corporate performance according to the level of profits earned, dividend distributed and market value of shares,

(b) *Senior management* will judge the performances of the juniors on the basis of established targets, or on what is the norm for the position or situation,

(c) *Customers* will evaluate a company using their own measures of the selling prices of products on offer, the quality and value of the products and associated services and reputation of the company,

(d) *The loan and investor groups* will judge corporate performance by taking account of longer term potential, risk profile, product market portfolio balance, market reputation and profitability.

(e) *Suppliers* will measure a company on its ability to meet its obligations at due dates, and the stability of its ordering pattern,

(f) *Governments and Institutional Bodies* will be concerned with the fairness of Behavior and actions, and the payment of taxes and other dues.

However, it may be asked *"Why is discussion on control so important in modern management literature in recent time?"* The answer to this pregnant question is not farfetched. The main possible reasons for the phenomenon include the following:

(a) *Limited Resources*: Resources are limited and therefore, there is the need for effective utilization of resources and materials by means of control. The primary function of management is to coordinate the resources of an organization effectively and efficiently.

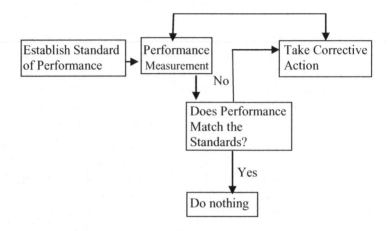

Fig. 5: The Control Process

(b)　*Attitude to Work:* Changing human beings (particularly employees) have the tendency to engage in random Behaviors. Control is therefore necessary to direct workers attention to the real objective of the organization.

(c)　*Change:* Change is an inevitable part of any organizational environment, market shift and new product emerges, new materials are discovered, and new regulations are passed. Through the control function, managers detect changes that are affecting their organizations products or services. They can then move to cope with the threats or opportunities these changes create.

(d)　*Mistakes:* Organization members inevitably make mistakes wrong part is ordered, wrong pricing decisions are made, problems are diagnosed incorrectly, and so on. A control system allows managers to detect these before they become critical.

(e)   *Delegation:* When managers delegate authority to subordinates, their responsibility to their superiors is not diminished, the only way managers can determine if their subordinates are accomplishing the tasks that have been delegated to them is by implementing a system of control. Without such a system, managers are unable to cheek on subordinate's progress.

In the mean time, the following is a list of the activities that are contained in the planning process

of   most modern organizations domestically or at the international scene:

(a)   Prediction (or forecasting) the anticipated future circumstances, problems and opportunities that lie ahead of the organization with particular references to the past, present and expected future social, technological, economic, political, environmental Behavior that are likely to affect organizational performance,

(b)   A concise predetermined performance standard or target which have to be realised on the basis of time specification. This would allow a control mechanism to be instituted especially if actual and standard performances are at variance. This means that there must be a concrete value to be achieved which should be quantified as far as possible to facilitate measurement and comparison of actual and standard performances,

(c)   There must be a procedure or mechanism for determining the appropriate strategy, method or technique to be applied (or employed) in the process of achieving the predetermined goal. This is tantamount to tactical, and strategic choice and development in planning,

(d)   A specification of basic tasks to be performed perhaps in tabular form or just in brief. This would generate a list (set) of activities to be performed serially, sequentially or concurrently in the planning process,

(e) A determination of the human, material and technological (machines and equipment) requirements for effective and efficient departmental and corporate performance during the planning period. This is tantamount to budgeting and budgetary process in planning, and

(f) A determination of the implementation or execution mechanism that will convert or transform the resultant plan into effect (and positive impact) on the organization. That is, a system of operation which will translate the plan so formulated into goal accomplishment for the organization.

According to *Ashiru (2001)*, planning is a primary function which comes before the manager intelligently can perform any of the other managerial functions. Without a plan in mind, a manager cannot properly and effectively Organize the operations of his department. A manager could not effectively or efficiently staff and supervise his subordinates, determine his goals and techniques, etc. However, with a good plan in place, these functions will be performed appropriately.

Consequently, as *Ashiru (2001)* puts it, planning is a managerial function which must guide every manager or supervisor. By planning, the manager realistically anticipates future problems, analyzes them, anticipates the probable effect of various forces and alternative courses of action, and decides on the courses of action which he believes will lead to desired results. To him, planning basically is mental work. This precedes operations in all departments or sections such that each division operates in a particular manner. For instance rules, regulations and common code of practice may be specified to guide the dos and don'ts of the organization, and this would serve to focus, direct and harmonies the operations throughout the organization.

The use of plans, which serve to specify operations far ahead of time, may be a potent weapon for coordinating operations and tasks in an organization. This allows work schedules to be developed and judiciously followed in consonance with the predestined order of the duties and tasks to be performed. This technique is particularly applied when activities tend to fluctuate and the chance of re-order than tends to be very high. Another technique of achieving coordination in modern organization is through conferences, seminars and similar procedures. In this respect, conferences or meetings are organized mainly for ironing out areas of disparities such as conflicting opinions so as to achieve conformity of organizational norms and code of practice.

This would naturally lead to adherence to rules and regulations and hence leading to coordination in the organization. However, modern managers must be made to realize that too much coordination may lead to dogmatism will would not allow initiatives to be practiced. For instance, there must be a mechanism for improving or adjusting operations to demands of circumstances. Hence, flexibility should be while too encouraged much rigidity should be avoided especially in order for the organization to react a appropriately to challenges of the global modern management.

From our discussion in this section, we would observe that planning is a decision making process. They include situational analysis, evaluation of alternative goals and plans, the evaluation of alternative goals and plans, the selection of goals and plans, implementation, and the introduction of monitoring and control systems. The planning process in modern entrepreneurial organizations should not constraint managers and organization; rather, it should promote flexibility, creativity, and understanding.

Planning takes place at all levels of an organization, strategic planning involves decisions about the organizations long-term goals and strategies. Strategic goals are major targets, or end results, that elate to the long-term survival, value, and the growth of the organization. a strategy is a pattern of actions and resource allocations designed to achieve the organization goals. Tactical planning translates broad strategic goals and plans into goals and plans relevant to specific portions of the organization. Operational planning identifies the specific procedures and processes requires at lower level of the organization.

The goals and plans that emerge from the overall process should be consistent and integrated. During the 1980s, many organizations in Nigeria recognized that their strategic planning activities could not be centralized and detached from the rest of the organization. As a result, strategic management involves managers from all parts of the organization in the formulation and implementation of strategic goals and strategies. Planning becomes an integral part of management in general.

The strategic management process encompasses the basic steps required in any planning process. These include internal assessment, environment analysis, strategy formation, strategy implementation and strategic control. It begins with a review of the current mission, goals and strategies of the organization and a thorough evaluation of internal resources and skills.

The environmental analysis examines all pertinent stakeholder and forecasts key trends in the forces operating outside the organization. Strategy formulation revises the organization's mission, goals and strategies as needed. Current evidence suggests some reversal in the extreme diversification trend of the past 30 years and an increasing focus on the development of competitive advantage at the business level. Strategic managers are beginning to realise that this advantage must be supported by a comprehensive set of internal mechanism for both implementation and control.

2.3   ORGANIZING

As another management function, organizing involves structuring activities, materials and human receives in other to perform a task. Oyedijo (1995:P. 8) states that organizing is the process of grouping activities among people, of assigning task, resources and authority to them and of systematically integrating the divisions into a unified whole. It is a process of dividing work into environment tasks or duties, of grouping such duties in the form of posts, of delegating authority to each post, and of appointing qualified staff to be responsible that the work is carried out as planned.

After the determination of the goals of an enterprise, it is necessary or mandatory to ensure that competent human resources are made available to implement and achieve them. There should be necessary materials; time must be allocated, etc. Even after these are done, each worker must be informed of his responsibilities, obligations and authority within the network. These are made possible through the organizing function of management. Organizing function in modern management is highly imperative because it is through it that various organs and sub-systems of the enterprise are synchronized or integrated together.

The main features of organizing as a managerial function may be exemplified in the following ways:
(a)   Organizing assist in determining what to be done. This involves the task, operation or assignment to be performed as well as goals and objectives to be achieved,
(b)   Organizing assists in the process of resources allocation, allocation of authority, and assignment of responsibility among members of the

organization. It allows individuals, groups and divisions to be aware of what exactly should be done and the rights, powers and obligations attaching to it,

(c)   Organizing helps to spotlight the various mix of resources that are required for optimal performance, how much of these are available within the enterprise and whatever the sources of the remaining outside the enterprise,

(d)   Organizing helps to establish relationships among living and non-living components involved in the normal working mechanism within the enterprise. Organizing functions help to determine the linkage among positions in the enterprise so that members in each group can work optimally collectively as a team. The formation of relationships can be achieved through building or developing certain norm in the form of rules and regulations that encourage team wok within the enterprise.

This in turn allows for the subordinates to work harmoniously in consonance with their leader's dictates under necessary circumstances. Organizing function helps to determine the channels of operations throughout the enterprise and it specifies the degree of authority and autonomy to be given to individuals and departments,

(e)   Organizing functions assists the manager to ensure that the right work is assigned to the right person. It helps to ensure that there is a place for everything and also that there is everything in its place within the network of the organizational mechanism,

(f)   It is through the organizing functions that procedures for accountability and performance strategy are specified thereby classifying who reports to whom in the enterprise,

(g)   It is through the organizing function that structures, processes and procedures within the enterprise are received and where necessary updated.

Meanwhile, it should be noted that in the process of organizing the work and duties in an enterprise, attention should be directed towards grouping activities and operations into meaningful and related sub-units and divisions while avoiding duplication of efforts and too much degree of specialization. The utmost aim of organizing function in modern organizations includes:

(a)   Achievement of understanding and minimization of goals and interests, conflicts as well as reduction or avoidance of confusion, unnecessary rivalry and jealousy among the members of the organization,

(b)   Giving direction and predictable pattern of activities and operations as regards the way tasks are to be performed. This leads to effective and efficient coordination at the work place and job satisfaction among the workers,

(c)   Defining or fixing the responsibilities and obligations attaching to each positions or positions holders as well as removing possible friction and misunderstanding among the staff,

(d)   Avoidance of duplication of efforts and resources in the enterprise,

(e)   Giving recognition to the persons in positions of authority in the enterprise,

(f)   Facilitating and encouraging the practice of delegation of authority and assignment of responsibilities for efficient and effective job performance,

(g)   Achievement of smooth, effective and uninterrupted communication, coordination and a balanced working mechanism for the organization. This manifests itself in the sense that a sound organizing function is the medium through which management directs, synchronies and control the efforts of the whole enterprise thereby making the tasks of modern management a lot less difficult, less liberal and more effective and efficient, and

(h) Facilitating effective and efficient corporate administration of the enterprise and its divisions, encouraging organizational growth and survival as well s stimulating diversification. This would help to improve the operations of the enterprise and its various organizations.

However, if appraised critically, organizing process may be divided into six fundamental phases. These are determining major tasks required which involves identification of the work to be done, designing jobs which involve a detailed analysis of the nature and content of each job and grouping jobs into departments which involve the design of the organization structure where related activities are brought together into departments.

Others are creating authority and reporting relationships involving each individual to be made to know what power he may exercise and who he is responsible to, delegating authority to subordinate managers since managers cannot function alone, some aspects of the work have to be delegated, and coordination which involves provision for synchronization that should be made in the organizational structure. This is made possible horizontally, vertically or even diagonally within the organizational mechanism.

2.4 STAFFING

If all other resources, money, materials machines, methods or techniques and time are available within an enterprise, without the human resources, nothing but eventual failure and subsequently corporate collapse can be made. Hence, staffing is an important function of a manager.

Staffing as a management function implies that the administrator or manager is concerned with the personnel activities of devising an efficient and effective system of staff recruitment, selection, placement, training and development as well as providing favorable conditions of work.

Staffing essentially is the personnel administration function which is especially concerned with the development of a highly motivated, smoothly functioning work force. This function is actually the responsibility of every manager, as suggested by the phrase "Management is People". The fact that staffing is the responsibility of one special department as well as of the entire organization makes the lateral relations between the personnel department and other departments particularly difficult. The features and activities of staffing function can be exemplified by the message conveyed by the Table 1. Traditionally, staffing function at work has been conceived of as a staff function that is secondary or subsidiary to the major line functions of business (such as manufacturing or sales). Line authority is the right to direct subordinates to work.

The role a staffing department plays in a firm depends on the authority granted to it by top management. As a staff department, it advises and helps line managers to recruit, select, train and motivate workers. Finally, decisions about personnel matters, therefore, are made by the line managers. In some firms, however, the personnel manager has functional authority over specified personnel activities. He or she, for example, may make hiring and promotion decisions.

Table 1:   *Responsibilities of the Staffing Function*

	Activities	Objectives	Procedures
1.	Determining human resource needs	To specify the firm's need for applicants	(a) Study company objectives (b) Study organizational chart (c) Forecast human resource (d) Develop management inventory (e) Perform job analysis (f) prepare job description (g) Prepare job specification
2.	Searching for and recruiting applicants	To attract applications to the firm	(a) Specify sources of recruits (b) Recruiting
3.	Selecting applicants for employment	To select the most desirable applicants	(a) Prepare job application form (b) Conduct preliminary interview (c) Administer Selection tests. (d) conduct in-depth interview (e) Conduct background investigation (f) Conduct final Selection Interview (g) Schedule physical examination

4.	Training and developing employees	To build and maintain a productive force	(a) handle job-orientation (b) Perform job-skill training (c) Aid in management development
5.	Appraising employee performance	To rate employee objectively	Develop performance appraisal system
6.	Compensating employee	To develop a fair and equitable system for paying employees	Wage and salary administration
7.	Promoting employees	To reward productive employees in order to utilize the human resources more effectively	Developing promotion policies
8.	Providing personnel services	To build and enhance employee moral	(a) Provide fringe benefits (b) Employee safety and health
9.	Performing other personnel activities	To advise and assists line managers in coping with social personnel problems	(a) Formulate employee discipline policy (b) Retrain employees (c) Share work among employees (d) Counsel employees
10.	Terminating employees	To facilitate the exist of employees from the employer's service	(a) Retirement (b) Resignation (c) Dismissal (d) Discharge

2.5. DIRECTING

Every manager in contemporary organizations, irrespective of nature, scope and objectives, direct the activities of individuals in his department as well as those of the organizations themselves. Again, the real definition of management is "achieving an objective through the efforts of others. If this is true, then, the goal-pursuing person titled, the manager, must direct others.Therefore, directing function is an integral part of the modern manager's job. Directing simply is the continuous task of making decisions, embodying them in specific and general directives or structures, and setting the pace and direction for the enterprise as the leader and *mover* of the enterprise.

Directing function, however, is usually achieved or carried out using organizational rules, regulations, procedures and policies. Consequently, without the directive function, an organization will have no focus, and individuals and groups in an enterprise will just be gambling perhaps working at cross-purposes. Directing therefore is an integral part of leadership task in modern corporate management and administration.

2.6   REPORTING

Whatever is the outcome of a managerial process, whether favorable or otherwise, must be communicated to the person or group of persons who are to make the final decision. By this, a manager or administrator has to report his performance and the basis of evaluation of the process. Consequently, reporting is a chief function of management. *Augustus Adebayo (1995, P. 34)* agreed that reporting is the all-important function of keeping those to whom the administrator is responsible informed of what is going on, while at the same time the administrator or chief executive keeps himself and his subordinates informed through reporting, the reporting process. Consequently, reporting is the managerial process through which all members of an enterprise are made familiar with the processes, procedures and operations of the organization.

2.7   BUDGETING

Budgeting as a managerial function is the overall hallmark of managerial position within an enterprise. Since finance and administration or management are inseparable, every manager or executive officer's act has its financial implications. Hence, the management of finance is one of the firs, and one of the inescapable, responsibilities of the modern mangers especially as budgetary allocations are concerned. To various departments such as personnel, production, marketing, research and development, etc. a manager who fails in this case is not worth calling manager at all!

2.8   LEADING

Leading is the act of influencing the Behavior of subordinate in such a way that they are persuaded to be willing followers. Actually, leading and directing combine to form what is called leadership. Leadership is the will to dominate the proceeding in which one finds himself in such away that subordinate are persuaded or encouraged to be willing followers. Oyedijo (1995:p.15) was of the opinion that leadership is the management task that is concerned with how to influence the Behavior of subordinates.

In practical terms, everyone who has some people, as his subjects, under his control is a leader. For instance, the governor of a state, the director general in a government ministry, the vice chancellor of a university, the Head of department in a polytechnic, the production manager in a manufacturing company, the marketing or finance controller in a conglomerate, the supervisor or foreman in a pharmaceutical firm, etc, are all leaders. Consequence, every manager, administrator, supervisor, foreman, etc, is expected to perform one form or the other of leadership roles. As a result, the principal responsibilities of a dynamic leader include the following

(a)   To identify, specify or formulate suitable aims and objectives which his subjects (or subordinates) should strive to achieve, and also to provide them with focus or direction towards the attainment of the goals,

(b)   To specify acceptable standards or codes of operational Behavior for his subordinates and to encourage good working habits while leading them by example,

(c)   To provide stimuli or impetus in order to motivate (stimulate) his subordinates to always want to put in their best into the work processes. This would serve as catalyst for good performance and encourage their innovation, resourcefulness and adaptability, by this, the subordinates would feel that their contributions are worthwhile and very significant,

(d)   To demonstrate to his subordinates their roles towards corporate goals accomplishment, indicating and suggesting clearly what is expected of them without them being driven,

(e)   To ensure that the tasks, activities and efforts of the individuals, groups and divisions in the organization are integrated or harmonized to resolve goal conflicts and other forms of unnecessary frictions, rivalry or competitions at the work place. This would naturally encourage *espirit de corps* (the spirit of solidarity) in the organization,

(f)   To determine who should do what job. This implies to select the right employee for the right job. That is, matching persons with jobs at the workplace,

(g)   To assist his subordinates in their career choice, development and actualization. This can be done by developing, encouraging and supporting them through appropriate training and development programs. By implication, a good leader should help his subjects to improve their knowledge, skills, attitudes and Behavior so that they can be more innovative, adaptive and resourceful,

(h)   To be committed and dedicated to resolving grievances, conflicts or differences among various categories of staff in the organization. This is tantamount to reconciling contradictory positions and opposing courses of actions in the organization. This, however, can be done through reconciling the needs and wants of individuals and groups in the system and hence resolving their goals conflicts,

(i)   To be ready and willing to present his subordinates demands and problems to top management and other relevant authorities for appropriate actions,

(j)   To represent and defend, where necessary, the interest of his subordinates at the appropriate levels of management especially in time of appraisal, promotion etc, and

(k)   To represent individuals, divisions, departments, etc. within the area of his jurisdiction formally at various ceremonies and occasions.

In the mean time, it must be crystal clear here that leadership Behavior is a function of many variables. These factors include the personality of the leader, his education, training and development, the nature of work and working environment, time and situation, etc. It is also dependent upon the social, economic, political and technological environment prevailing at the moment. Hence, there are various leadership styles such as democratic, autocratic, benevolent and situational styles. However, the most common leadership styles in the Nigerian society are:

(a) *Autocratic Leadership*: Autocratic leadership reflects a narrow span of management, tight supervision and a high degree of centralization (task-oriented). Managers who utilize this style tend to be repressive and hold communication other than that which is absolutely necessary for doing the job. Autocratic leaders unilaterally make decisions, vesting little, if any, and participative rights in the group. This style is *demotivating* because it tends to minimize the degree of involvement of groups and individuals in the job decisions-making process.

(b) *Democratic Leadership*: Democratic leadership (employee-centered) emphasizes a non-pressure orientation that maximizes group and individual participation in the decision- making process. As a motivating factor, a free flow of communication is encouraged among all members of a department so that a climate of understanding can be built on a foundation of honesty and trust. The democratic style is fully consistent with a decentralized organization and a wide span of management.

(c) *Free Rein*: Under the free rein, or *laissez-fairs* style of leadership, the organizational climates such that people, assumed to be self-motivated, do their jobs virtually without much supervision. However leader is available in a consultative capacity to help if requested. The type of leadership style is motivational to employees.

However, autocratic leadership style can be effectively utilized in motivating workers in certain circumstances. This follows that effective influence means better motivation of workers which requires matching leadership style with the situation.

2.9 FORECASTING

An important function of management, which precedes and very closely related to, planning is forecasting. Forecasting is actually the mechanism through which past and present events and experiences are brought together through a thorough analysis of qualitative and quantitative data (facts, figures and evidences). Such a thorough analysis, as in this case, naturally leads to prediction, projection and predetermination of anticipated future developments paving way for planning functions. However, the ultimate aims of forecasting in management include the following:

(a)   To identify and clarify anticipated problems, opportunities and even weaknesses of the organization,

(b)   To predict, project or estimate the future character and trend of future performance and constraints of the organization,

(c)   To predict and think over setting realistic goals and outputs of the organization in concrete terms,

(d)   To estimate trends, through trends analysis and to establish possible programs of action for the organization,

(e)   To forecast and predict the organizational resources such as men, money, materials, machine, methods and time (5Ms + T) needed to implement successfully the corporate and departmental plans,

(f)   To assist the manager or administrator to anticipate and prepare for alternative courses of action, control and results, and

(g)   To anticipate and prepare to capture the likely dysfunctional effect of a faulty plan before, during and even after its implementation.

Forecasting actually pertains to predicting in advance, visualizing and evaluating the possible problems and opportunities that may be open to the organization in future: say, next year, five years or ten years time. The reality of forecasting would definitely affect organizational planning processes and hence the plans themselves. If forecasting and predictions are carefully made about the organizational performance, the chances are that the organizational plans would be successful and vice versa.

2.10 MOTIVATING

Motivation is the management task of providing impetus or stimulus to a person for him to respond positively toward an intended or predetermined performance. It is a stage of encouragement to perform a specified task or activity. *Oyedijo (1995:P.2)* defines motivation as "the act of influencing a person to do something or behave in a particular way by providing an incentive with which he could satisfy his desire or need".

By implication we would observe that motivation implies to provide the person with an incentive, an urge or a drive, to propel and incite the person so that he can direct his responses towards a valued goal, want or need. Consequently, motivating organizational employees involves encouraging them through various forms of incentives in such a way that they perform willingly certain activities or operations leading to efficiency and effectiveness in goals accomplishment in their respective organizations.

2.11 COMMUNICATING

Communication, as a management function is the process of creating, communicating and interpreting ideas, facts, opinions and feelings about work performance, organizational effectiveness and efficiency as well as goals attainment in organization. It is through communication that modern managers carry out their planning, organizing and control functions. Hence, a manager or an administrator must be an effective communicator. Otherwise, he will not be able to carry out his managerial duties and responsibilities through issuing orders, directives, instructions and the likes. These he usually does through internal memoranda, minutes of meetings, notices, company manuals, and others. Hence, communication is an integral aspect of modern management functions.

REVISION QUESTIONS

1. What is Management? Enumerate and explain in details the main functions that are likely to be performed by a manager in one of the large scale industrial organizations in your country.

2. What is *personnel administration*? Explain with possible illustrations, the chief personnel functions in a named establishment in your locality.

3. Explain the following terms pointing out clearly the main activities or tasks involved in each of them:
   (a) Leadership,
   (b) Motivation,
   (c) Planning,
   (d) Decision making, and
   (e) Communication.
   Which of the above management functions would you consider the most important and why?

CHAPTER THREE

ORGANIZATION IN MODERN MANAGEMENT

Things to Consider:
* Nature of Organization.
* Classification of Organizations.
* Forms of Organizations.
* Organization Structure.
* Characteristics of a Good Organization Structure.
* Forms of Organization Structure.
* Organizational Charts.
* Centralization and Decentralization.
* Forms of Organization
* Line and Staff Organizations.

3.1   NATURE OF ORGANIZATION

The activities of any enterprise can be divided into a number of different types of work or jobs. In a small business, the owner, perhaps assisted by one or more of his relatives or staffs, will do all the work necessary to keep the business running: ordering goods for sale, storing goods, selling to customers, collecting payments, banking, keeping Accounts records and Books of Account, paying bills, and so on.

As the business grows, different people will be made responsible for different jobs or groups of related jobs. For example, one person may be made responsible for ordering stocks of goods, looking after them in the store, and issuing them when they are needed. Another person may be made responsible for all matters concerning money; paying it into the Bank, keeping accounts records and books, paying bills, preparing sales documents, and so on. Another person may be made responsible for all matters concerning the sales made by the business.

As the business continues to grow, each of the people mentioned will probably need one or more assistants, and so gradually, a "Stores Section", an "Accounts Section", a "Sale Section" and other "Sections" will come into being. The staff in each Section will still be responsible for a number of related jobs, but it is likely that as time progresses, different people in the Section will *specialize* in certain jobs; that is, in the Accounts Section, one person may be responsible for preparing all the sales documents needed (a Leger Clerk), another for collecting, safeguarding and banking all money received by the business (the Cashier), another for keeping the Accounts Books (the Bookkeeper) and each of these *specialists* may even have assistants.

If the enterprise continues to expand, and more and more staffs have to be employed, each Section will grow into a "Department" comprising a number of Sections. For example, the Finance Department would have a ledger or customer's Accounts Section to prepare all the sales documents necessary and to collect payment when it is due; a Cashiers Section to deal with all the business money, a Book Keeping Section to keep the books of the business, a Payments Section to check and pay all bills including salaries; and so on. The Department would be in the charge of the Chief Accountant, who would thus be a Departmental Manager, and each Section would have its own Section Manager, with different designations: the Head Bookkeeper, the Chef Cashier, etc. There would also be more junior managers, like Cashiers and Assistant Cashiers, and so on.

In many modern organizations, there are usually a number of *divisions*. Each Division will be made up of a Department, and each of these Departments will be made up of a number of sections.

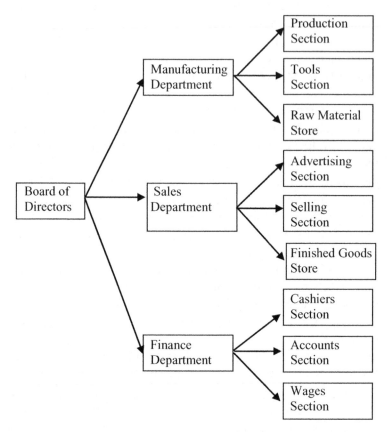

Fig. 6: A Horizontal View of a Business Organization

Enterprise becomes the more complex its organization has to be. The basic organization of a business, for example, can be laid out in a diagrammatic form whether horizontally, vertically or in circular form.

However, many people find the horizontal type easier to understand. Each business will, however, evolve its own organization, and some businesses, because of their size, will need far more complex diagrams to show how they are organized. Meanwhile, it is important to remember that each undertaking will be organized to suit its individual requirements. Although there are *basic* types of organization, like the one which we have shown in our diagrams; they will be adapted by different organizations according to their needs. Even two organizations dealing with the same or similar items may be organized differently.

It should also be remembered that from time to time a business may have to alter some or all the parts of its entire organizational structure because of changes in the work it does or other factors. Once the basic organizational mechanism has been laid down in the form of a diagram, it can be expanded into what is called an organization chart; to show the responsibilities of the various persons who work within the system. By implication, immediately the vision, mission and goal of an organization have been established, it becomes necessary to create an avenue which ensures that competent hands are available to pursue and implement them.
Appropriate human and non-human resources are needed as inputs into the mechanism in order to implement the policies and strategies, and also to realize the organizational goals; hence, all these should be provided. Even after these are made ready, each and every one of the participants should know the roles expected of him or her within the arrangement, and the relationship of his position and responsibilities along the organizational hierarchy; this phenomenon necessitates the study of organizations in the contemporary industrial society.

To a layman on the street, organization means *putting things together in certain order*. Technically speaking, however, the concept of organization may be considered from two distinct approaches as can be observed. The first is to perceive an organization as a structure, or a network of specified relationships among given individuals or groups. An alternative to this is to consider an organization concept as a process or as an executive function in which the dynamic of organization changes and growth are central or pivotal.

The two aforementioned concepts are of paramount use in the study of theory and practice of management. For instance, the structural concepts enables both the managers and administrators alike to observe, describe, explain and classify the principal features of the anatomy of organizations and to recognize the differences and similarities (variations) between one organization and the other while the concept of Organization as a process facilitates the discernment of the various types of the executive Behavior that lead to structural changes in the organization.

It must be observed that an organization as an entity or *person at law* exists because one or more individuals cannot perform a job-task themselves. This idea is supported by *McFarland's* view that *organization refers to a particular company or group of persons working together*, towards achieving a common objective. As have been said earlier, organization may be considered as one of the management functions which involves structuring and re-structuring activities, operations, materials, personnel's and positions to perform assigned managerial functions.

Organization is the mechanism through which the flow of operations, materials and employees are arranged in order to effectively and efficiently realize predetermined goals with minimum inputs consumption. It can also be considered as a mechanism for grouping and harmonizing operations among people, assigning responsibilities and delegating authority to them, and systematically integrating the various segments (or divisions) of the organization into a unified whole consequently, organization can be considered as the process of identifying, clarifying, grouping, synchronizing and harmonizing the operations to be carried into effect, assigning responsibilities and delegating authority necessary to perform the operations, and establishing various relationships required in order for the people to operate harmoniously towards the accomplishment of corporate goals. By implication, organization simply means arrangement of parts in such a way as to get a complete, coherent, unified and effective whole.

Urwick in his concepts of organization in a *British Institute of Management* proceedings pamphlet described *an organization as a process consisting of divisions of all the activities necessary for any purpose. These divisions, according to him, involves the arrangement of all the activities into growths, each group is assigned to an individual or a group of persons acting in a corporate capacity as a position or post. Every such position carries responsibility for the supervision of others.* From this discussion, it would be crystal clear that organizations define and illuminate the part which an individual in an undertaking is expected to play and the place of such an individual among other places in the system.

However, to make it more general, *an organization may be defined in terms of corporate entity concept. In this respect, an organization is any institution or production establishment that is formally set up for the attainment of well defined predetermined goals.* With this definition, one would also be able to include a university, a ministry in the public sector, a political party, a manufacturing company, banking or other services delivering companies, etc in the bracket of organizations; since each of these was established to achieve identified goals. Again, a religions movement like the Muslim Association of Nigeria, Nigerian Muslim Students Society, etc, would be regarded as organizations as they were established to inculcate moral values in their members and the society.

The above conception of organization which appears to be at variance with *Urwick's* perspective is, however, necessary because *Urwick* and his contemporaries who share his perspective considered an organization in a narrow sense as being synonymous with management or as one of the management functions. However, the examination, explanation and description of the aspect of the general management which deals with the structuring of work organizations can be said to be in its growing or developing stage in Nigeria under what is called organizational reengineering, restructuring or repositioning. Hitherto, the contributors in this sphere of knowledge include the classical theorists such as *Henry Fayol, Urwick* and *E. F. L Brech*. Also, it was the source of inspiration for *Max Weber's* theory of bureaucracy and it is now a burning issue for, and features of, the contemporary theorists of complex organizations: the contingency school who view organizations from various perspectives

.   Meanwhile, organization as a managerial process has six fundamental stages or phases. These are:

(a)   Iden*tification of tasks to be performed*. This involves determination of the operations that is needed to be done,

(b)   *Job designing*. This involves detailed and objective analysis, investigation, and design of the full implication of each job task or activity,

(c)   *Grouping the organizational activities and operations* into related groups and putting them into departments or divisions. That is, related operations are grouped together and put into departments,

(d)   *Development of authority and reporting mechanism* in which case each individual is allowed to know what power, authority and responsibility he has and to whom does he report in the organization,

(e)   *Delegation of authority and assignment of responsibilities* to subordinate officers. Because of the fact that individual managers cannot perform all duties and activities alone, they have to delegate some of them to their subordinate officers while taking full responsibility for their performance, and

(f)   *Coordination and integration.* This has to be done in such a way that all efforts are focused, directed and channeled towards the attainment of organizational goals,

3.2   CLASSIFICATION OF ORGANIZATIONS

Despite the fact hat organization as management function, is a process (a set of activities), an organization as a corporate entity is a consciously established and coordinated social unit, composed of two or more individuals, that operates on relatively permanent basis in order to accomplish a goal or a set of objectives. In this case, there are various types or classes of organization depending on certain criteria. This classification or distinction however becomes highly imperative in order to reveal the nature of the groups and peculiar characteristic of various organizations. The distinction is also necessary in order to reveal the divergences and similarities in the structure, composition and objectives of various organizations.

Meanwhile, the man criteria to distinguish between the various classes of organizations in the modern industrial society are ownership, purpose or goal of the organization, its size, its contribution to the society, prime beneficiary, membership, industrial affiliation, nature of authority, market orientation as well as the management principles and practice of the corporation. Let us now consider the various possibilities as contained in the following table:

Table .2: Classification of Organizations

CRITERIA	COMMON CLASSIFICATION	EXAMPLES
Ownership	Private organizations comprising all privately owned organizations	- Sole Proprietorship - Partnership - Limited liability Companies
	Public organizations which are composed of all public corporations and extra-ministerial organizations. Also included are other organizations established jointly by both private and public sector. Such companies are controlled financed and managed by or on behalf of the government	
Purpose or Objective	Profit making organizations. These are organizations whose main objectives are profit maximization	- Sole Proprietorships - Limited Liability Companies -. Other business enterprises both in the public and private sectors
	Non-profit oriented organizations. These organizations have welfares orientation, and they are usually set up by government for the upgrading and improving the welfare of the masses.	-
Size of the organization	Small Scale Organizations	- Sole traders. - Partnership

	Medium Scale Organizations	- private Limited Liability Companies - Public Limited Liability Companies
	Large scale organizations	- public Limited Liability Companies -Public Corporations
Contribution to society	Political organizations having the machinery of government.	- political parties, - pressure groups and non-governmental organizations
	Religious organizations whose principal objectives to produce a well mannered and spiritually advanced society of a high moral value citizens	
	Academic and professional organizations	- Universities, Colleges and Schools - Professional Organizations like the Institute of certified management scientist, chartered institute of administration, institute of cost and executive accountant, institute of corporate affairs management, , etc

	Business and economic organizations	Manufacturing and services Companies
Beneficiary	Common weal organization	
	Service Organizations	- National Television Authority Federal and State Ratio/Broadcasting Corporations Hospitals Insurance Companies, Barbing and Tailor Organizations, etc.
	Mutual Benefits Organizations	- Political Parties, Clubs and Societies such as Cooperative Societies
Memberships	Voluntary organizations	Red Cross
	Industrial firms which admits only the employees and employer of a particular industry	-A Manufacturing Company - A Banking Company

From Table 2, one would observe that using the size as the criterion for classifying organizations, three classes have been identified. These needs to be clarified because what is a small, medium or large scale organization is a function of many factors such as the capital bases of the company, scope of operation, risks involved in setting up and running the organization, the nature and level of technology being employed, the extent of the market share of the company, as well as the personal ability of the owners or operators. Such personal traits of the operators include technical know-how, managerial acumen, as well as the popularity and influence of those who are behind such an organization.

For instance, P. Z industries Plc. may be considered as a large organization if the company dominates the market for detergents in Nigeria or if those who constitute its Board of Directors are mostly the economic powers in the country. However, it should be made clear at this juncture that there is no hard and fast (water-tight) line of demarcation as to which group should an organization belongs. As we can observe from the presentation in Table 3.21, an organization may be included in more than one category or class depending on what criterion becomes operational, individual judgment, reasoning and perception.

3.3   FORMS OF ORGANIZATIONS

Apart from classifying modern organizations in terms of their objectives, membership, size, etc, as we have done in Table 3.21, organizations may also be categorized on the basis of the forms which they take by mere inspection. In this case, it is apparently clear that contemporary organizations may be classified again into strictly formal organizations, spontaneous growth organizations and hybrid organizations. This fundamental division of contemporary organizations becomes inevitable because of the different approaches found towards the study of these organizations. Hence, attempts have been made to classify the organizational styles here on the basis of the main characteristic features as in the following sub-sections.

3.3.1   STRICTLY FORMAL ORGANIZATION

The strictly formal organizations refers to planned, coordination and integration of organizational operations performed by people for the achievement of common predetermined explicit goals as well as the relationships within the organization on the basis of rules, and procedures, through a hierarchy of authority and responsibility.

Formal organization may also refers to the arrangement of divisions, individuals with predetermined duties and hierarchical stable structure and defined authority towards the accomplishment of certain corporate objectives such as specialization and division of labor for better performance, to allow peace and progress to prevail, establishment of efficient and logical patterns among divisions and individuals, and to coordinate and integrate specialists for the attainment of organizational goals.

Allen Louis agreed that formal organization is the organizational pattern as defined by management or the pattern of division of tasks and power among the organizational positions, and the rules expected to guide the Behavior of the participants as defined by management. To him, the formal organization is a system of well-defined jobs, each bearing a definite measure of authority, responsibility and accountability, the whole consciously designed to enable the people of the enterprise to work most effectively together in accomplishing their objectives.

Again, *Kinard (1988: P. 292)* was of the opinion that every formal organization is characterized by well-defined authority-reporting relationship, job titles, policies and procedures, specific job duties and a host of other factors necessary to accomplish its respective goals. Typically, according to him, the formal structure is represented by a printed chart that appears in organizational manuals and other formal company documents. In their study, *"The Management of Innovation"*, *Tom Burns and G. M Stalker* introduced the term *"mechanic"* to describe the formal type of organization. They noted that such a style would be the most suitable for stable conditions whereas an organic organization would normally adopts a more flexible approach.

When change is very slow, the formal type of organization has much to offer, especially when adapted to suit specific circumstances. For example, the unity of command may be varied under specific circumstances. Undoubtedly, the formal style of organization shows quite clearly who is responsible for each job area. It should however lead to clear commands being given and the avoidance of misunderstandings. The main objection of the styles of organization is its possible rigidity, if truly mechanistic; the structure is regarded as being more important than the people within the business.

Meanwhile, it is worthwhile at this point to recognize the fundamental characteristics of strictly formal organizations as follows:

(a)   In formal organizations, strict rules are followed;

(b)   Organization charts depict reality;

(c)   Each person knows his responsibilities which is shown in job description;

(d)   Strict channels of communication are followed;

(e)   No changes can be made in responsibilities without proper planning and authorization;

(f)   The unity of command is followed without departure;

(g)   Standards of performance are established and jealously followed;

(h)   Well-defined structure of tasks and responsibilities which is clearly observable; a formal organization is easily recognized in terms of its formalized leadership, follower and the schedules of operations;

(i)   Well-defined set of individual rights and responsibilities;

(j)   There is a kind of relatively permanent organization that is supported by organizational growth and development;

(k)   Such an organization has been formally established and structured for the attainment of predetermined objectives through the performance of certain operations under a formal leader.

3.3.2 SPONTANEOUS GROWTH ORGANIZATIONS

Organizations in this category are also known as informal organizations, and they are usually formed or developed as a result of social relations among members of an organization, both employees and employers. The Behavior, responsiveness and relationships that exist among such organizational members are not formalized that is, they are not based on formal rules, regulations and procedures. In actual fact spontaneous growth organizations usually spring up among the organizational members in the course of their daily operations. This is what *Keith Davis* referred to as network of personal and social relations that is not established or required by the formal organization but arising spontaneously as people associate with one another.

Oyedijo   (1995:P.124) said that informal organizations (groups) are collectively known as bureaucracy's other face not established by the management of the company. They are not easily identifiable because an organizational chart cannot be drawn to show their structure and hierarchy of positions since their structure are not rigid. He, however agrees that informal organizations exist in all formal organizations although they do not have a permanent character in terms of leadership and membership. Typical instances of spontaneous growth organizations also known as *informal groups* are all associations or unions of employees whose membership are optional, and that are not established or formed for a particular predetermined goal other than to serve the peculiar interests of their members.

However, irrespective of their objectives, membership and other peculiar characteristics, the informal organizations usually spring up through the interactions and sentiments among organizational members; as a result of their psychological and social needs and also the development of groups within their own relationships and mode of Behavior, not withstanding those defined within the formal set up.

Ariyo (2001) identified four major areas of differences between formal and informal organizations as follows:

(a) *Interpersonal Relations*: That is, relationships in a strictly formal organization among their members are pre-described whereas in a spontaneous growth organizations, relationships are largely dependent upon the needs of the people,

(b) *Leadership:* Leaders of the strictly formal organizations are designated whereas, leaders of informal organizations usually emerge out of interactions and sentiments,

(c) *Behavioral Control*: Strictly formal organizations control employees' Behavior through rewards and punishments while informal organizations control their members through pressure, and

(d) *Dependence*: Subordinates are more dependents in formal organization than are members of spontaneous growth organizations because of the formal leaders' ability to reward and punish their members.

However, it should be realized that spontaneous growth organizations style attempts to give prominence to the informal working groups, regarded by many industrial sociologists as the most important aspect of management. They argue that the formal structure is simply a representation of the ideal which is rarely achieved. Accordingly, a natural organization is regarded as being more acceptable, being based upon what is actually occurring. Unfortunately, whist there is no doubt that the informal group is important and the grapevine is often a vital channel of communication, this does not necessarily imply that the best type of organization is one which grows without guidance or plan. Indeed, it can be argued that the setting up of profit centres and cost centres would be virtually impossible unless there is a formal organization.

Possibly, with the small to medium size business, the spontaneous growth organization structure can work quite well. Even so, there must still be guidance on what the business is trying to achieve and how is it to be done: often too formal a structure can restrict managers and stifle initiatives; without recognition of a positive organization, there are bound to be problems. Occasionally, there are stories of chief executives with excessive powers who carry out personal policies without regard for the well-being of the organization as a whole whilst acknowledging inevitable bureaucracy which accompanies control. Provided this can be maintained with the appropriate degree of flexibility, the best approach will usually be the setting up of a formal organization, but with provision for meetings and other means of exchanging ideas and opinions.

According to *Ariyo (2001)*, it would, however, be wrong for managers to feel that the formal and informal organizations are separate and distinct from each other. They usually cut across formal organizations boundaries. He maintains that informal organizations can make or mar formal structures depending on the type of relationship and group values that develop and operate. He also asserts that it is possible for an informal group to be the same as formal group in an organization or just a part of the formal group. Hence, he concludes that the informal organization has an important influence on the morale, motivation, job satisfaction and performance of managers and their employees.

Meanwhile, it should be understood that the spontaneous growth organizations have important roles to play in modern organizations; the prominent ones among these are as follows:

(a) They enable the social, psychological and sentimental needs of their members such as recognition, group acceptance and other needs to be satisfied,

(b) They bring about a sense of belonging and identification to their members thereby making the work place quite interesting and enjoyable,

(c) They allow the acceptable and unacceptable Behavior to be formed among their members through compliance to group norms and code of practice and also through socialization of their members,

(d) They give their members sympathetic hearing and support in times of needs especially when the later experience any form of difficulty on the job,

(e) They assist their members to meet personal economic, social and psychological needs. Such as financial support, advice and encouragement as may be appropriate from time to time,

(f) They represent additional channel of communication especially through provision of soft (or informal) information among the group members,

(g) They may influence formal decisions as much as they may influence the implementation of acceptable informal formal decisions, and

(h) They can support the attainment of corporate goals through assistance which they sometimes give to managers who may experience difficulties in certain aspect of their jobs.

However, despite all these contributions which spontaneous growth organizations could make to assist their organizations successful, they can also serve as stopping blocks to their organizations in certain circumstances. For instance, informal groups can encourage rumor mongering and information distortion. They can also encourage ferocious resistance to changes especially if such changes would affect their group norms adversely. Finally, the potency of informal groups' power and their group cohesiveness sometimes serve as deterrent factors imitating against the attainment of the goals of the strictly formal organizations.

3.3.3   HYBRID FORM OF ORGANIZATIONS

A number of approaches, which may be regarded as styles in their own right or simply modifications of the strictly formal organizations and the spontaneous growth organizations are also in existence in the contemporary organizations. These are called the hybrid forms of organizations. The common examples in this respect are as follows:

(a)   *Centralization*:   This means that all authority stems from the Head Office, and all the remaining parts of an organization must receive instructions from that source being given little or no power themselves,

(b)   *Decentralization*: This break up an organization into manageable units such as profit or cost centres, thereby giving autonomy with the minimum of control from the centre. In recent times this approach has found favor in most organizations. It cuts down bureaucracy and responsibility,

(c)   *Participation*:   This attempt to involve workers and managers in the decision making processes of the organization. The main impact on organization is through consultative committees and even by having workers-directors, although this concept is far from being clear cut or generally acceptable,

(d)   *Making full use of specialists*:   In this case, specialists such as accountants, personnel managers, marketing managers and production managers are fully involved in organizational management. This particular concept has long been

accepted from the times of Adam Smith, F. W.
Taylor and others. However, one modern management
philosopher who does not agree entirely with the
approach is *Peter Drucker* who feels that
specialization may be carried too far. Certainly, if
taken to the point where a worker carries out a
specific operations which is repetitive, there may
be monotony and there will be much stress in the
operation,

(e)   *Autocratic and Total Control*: Autocratic and total
control of the means, objects and implements of
producing and selling the product is an extreme
mechanism but it may operate quite successfully.
Although apparently opposed to modern ideas on
participation,, the approach is not as unusual as if it
might be supposed. Many production control
mechanisms rely upon strict planning and control
without which a high degree of success would not
be easily achieved; if it would be achieved at all.

3.4   ORGANIZATION STRUCTURE

The structure of an organization can be best
explained in terms of the skeletal analogy that enables an
organization to "stand erect"! Without the structure of
events, positions and activities demarcating individual's
responsibility area, the organization will not "stand". The
structure of an organization, therefore, implies the pattern or
network of relationship among the various position and the
position holders. It shows the ways each position holder
relates to others vertically, horizontally and even diagonally
as it often happens when a manager tries to intervene in
matters at lower levels outside his own department or
section.

Any organization, whether formal or otherwise, has
inherent in it, a form of structure. In the case of the formal

organizations, the structure is clearly and systematically defined arising from the planning efforts of top management. However, this does not obviate the fact that occasionally, some elements of formal structure may spring up spontaneously. Despite the efforts of the management in discouraging formation of informal structures as they tend to disrupt or jeopardize the efforts of the management, the structures often develop out of the needs of informal groups members such as norms, beliefs and group acceptance.

Typically, key executives in every organization normally decide the basic patterns or structures that they feel will enhance effective and efficient performance of their daily duties. That is, it is the top management that decides the particular structure to be adopted in particular organizations as structure should follow the pattern of corporate strategy of the organization.

> "...key executives in every organization normally decide the basic patterns or structures that they feel will enhance effective and efficient performance of their daily duties"

According to *Lawrence and Lorsch* (two Harvard researchers), "most organizations are in a state of tension as a result of the need to be both differentiated and integrated". Once an organization has grown beyond the point when the owners can exercise direct control, some degree of differentiation or specification becomes inevitable.

Hence, most organizations have to face up to a member of crucial issues that will best sustain the success of the enterprise. Some of the most frequent issues in this respect are:

(a) To what extent should we encourage the specialization of roles?

(b)   What degree of standardization should be imposed on Behavior and methods, or put in another way, what degree of discretion should be allowed to individual job holder?

(c)   How much formality should be encouraged?

(d)   How many levels of authority should we establish?

(e)   To what extent should decision making be centralized or decentralized?

There is no one perfect answer to any of these questions, but there are a number of possible options, which, taken together, can produce an optimum design for an organization. From the above analysis, it can be concluded that an organization structure or *organogram* is the way and manner in which the functions, tasks, responsibilities or activities in an organization are divided, shared or grouped. This division of work and responsibility assignment also includes the way and manner power, authority and influence are shared, assigned or allocated among various individuals and groups in the organization, as well as the various relationships within the whole system. That is, the *organogram* of an organization shows the formalized relationships and position networks of the organization among the employees in carrying out of their respective duties individually and collectively.

3.5   CHARACTERISTICS OF A GOOD ORGANIZATION STRUCTURE

There are certain critical conditions which a good organization structure must satisfy and these may also be referred to as the main features or characteristics of the modern organizational organograms. *Oyedijo (1995, P. 79 - 82)* provides a list of these features as follows:

(a)   *Clarify of goals and duties.* This implies that within a good organization system, corporate and individual objectives must be clearly formulated and stated, and also the means and manner of achieving them must be clearly stated.

(b) *Purposive Activity*: All efforts in the organization must be focused, directed or channeled toward the accomplishment of the predetermined individual, department and corporate goals,

(c) *Individual Consideration*: Individual and divisional differences must be thoroughly considered when decisions are being made as to jobs, tasks, activities or responsibilities or assignment,

(d) *Similarity of Duties*: That is related activities or operations must be grouped together and put under a common divisions or department,

(e) *Unity of Command*: This implies that each member of the organization must respond, and be made responsible, to one person on one particular issue at a time in the system,

(f) *Evaluation Criteria* : There must be a predetermined standard against which individual and group performances are measured so as to determine operational efficiency or productivity at an appropriate time,

(g) *Span of Control*: This implies that the number of subordinates who should be in a department under an executive officer must be limited to those the executive officer can effectively monitor and control for the betterment of the corporate performance. In this case, the optimum number is usually between 4 and 6 subordinates,

(h) *Adequate Resources*: This implies that each individual or division must be provided with adequate mental, physical and material resources to carry out his/its assigned duties or responsibilities,

(i) *Commensurate Authority*: This implies that it is not enough to assign responsibilities among individuals and departments, it is also important to delegate appropriate and adequate authority to those who will perform the tasks for their effective performance,

(j)   *Possibility of Coordination*:   Although each individual and group have a specific function or a list of related activities to perform, there must be a way by which the activities of all individuals and departments would be coordinate and integrated in the organization,

(k)   *Flexibility in Operations*: Every organization should be flexible enough in such a way that unanticipated changes are accommodated. This would not allow the organization to suffer from any form of adjustment lag,

(l)   *Consultation and Participation*: This implies that every organization structure must encourage (or give room for) consultation among the organizational members and their participation in decision-making processes,

(m) *Specialization*: This implies that specialization must be allowed as much as possible among the organizational members so that they do not become jack of all trades, master of none,

(n)   *Delegation:* This implies that operations and activities must be well assigned, appropriate authority must be delegated for their effective performance while adequate allowance must also be provided for as safeguards for management control,

(o)   *Differentiation*: This implies that within the structure, line and staff functions and responsibilities must be well differentiated and techniques of inter-divisional communication clearly determined, and

(p)   *Clear Line of Communication*: This means that there should be a clear, short and direct line of communication between a job holder and his superior officer who is responsible for the supervision of the work. In addition, there must be clear line of authority and of information among position holders in the organization. This guide against conflict, friction and unnecessary rivalries among the staff.

3.6 FORMS OF ORGANIZATION STRUCTURE

Although there are various alternative forms which an organization structure can take, most organizations structures are based on criteria such as the company products, location of factory plants, function being performed in each divisions or departments of the organization. However, the choice of criteria to use is dependent upon the choice of management. Hence, the common structures in modern organizations are:
(a)   Functional Organization Structure,
(b)   Product-based Organization Structure,
(c)   Regional or Geographical-based organization structure, and
(d)   Market or Customer Oriented Structure.

3.7.1   Functional Organization Structure

This approach is the system in use if an organization is structured on the basis of the basic managerial functions such as production, marketing, financial or accounts, and personnel functions. This approach is also known as lateral structure in which each functional division is headed by an expert and the staffs there perform certain kind of job or operations day-in, day-out. This type of functional arrangement is suitable where an organization operates in a small and unique market, where there is a limited number of product, where the scope of operation is limited to a single geographical location, and where the organization is some how small,

Meanwhile, the major merits of this type of arrangement are:

(a)   The structural arrangement is simple to determine, understand and operate. This is because there is only one line of authority and clear channel of communication which are usually short and do not available at cross-purposes,

(b)   Functional organization structure gives room for easy coordination, harmonization and integration of the operations of various divisions in an organization owning to the fact that related activities are usually grouped together and put under the control of an expert as a functional department,

(c)   The task and duties of individuals in the organization are well-defined, concentrated and differentiated from those of another person. This encourages division of labor and specialization among the staff in the organization,

(d)   A functional organization structure helps to drastically reduce the problems arising from top management control and coordination as responsibilities for goals achievement are clearly defined and put directly under the manager in each functional division,

(e)   There is uniformity in operations and conformity to standards since operations can be easily standardized and formalized. Again, each expert is placed directly in a division where he can perform optimally,

(f)   A functional arrangement ensures that there is adequate representation of each vital functional division in top management deliberations,

(g)   The arrangement helps to reduce or even eliminate duplication and overlap of executive staff and experts as well as scarce resources in the organization,

(h)   Functional arrangement allows for judicial use of technical know-how and hence assists the enterprise to place emphasis on operating efficiency gains arising from the use of experts as human resources as well as specialized requirement, and machinery,

(i) This structural arrangement is economical because all products are produced by only one division, marketed by only one division, etc. This encourages an optimal use of available resources in different departments, and

(j) The arrangement encourages flexibility in internal and external adjustment in the type and scope of operations in the organization. For instance, each division may be adjusted (reduced or enlarged) appropriately and also the size of the entire organization may be so adjusted with ease.

However, despite the above chain of merits, the functional structural arrangement also suffers from the following shortcomings:

(a) Each division may consider its objective as the ultimate rather than a part of the corporate goal which must be achieved together. This may lead to the situation where each department may be working to the detriment of others which is tantamount to sub-optimization.

(b) Where a company deals in many products, each product may not be given adequate attention on the scheme. If structure were to be arranged on products basis, as in the case of product structure, this problem would be eliminated,

(c) Functional organization tends to look improper and narrow to allow the practice of modern management techniques especially when consideration is given to size and coverage of contemporary industrial private and governmental organizations: majority of them are large in size and operates as multi-product enterprises,

(d) In functional organizations, the opinions, viewpoints, orientations and decisions of divisional managers may look myopic due to concentration on specialized operations over time,

(e) In functional arrangement, the Chief Departmental functionaries may be overloaded with many duties because they are responsible for the attainment of corporate goals,

(f) The discharge or disengagement of a divisional manager may spell doom for the organization. This may even sink the efforts of the entire organization ultimately, and

(g) Functional arrangement may lead to unhealthy competition, conflict, friction and rivalry among various divisions and departments creating problems of coordination and control for top management.

In practice, the common functional arrangement in modern organizations may be depicted as in Fig. 7.

3.7.2 Product Organization Structure

A product based organization structure is the one in which a separate and distinct division, section or department

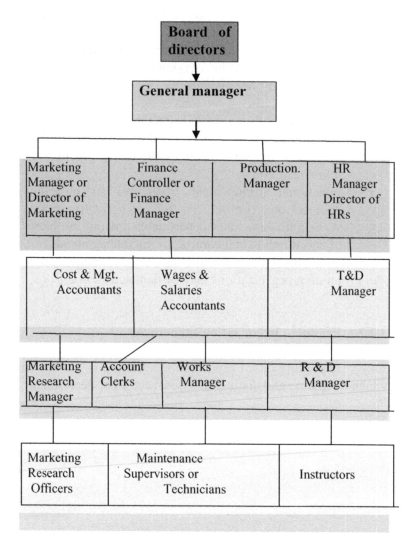

Fig. 7: A Functional Organizational Structure

is created for each and every one of the products of an
organization. This mechanism is only useful and relevant if
and when a particular organization is dealing (or is involved
in) many products. That is, this type of structural

arrangement becomes highly imperative whenever a company has grown enough to the states of multi-product organizations. *Oyedijo (1995: P. 87)* agrees that product organization structure is normally adopted where the product lines of the company are many and are heterogeneous, where the functional structure is inefficient to cope with the peculiar needs of each product, and where the product range generates sufficient sales volume to justify the inevitable duplication of marketing personnel and services.

The major benefits of product-based organization structure in the modern industrial settings include the following:

(a)   Adequate attention is given to each and every one of the product lines of the company without a total neglect of anyone,

(b)   The organization is able to be responsive to immediate changes in market situations in respect of each product and necessary, adjustment is made appropriately,

(c)   It makes for development of products specialist into generalists that would be willing, ready and able to take up the job and responsibilities of top level management positions as and when the need arises in future,

(d)   Product-based organization structure encourages specialization of managers on the basis of product lines. This in turn encourages operational efficiency and hence enhances higher corporate performance or productivity,

(e)   This kind of organization allows for product growth, development and diversity which would naturally enhance better chances of organizational performance at the market places,

(f)   Because of the fact that each product unit or division is given an appreciable level of autonomy, top managers are able to concentrate on strategic managerial activities with less concern for tactical and operational problems and responsibilities for individual product lines, and

(g) Product-based organization structures provide motivation and self respect to individual product managers as they are provided with overall authority, responsibility as well as autonomy to deal with their product lines with little or no interference from top management.

However, despite this chain of advantages ascribed to a product-based organization structure, the mechanism still suffer from the following disadvantages:

(a) The structure is more expensive, time consuming and somehow laborious. This is because different staff and office premises have to be maintained and sustained for each product line especially in respect of store houses and marketing operations,

(b) Product managers also tend to become narrow-minded as each of them tends to develop himself in one product line only. This may limit his chances of advancement into the general responsibility level,

(c) Product-based structures may encourage conflict, friction and unnecessary rivalry among different product managers and even between a product manager and the general manager. For instance, a product manager may want to perform an action which may lie outside the area of his jurisdiction and which may be challenged by the general manager. For illustration, a product manager can request for, but cannot order beyond a certain volume of advertising for his product. This can only be done by passing through the General Manager which may cause some disagreements between both parties,

(d) This mechanism of administrative management requires a large army of staff with general management skills and activities that may be very

difficult to recruit and/or retain in certain
circumstances,

(e)   Product-based mechanism naturally leads to more
        problem of control and coordination on the part of
        top management as each and every one of the various
        product divisions has to be harmonized into the
        whole scheme of things.

For more clarification, a typical product-based
organization is presented in Fig. 8 that follows:

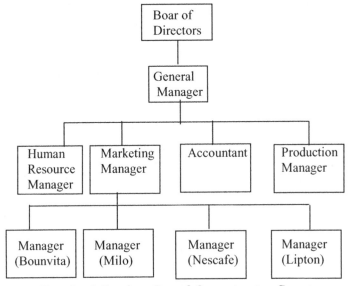

Fig. 8: A Product-Based Organization Structure

3. 7.3 Regional-Based Organization Structure

Immediately an organization grows or develops to a
level of operation which spreads over a wise geographical
location, it becomes imperative for it to adopt a geographical
or regional-based administrative structure. Under this
managerial mechanism, the firm needs to set up local or

foreign branches or regions with a set of complete facilities for production, distribution and services in each of the different offices. However, coordination, control and responsibilities for finance are usually retained at the Head Office. Meanwhile, the regional structure, for its effective and efficient application, is dependent mainly upon an overall corporate plan, strategy, policy and very strong supervision from the Head Office, so as to maintain a thoroughly harmonized management effort.

The common five conditions under which geographical organization structure becomes imperative are as follows:

(a)   Where their are important socio-cultural differences between markets/consumers that need to be taken care of by a geographic division of work,

(b)   In international marketing where marked differences in national cultures make local knowledge essential for effective design, pricing, promotion and distribution of products or services,

(c)   Where the product is intensively distributed and its volume is large. This is necessary because the product must generate sufficient sales volume in order to justify separate area offices,

(d)   When there is a need to encourage local participation in decision-making and to take the benefit of the economy of localized operation, and

(e)   When communication is poor and there is a need to reduce transportation costs and also to reduce the time required for product delivery.

As in the case of the other types of organization structure, geographical organization also has some merits. The most common one among these are:

(a)   It allows sufficient first-hand information to be collected and utilized particularly through local branches in the ease of a domestic business or through foreign branch offices in the case of international, multinational or transnational organizations pertaining to marketing operations of the organization,

(b) It encourages periodic measurement and comparison of operations and performance among various branches of the organization making use of information generated from exchange of knowledge, mechanisms, and experiences among the staff in such branches. This naturally leads to better managerial decisions,

(c) Geographical arrangement allow top managers at the Head Office to concentrate on strategic management without a serious distraction,

(d) It encourages the opportunity for economics of local operations such as minimum transportation expenses as well as economy of large scale operation as a corporate entity,

(e) Geographical arrangement is highly flexible and allows for adjustment of corporate information, knowledge, strengths opportunities, weaknesses and resources to suit local or branch offices environment,

(f) Regional organization structure allows for better and improved inter-personal communication with various interest groups at various locations of company branches,

(g) It creates goodwill for the enterprise through provision of employment opportunities for inhabitants of the locations where branch offices are sited and also by embarking on various corporate social responsibilities such as scholarship, games sponsorship, etc,

(h) The mechanism of administrative management encourages profit and/or loss responsibility to be assigned to the lowest strategic levels,

(i) The mechanism encourages functional coordination and integration within the predetermined market, and

(j)   Branch offices and their geographical locations usually constitute conducive environment for educating, training and developing future top level management personnel.

However, this structural arrangement possesses the following disadvantages:

(a)   The mechanism is very expensive as it involves duplication of offices, resources and personnel at each of the branch offices,

(b)   Changes in or modification to organizational policies, strategies and procedure may be communicated late to branch offices. Likewise, there may be delay in communicating reports to the Head Office from the local branches, etc. This may have a serious consequence for the organizational corporate performance,

(c)   It discourages maintenance and sustenance of cheap and economical services across various branch offices,

(d)   The mechanism increases and complicates the problems of control and coordination for top level managers,

(e)   Using this mechanism, it is always problematic or difficult to sustain a consistent and coherent organizational goodwill as well as reputation across the various local offices as each branch manager tend to enjoy certain degree of autonomy, and

(f)   The mechanism tends to prolong the administrative structure by at least one more layer of management through which the various local branches are run.

3.7.4 Market-Oriented Organization Structure

An organization is said to be structured on the basis of its product market or its customers when different sales force with different qualities in terms of skills, experience and technical know-how about the product are considered against different categories of buyers when its structural decisions are being made.

Consequently, the mechanism is also referred to as customer oriented organization structure from this explanation, it would be crystal clear that only the marketing department or division is decentralized (i.e., sub-divided), while every other divisions of the organization remains un-effected. However, market organization structure applies when a company deals in durable goods which may be distributed to both consumer and industrial buyers; it is also used when consumers are different in their fundamental characteristics and their buying Behaviors.

However, the mechanism allows for some division of labor and specialization in modern organizational administration particularly in handling issues with various buyer categories. In this case, the problems of each customer are ironed out immediately without much delay. On the other hand however, the mechanism involves duplication of efforts, but this is inevitable. The mechanism also brings about difficulties in coordination, control and decantation of information among the various customer groups. This particular problem can, however, mitigated or completely surmounted the use of inter-departmental committees whether had hoe or standing ones.

3.7.5 Matrix Organization Structure

This organization arrangement may also be called complex or project organization structure. The mechanism of this type of structure is that two-way flow of authority and responsibility is involved. That is a matrix organization structure involves both vertical and horizontal flow of information, authority and responsibility across various divisions of the organization. In this case, the vertical authority beyond to each functional managers, supervisors and foremen while the horizontal authority belongs to probably coordinators of programs and other general overseers in the organization.

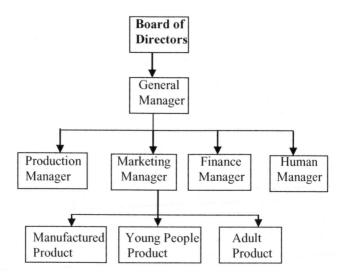

Fig. 8 A Customer-Based Organizational Structure:

However, the matrix type of organization arrangement is practiced in the following circumstances:

(a)   When the operations have little or no knowledge of the operations duties or activities to be performed and hence there is a need to appoint a coordinator or general overseer. Hence, in this link between the operations and the operators,

(b)   In construction and developments projects where individual projects are tome-band at the end of which the executor are re-assigned to other functions of different nature and/or scope,

(c)   When there is an urgent need to achieve a target while meeting specified constraints such as quality and time standards simultaneously through traditional means. In such a case, a project director may be appointed to supervise and coordinated to supervise and coordinate the efforts of the particulars. Such participants are therefore subject to the directives of their functional managers and those of the project director or coordinator,

(d)   When particular project or program requires skills of a specific or specialized nature which cannot be obtained from among the functional staff both operatives and their managers. Here, there is a need for a general overseer who will be particularly dedicated to the success of the project   in all ramifications

(e)   When there is a need to reduce operational cost to the barest minimum. Under this condition, the project director is able to relate all operations with their cost implications and thereby come out with suggestions as to means and ways of minimizing the total cost of the project to the enterprise.

As with other types of organization structure, matrix organization arrangement also has its own merits and demerits among its merits are:

(a)   The mechanism tends to satisfy majority of the customers or clients because operations and activities are largely effectively harmonized integrated and coordinated,

(b)   More continuous support is provided for the operation concerned through effective and efficient supervision and monitoring by the project director or general overseer,

(c)   The mechanism creates and promotes adequate checks and balances among completing viewpoints and perspectives with individuals and divisions for various strategic development practices,

(d)   The arrangement encourages concurrent pursuit of varying forms of strategic perspectives, projects and programs,

(e)   The arrangement also facilitates conflict and friction-free environment while encouraging coordination and control of related operations,

(f)   Matrix organization structure allows for different and district factors to be articulated and managed directly within the organization, and

(g)   The system allows appropriate and adequate attention to be given to each critical factor within the organization structure for effective and efficient corporate performance.

Meanwhile, despite all the aforementioned advantages of the matrix organization structure the mechanism is faced by the following short comings:

(a)   The choice and determination of criteria to be used in forming varying work groups and teams usually constitute great problem and teeth to top management,

(b)   Matrix organization structure in most cases leads to conflict friction and rivalry among between managers and project/program directors and coordinators these problems may be insurmountable due to the two competing lines of authority and responsibility,

(c)   The frequency of development and dissolution of project groups may not allow stability of work team and this may in turn may discourage the development of interpersonal relationships,

(d)   Matrix form of arrangement of organizations may not permit in depth functional skills to be developed in employees which may adversely affect their long-term career and personal advancements,

(e)   The mechanism is always very complex and hence difficult to manage. Participants in most cases resort to confusion as to whom they should report to and who should report to them as well as for what purpose. This would help in maintaining balance between the vertical and horizontal lines of authority and responsibility,

(f)   Due to the multiplicity and varying authority the mechanism makes it somehow difficult to respond quickly and decisively without first taking care of many alternative view points and perspectives and also getting the approval of varying interest groups which may eventually paralyze actions,

(g)   There is often delay and time wastages on communication due to the matrix tendency that every activity and operation is considered significant meaning that every participant needs to communicate with every other participant apparently for perceived equality, justice and fare play, and

(h)   There are usually high operations cost, inefficiency in communication and delays in decision-making resulting in late project and program completion.

The following diagram illustrates a better explanation of matrix structures.

3.7.6   Hybrid Organization Structure

From the discussion so far, we have seen that there are many approaches to organizing an enterprise. Particularly, an organization structure may be of the type functional structure, product-based structure, geographical-based structure or it may be of the matrix type. Particularly, there are many situations when an organization may decide to combine two or more of the structural arrangements. This is known as hybrid organization structure, and it is a typical feature of very large, complex, multi-location or multi-product organizations. The common examples are multinational and translational organizations that are somehow giant enterprises of the modern time. However, it should be noted that there is no one best structure for a particular organization. Consequently, the structure of administration adopted by an organization is a function of many criteria or variables .

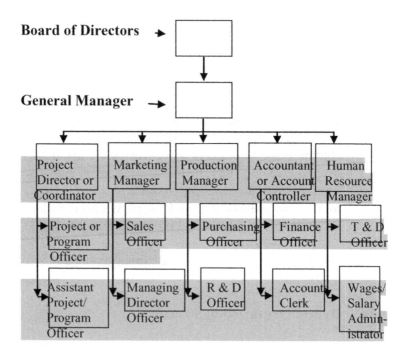

Fig. 9: A Matrix Organization Structure.

3.7.7   Choice of a Good Organizational Structure

As mentioned in the just concluded section, there is no one way approach to designing a good organizational structure. The structure adopted by any organization is completely dependent upon several factors. Among such variables are the origin and history of the enterprise its ownership and control structure, corporate and divisional resources, its goals operations or activities, its size and market coverage or scope, its stage and type of technology as well as its strategy and policy etc.

To clarify these criteria, one would agree that the structure of an organization be it public and private, small or large, is dependents on its strategy and policy, and on whether it is a small company, a subsidiary of another giant one or a public sector organization. Also, the method or approaches by which an organization is structured and the reporting pattern adopted are all functions of the nature of the organization. By implication, it depends on whether the organization belongs to the government or private individuals.

Next, it is crystal clear that a large organization with several branch offices can use a regional arrangement while a relatively small company with just few numbers of staff and perhaps no other office other than the Head Office cannot go into the difficulties of running a geographical arrangement. Again, some organizations are primarily concerned with production of physical goods while some others are mainly concerned with services delivering such as banking, construction and the civil service. These differences directly or otherwise affect the way and manner organizations are structured or arranged.

Furthermore, the size and scope of an organization serve as the primary criteria for structuring the organization. The larger the size and coverage of an organization, the more difficult and complex in structural arrangement the organization becomes, the more demanding the management of the enterprise. In addition, the degree or extent of complexity, dependability, stability and adaptability of the technology and techno-structure of an organization will naturally dictate the way and manner the operations of the enterprise are distributed. By implication, the technology of an enterprise always dictates its span of control authority levels and extent of delegation, responsibility assignment, and number of steps along the ladder of responsibilities and so on. It also prescribes the operations and responsibilities that could be integrated together and this naturally determines the structural designs due to its impact on coordination, monitoring and control.

Finally, *Alfred D. Chandler* says that the structure of an organization follows its strategy. Consequently, it should be expected that the strategy which a company has chosen toward its goal accomplishment will normally prescribe and closely relate to the structural design it adopts. Because of this, an organization that pursues a product diversification strategy will adopt a based structural design. The one that pursues a market growth and expansion strategy will engage a geographical structural design while a one-product company perhaps within a small area will employ the use of a functional structural arrangement. For better illustration, the principal determinants of the most appropriate organizational structure in the contemporary organizations may be presented diagrammatically as follows in Fig. 10.

3.7   ORGANIZATIONAL CHARTS

Closely related to the concept of organization structure is another popular concept known as organization chart. In fact, all the diagrammatic representations in section 3.6 used to depict organization structure are typical examples of organization charts. Invariably, an organization chart is therefore a diagrammatic representation of the structure of an enterprise. Such a diagrammatic representation shows the process of dividing work or operations into convenient duties, such duties are grouped in the form of posts, and the nature and extent of responsibility of each person and division can be indicated. It shows the lines of authority and responsibility whereby vertical lines show the downward flow of authority and the upward flow of accountability.

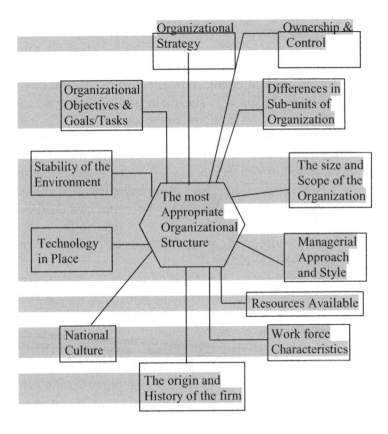

Fig. 10: Determinants of Appropriate Structural Design in an Organization.

In other words, an organizational chart is a systematically and schematically planned diagram of lines connecting various levels of authority responsibility and accountability relationships within an organization. It is a crystal clear picture of networks of divisions of duties and activities to be performed and of line of responsibility and accountability. However, an organization chart may be presented in vertical horizontal and circular forms depending on the preference of the person presenting it. These are explained as follows:

(a) *Vertical Organization Charts:* All the charts in this section are   examples of vertical organizational charts. Hence, vertical charts show direct lines of authority.

(b) *Horizontal Charts*: The main aim of this type of charts is to avoid over-emphasis on levels of authority in an organization. Such a chart is normally read from the left to the right with the most senior officer on the left and the most junior officer on the right. This type of organizational charts is naturally preferable to the junior employees as they do not usually see themselves as belonging to the bottom cadre of their organizations as clearly shown by the vertical chart.

(c) *Circular Chart:* This type of charts is also known as spherical chart and its main goal, as in the case of horizontal charts, is also to eliminate or reduce over-emphasis on level of authority. By implication, both the horizontal and circular organization charts tend to water down the dysfunctional effects of hierarchical mechanism in formal organizations. In circular charts, positions are indicated in circular forms, and within each circle of a senior staff, other circles belonging to his/her subordinate officers

From our discussion so far, we would observe that organization charts are deliberately and systematically planned diagrammatic representation of different positions and position-holders in a formal organization. Such a representation is a connection of lines indicating the levels of authority, responsibility, accountability or the structure of formal reporting relationship that exist within an organization.

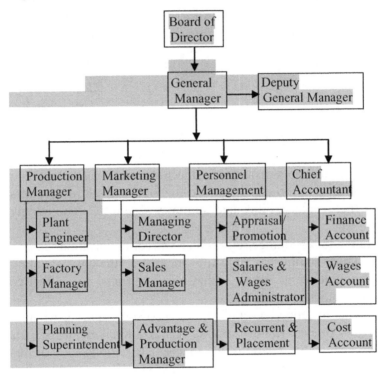

Fig. 11: A Vertical Organizational Chart

The major functions (or merits) of having an organizational chart in place in contemporary organizations include the fact the such an arrangement:

✓ Assists to identify and pinpoint activities, responsibilities or operations to be performed and those who should do the job. Hence, it assists organizations to avoid duplications and wastage of resources while still enhancing effectiveness and efficiency,

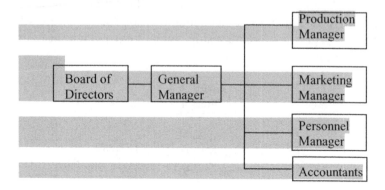

Fig. 12: A Horizontal Organizational Chart

✓ Assists to know at a glance the position of leadership and those of *followership* in an organization without much stress so that responsibilities and authority would be appropriately placed,

✓ Helps to encourage clear line of communication among various administrative staff members thereby avoiding communication noise (that is, barrier to effective communication),

✓ Assists to reduce or eradicate unnecessary conflict, friction, rivalry or even jealousy among organizational members. This is because the relationships that subsist among the various divisions and the entire organization is well every individual is aware of his position, duties and responsibilities as a

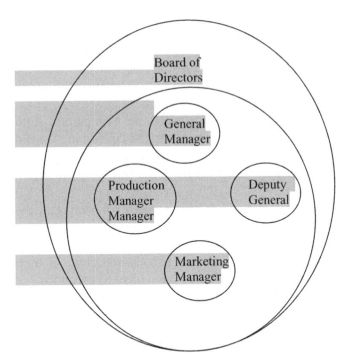

Fig. 13. A Circular Organizational Char

member of the system,

✓ Encourages effective and efficient resource and facility coordination and control. By this several operations and activities are carried out without damaging (or passing a threat to) the organizational unity and cohesiveness,

✓ Helps to identify and pinpoint sources of actual and potential problems difficulties or errors that would otherwise sink the efforts of the organization if care is not taken,

✓ Serves to provide vital information about the management and administration of the organization to which they relate to all interest groups such as the employees, management, government, general public consultants, clients and customers, etc,

✓ Helps as a starting point for organizational reengineering, adjustment or development. This is because, any change or modification of an organization starts from a study and understanding of the existing structure of the organization which is depicted by the organization chart, and

✓ Serve as important tool for inducting new entrants into the organization and also training and developing the old staff. Hence, organization starts helps a lot in the process of managerial understanding of the entire organization.

However, in spite of this series of advantages, the following disadvantages have been ascribed to most organizational charts as follow:

✓ Most organization charts are usually too rigid in their design. They usually do not take cognizance of unexpected changes and new developments. Hence, they need reworking and redesigning or modification as new tasks or activities emerge,

✓ Over concentration on a rigidly drawn organization chart may lead to delay of actions and even communication. This is because organizational members may be forced to wait for further instruction or directive once they have performed their own side of the job even when jobs are piling up in preceding sections,

✓ The mechanism of organization chart is not humane. The mechanism is to mechanic. Such a mechanic approach to the study of organizations may not be real as no room is given to social relations (i.e. informal selling's and interactions) within the system,

✓ The use of organization charts may lead to unnecessary conflict, friction, jealousy or even rivalry among organization members if care is not taken,

✓ Organization members may limit the scope of their operations and activities to their specific divisions or positions. Consequently, organization charts tend to lead to narrow interpretation or conception of duties and responsibilities,

✓ Organization charts do not give adequate room for workers' initiative. Hence, workers initiatives and morale may be killed as every individual has to perform his assigned duties in the predestined manner, and he has to dance to the tune of work within the chart. Such a situation naturally lead to judicious adherence to rules, regulations and procedures killing initiatives, and

✓ Organization charts usually show a static structure of an enterprise without due regards for continuous changes and dynamic nature of modern organizations. Changes of various forms do occur within an organization from time to time arising from decision-making, communication, corporate adaptation and adjustment, organizational reengineering and restructuring, etc. these have to be reflected in the organization structure and hence organization chart which would not be possible in the way various charts are drawn.

Consequently, for proper understanding of contemporary organizations, it is generally believed that a schedule of responsibilities of each position or position-holder (organization schedule) showing organizational relationships should be attached to organizational chart probably as the key. This would serve to clarify and illuminate the time picture of the organization charts. This is necessary because organization charts do not normally contain important aspects of management and organizational processes and schedule of work relationships, information flows and communication network, decision criteria and procedures, the nature of operations, etc. all these would be made crystal clear by organization schedule which should be attached to each and every one of the organization structure.

3.8 CENTRALIZATION AND DECENTRALIZATION

Organization in the modern age cannot be judiciously be discussed without making adequate reference to the concepts of centralization and decentralization. Centralization is a mechanism of administrative management whereby control is exercised from the center on the activities of all divisions, departments and braches. Consequently, in the contemporary enterprises, employees are appointed to the clerical staff of the whole organization, and not merely to one division or office. In this case, detailed instructions on methods and procedure to be followed are issued from Head Office. Services that can be centralized however, are filling, typing stationery supplies and duplicating.

By implication, centralization is a form of organization in which authority responsibility and duties are located in one place and on one person or few persons in such a way that decision making is concentrated in or restricted to top management. This type of administrative mechanism implies that those that are responsible for carrying out an assignment are not made responsible for decision making as to when and how the actions involved are to be performed. The system is the deliberate, planned, systematic and consistent concentration of authority and responsibility at a central place within the understanding or enterprise.

Centralization becomes relevant and practicable where management think that certain degree of it is inevitable to harmonize, unify, integrate and focus the entire operations of the organization. This is apparently because such an effort would naturally provide a kind of central direction required to keep all divisions of the enterprise functioning harmoniously toward a common predetermined corporate goal which may not be possible from a high degree of decentralization.

Many management experts nowadays are of the opinion that centralization has the following advantages:

(a) It encourages uniformity of policies, strategies, techniques and standards of operations in the enterprise,

(b) It encourages optimal administrative coordination and control through adherence to laid-down rules, regulations, policies and procedures,

(c) It leads to organizational effectiveness and efficiency through centralization of authority and responsibility in one place on one person or a few number of individuals in the organization,

(d) It reduces or prevents conflict, friction, jealousy or unhealthy rivalry and competition for power and authority among members of the organization,

(e) Individuals and groups in the organization are prevented by centralization from developing a narrow-minded and parochial perspective of the enterprise,

(f) It allows emergencies to be handled without unnecessary delay by top management as just a few consultation would be needed

(g) The specialized staff can perform the work more quickly and easily with proper facilities which are utilized more fully. Hence, there is economy of staff and other resources because of its flexibility,

(h) The mechanism of centralization is cost effective. Costs would be drastically reduced because machines and equipment would be more fully employed with little or no duplication,

(i) As the centralized room or office would be used strictly for one purpose, it could be designed and equipped specifically for that purpose,

(j) Increased efficiency and effectiveness would result from the use of specialized staff particularly as the supervisors would also be specialized, and

(k)   There would be better supervision and training of staff which would definitely lead to effective control in maintaining standards of work or operations.

On the other hand, the following points constitute some of the major criticisms of centralized operations in modern corporate organizations irrespective of their purposes, orientation and the sector to which they belong:

(a)   Some of the gains in economy of operations are lost as frustrated members of the organization would be resentful of the impersonal nature of their operations or duties,

(b)   There is possibility of delays occurring because of the fact that where departments are interconnected in such a way that each depends on cooperation from others, the growth or formation of inter-departmental committees and other time-consuming bodies are inevitable,

(c)   The remoteness of managers or supervisors from the actual scene of operations can lead to some procedures being unworkable or inappropriate,

(d)   Employees in centralized divisions may have little or no interest in the activities or tasks they are performing for other divisions perhaps for sentiment or other reasons best known to them,

(e)   Many of the routine office practices which are mostly centralized use female labor such as the typing pool, and segregation of female staff is often disliked by girls,

(f)   The routine work of the centralized divisions retards the training and development of human resources,

(g)   Centralization stifles creativity of employees because little or no opportunity is given for workers to use their discretions. Employees are forced to perform their duties in line with rules and procedures,

(h)   The mechanism leads to delay and operational inefficiency as orders, instructions, directives, etc, have to come from the top or centralized office,

(i)   Too much remote administrative control may lead to autocratic, inflexible and impractical rules and regulations that are made by the executive officers that are far away from the shop-floor,

(j)   It may increase the volume of work at the center thereby reducing managerial and administrative effectiveness and efficiency,

(k)   It increases paper work and record keeping, and consequently enhancing bureaucratic system of administration,

(l)   It encourages extreme form of uniformity and adherence to work rules, regulations, procedures and methods thereby discouraging any form of adjustment or modification in response to varying needs at each operational level and the turbulent and dynamic modern management environment.

However, the direct opposite of centralization is decentralization and this is also called divizionalization or departmentalization. It is a managerial organization in which authority, responsibility and accountability for certain or specified operations are developed and distributed from the center, and put directly at the point of operative activities. In this respect, such authority, responsibility and accountability are respectively delegated, assigned and attached to somehow independent and autonomous divisions of the enterprise thereby creating more departments and sections where initiatives and powers can be exercised.

Meanwhile, despite the fact that administrative or managerial functions such as recruitment, selection and placement, accounting, marketing, etc, are shared among varying divisions, central administrative control particularly for corporate planning, governance and general management still remains top management affairs. By implication, decentralization or divisionalization simply refers to the deliberate, systematic and schematic mechanism to delegate and share to the lowest levels possible all authority and responsibility apart from those that are particularly reserved for the top management as part of corporate governance. Consequently, it is quite appropriate and adequate to assert that divisionalization is the process or act of placing authority appropriately in relation to responsibility for performance.

In the contemporary industrial and even governmental organizations, the following advantages have been found for decentralization as a mechanism of modern management:

(a)   Individual and group training and skill development as well as encouragement of initiatives are more enhanced through significant involvement in work activities,

(b)   There would naturally be improvement in communication arising from reduced inter-personal distance as members of the organization usually work more closely when operations are decentralized,

(c)   Conflict, friction, rivalry, jealousy and unhealthy competition are drastically reduced between and among staff at the corporate and departmental levels in the organization,

(d)   The number of levels along the ladder of responsibility in the hierarchical structure of the organization is also minimized resulting in better delegation of authority and assignment of responsibility,

(e)   Decentralization encourages individual and group motivation particularly through employees' participation and involvement in decision making process,

(f)   Divisionalizing operations encourages and stimulates employees initiative, creativity, inquisitiveness, self-expression and self-confidence through continuous work involvement and commensurate level of work autonomy or freedom as to the choice of ways and means of operations,

(g)   Divisionalization reveals the weaknesses of ineffective managers and administrators thereby allowing training and development needs, whether stated or un-stated, to be identified and also it allows initiatives for appropriate program of action for employees' training and development in the organization,

(h)   Decentralization encourages training and development of a large army of trained executive officers and hence it reduces the difficulties involved in executive successions and human resources planning,

(i)   It encourages sharing and spreading of work activities or operations among a large number of staff members for fast and quick executions and rapid decisions or results necessary to solve immediate problems of the enterprise. This is made possible probably because administrative paper work in the forms of memos, drafts, letters, etc, is drastically reduced at successive level of operations,

(j)   Decentralization as a form of democratic governance in modern organizations encourages employees' participation. Hence, it brings workers so close to management that they feel that they are working with rather than working for the management. This becomes possible as they are involved substantially at every stage of operations and decision making process,

(k)   Decentralization reduces, and makes easy, routine operations for top management and allows them enough time to concentrate on strategic matters of corporate governance importance,

(l)   Decentralization encourages job enrichment, enlargement as well as job satisfaction for employees, whether managers or operatives, as it allows them to exercise their own initiatives, judgment and to use their own experience in their job performance, and

(m)   Departmentalization in whatever form allows every division of the undertaking to meet specific requirements of its operating units without the intervention of the central administrative authority.

This implies that decision at every division or department would naturally reflect the local peculiarities of the department.

However, in spite of this long chain of merits or benefits of departmentalization, the mechanism is also prone to at least two major drawbacks. These consist of the fact that the system usually creates variations and diversity in policies, mechanisms and standards of performance in the enterprise. This however poses a significant problem of central coordination, integration and control simply because each division may see itself as an autonomous unit and may not be following the same pattern or procedure judiciously as expected of it.

Alternatively, in *divisionalization*, executive officers may decide to make decisions which favor their own divisions rather than those which are at congruent and consonant with corporate directives, this is quite unlike the centralization of executive functions which usually create unhealthy competition, rivalry, conflict and friction among departmental managers or even sub-divisional heads. From the look of things in this sections, we would observed that the concept of centralization applies mostly to small scale organizations whereas decentralization is mostly adopted by large ones such as multi-products, multinational and translational conglomerates.

However, in organizations where decentralization is practiced, it is still the responsibility of top management to decide on critical aspect of corporate governance and administration such as policy formulation, goal determination and strategy development. Meanwhile, irrespective of the nature, orientation, scope and size of an organization, certain determinants dictate the choice between centralization and decentralization. These are usually based on organizational peculiarities and some of them are:

(a)   The effectiveness and efficiency of communication mechanisms in the enterprise including communication channels, feedback and control,

(b)   The size and scope (or coverage) of organizational operations,

(c)   The availability of the required caliber and grades of human resources to handle the authority to be delegated and responsibilities to be assigned,

(d)   The degree of managements need for uniformity and formality in corporate and divisional policy and performance standards,

(e)   The importance of or necessity for decisions to long-term corporate growth and survival of the enterprise,

(f)   The appropriateness and adequacy of control mechanisms by which the performance of the executives and other key employees can be measured, monitored and controlled, and

(g)   The time span or period of any important anticipated change in the organization.

3.9   FORMS OF ORGANIZATION

In the modern industrial society, organizations exist in various forms. This phenomenon is inevitable because of the different approaches that are available for the study of organizations in the present time. Consequently, the common forms or classifications of modern enterprises are *strictly formal organizations* also described as *formalism* or *mechanistic organizations, spontaneous growth organizations* or *informal organizations*, and the modifications of these. Strictly formal organization using *Louis Alien's* words is a mechanism of well defined jobs, each bearing definite measures of authority, responsibility and accountability, the whole consciously designed to enable the people of the enterprise to work most effectively harmoniously together in accomplishing their goals.

The formal organization is characterized by being well-defined, bound by delegation, and relatively stable. It is a more or less arbitrary structure to which the individual must adjust for him to do certain things in a predestined manner, to obey orders from designated individuals, and to work cooperatively with others. Because of these arbitrary requirements, the formal organization tends to restrict and circumscribe the activities of individuals. It sets up boundaries, signposts, and pathways which must be followed.

Oyedijo, (1995: P. 122-123) quoting *Glover and Rush Brooke* says that formal groups are deliberately and officially Organized, membership is pre-described and there is usually a hierarchical structure with explicitly regulations and procedural rules together with clearly defined tasks, roles, authority, pre-established official objectives and rules and regulations about wages, fines, etc, which specify the way people are expected to behave in the organization (*Glover and Rush Brooke, 19971: P. 21*). Quoting *Louis Alien* again, *Oyedijo (1995)* described formal organization or formal work group as "the planned organization and the relationships within it as defined and laid down by official rules, regulations and an organization charts technically defined. Formal organization is the organizational pattern as defined by management or the pattern of division of the organizational positions, and the rules expected to guide the Behavior of the participants as defined by management".

However, the main features of strictly formal organizations include the following;

(a)   Organization charts depict reality,

(b)   Each member of the organization is aware of his responsibilities as shown in job description,

(c)   Strict channels of communication are followed,

(d)   No change can be made in responsibilities without proper planning and authorization,

(e)   The "unity of command" principle is followed without departure,

(f)   Standard of performance are established and followed,

(g)   The structure of activities is clearly defined for an observer to see. There are usually a clear leader, the subordinate officers, the specific operations to be performed and the place for the operations,

(h)   There are well-defined duties, rights, responsibilities and rights of the organizational members individually and collectively,

(i)   There is usually a relatively permanent relations and organizations which are complemented by organizational growth and development,

(j)   A formal organization is usually established to accomplish specific tasks and goals towards which such an enterprise must strive, and

(k)   A formal organization usually has an appointed leader.

In their *Management of Innovation, Tom Burns and G. M. Stalker* introduced the term, *mechanic* to describe the strictly formal type of organizations. They noted that such a style would be the most suitable form of enterprises for stable conditions, whereas to them, an *organic* organization adopts a more flexible approach. They agreed that when change is very slow, the formal type of organization has much to offer especially when adapted to suit specific circumstances. For example, the unity of command may be varied under specific circumstances. Undoubtedly, formalizing shows quite clearly who is responsible for each job area; hence, it should lead to clear commands being given and the avoidance of misunderstanding. However, the main objection to formalism in modern organizations is its possible rigidity. If truly mechanic, the structure of formalism is regarded as being more important than the people within the enterprise.

On the other hand, spontaneously growth organizations, or informal organizations, attempt to give prominence to the informal working groups, regarded by many industrial sociologists as the most important aspect of management. They argue that the formal structure is simply a representation of the ideal which is rarely achieved. Accordingly, a natural organization is regarded as being more acceptable, being based upon what is actually occurring. Unfortunately, whilst there is no doubt that the informal group is important and the grapevine is often a vital channel of communication, this does not necessarily mean that the best type of organization is one which grows without guidance or plan. In deed, it can be argued that the setting up of profit centers and cost would be virtually impossible unless there is a formal organization.

Possibly with the small to medium size enterprise, the spontaneous growth organization structures can work quite well. Even so, there must still be some guidance on what the enterprise is trying to achieve and how this is to be done: often too formal a structure can restrict managers and administrators and also encourage inactive performance and discourage the use of discretions, but without recognition of informal position in organizations, there are bound to be some problems. Occasionally, there are stories of chief executives with executive powers and authority who carry out personal policies without regard for the well being of the company as a whole while acknowledging the inevitable bureaucracy which accompanies control, provided this can be maintained with the appropriate degree of flexibility, the best approach will usually be the setting up of a formal organization, but with provision for meetings and other means of exchanging ideas.

From this analysis, it seems apparently clear that informal organization is the one of social relations product and interactions at the work place among members of the enterprise, their attitudes and Behavior, their relationship and all other informal ways of conducting a business other than in terms of rules, regulations, procedures and policies. Hence, it is because such groups are spontaneous, unplanned, and unofficial that they are generally refereed to as spontaneous growth organization. Spontaneous growth organization are the type which have been described by *Keith Davis* when he described an informal groups as *a network of personal and social relations not established or required by the formal organization but arising spontaneously as people associate with one another.*

Oyedijo (1995: P. 124) states that *informal groups are known as bureaucracy's other face because they are not established by the management of the company. They are not easily identifiable because an organization chart cannot be drawn to show their structure and hierarchy of positions since their structures are not rigid. in spite of this, informal organizations exists in all formal organizations although they do not have a permanent character in terms of leadership and membership.*

However, the following benefits or advantages have been directly ascribed to most spontaneous growth organizations in the modern time;

(a)   They assist their members to satisfy their social and affiliation needs in the form of the need for group acceptance, recognition and any form of social affiliation requirement,

(b)   They give to their members' social identification and sense of belongingness and serve to arouse their members, interests at work. This encourages willingness to participate in organizational matters and proceeding by the employees and hence it reduces labor turnover, absenteeism, etc, since work becomes more enjoyable,

(c)   They serve to assist their members in cases of economic, social and personal needs. For instance, cooperative societies may be formed among informal groups. Informal groups help a lot in upgrading the financial status of their members,

(d)   They may sympathize with their members during difficulties and they may contribute toward emancipation of such members from work and other social related problems,

(e)   They may assist their members in determining and conforming to, acceptable and unacceptable forms of work and societal norms and code of practice. Hence, they may assist their members to understand, appreciate and uphold their organizational rules, regulations, policies, ethical standards and procedures,

(f)   They usually provide supplementary channels of communication to their members as useful information may be provided through the unofficial or unauthorized sources,

(g)   They may assist their members in many respects by influencing formal decisions and policies though informally in such a way that their individual and group interests are adequately protected while still making such processes workable, effective and efficient toward accomplishment of the predetermined corporate goals, and

(h)   Spontaneous growth organizations can also assist their enterprise by serving to compensate for, or complement the, effort of weak or ineffective executive officers.

This may lead to improvement in corporate productivity or performance through various mechanisms of groups and individual participation in work procedures. However, despite this long list of benefits and positive contributions of the informal or spontaneous group organizations, informal groups also have some dysfunctional effects on modern organizational life. For instance, spontaneous growth organizations encourage rumor mongering, information distortion and, at times, they may work to the detriment of corporate interests just on the basis of their group sentiments most especially to project their group norms in certain circumstances. They can also put up resistance to change in formal organizations.

In the mean time, the main characteristics of the spontaneous group organizations include the fact that they are mainly independent of their groups by being autonomous, they usually regulate the attitudes and Behavior of their members through their group norms while also influencing the Behavior of their formal organizations. In certain respects, members of such a group usually maintain their intimacy by being familiar with one another as they are somehow homogenous: that is, they are familiar and similar in terms of their personal characteristics such as attitudes, Behavior, sex, age, orientation, and so on. Again, members of such informal organizations act to polarize and divide the formal organization into uniquely identified autonomous groups or clusters on the basis of group identify sentiments and common goals.

Consequently, the group may decide to function as an independent unit which naturally led to ferocious cohesiveness while still retaining their *loud* tone: that is, members usually enjoy being associated with the groups. Furthermore, it is often difficult for new members to break into the groups unless with the consent of the existing ones implying that spontaneous growth organizations usually maintain certain degree of cohesiveness. Finally, they are in most cases in existent with different and distinct status levels within individual groups. By implication, each of the spontaneous growth organizations are naturally stratified into different status strata.

However, in between the two extreme points of formalism and spontaneous growth organizations exist some kinds of hybrid organizations which are usually modifications of the two *extremists*. That is, a number of other approaches which may be referred to as styles in their own rights or simply modifications of the formal and informal organizations abound in management and administrative parlance and some of them are:

(a) *Centralization*: This implies that all authority stems or emanates from the Head Office and the remaining parts of an enterprise must receive instructions and directives from that source being given little or no power themselves,

(b) *Decentralization*: This refers to the breaking up of an enterprise into workable and manageable units and divisions called profit centers or cost centers thereby giving autonomy with the minimum of control from the center. In recent times, this approach has found a significant favor as it cuts down bureaucracy and responsibility,

(c) *Participation*: These attempts to involve workers and managers in the decision making processes. The main impact of this style on organizations is manifested through consultative committees and even by having workers-directors forum, although this concept is far from being clear cut or generally acceptable,

(d) *The full use of specialists*: This concept of making full use of specialists such as accountants, personnel managers, marketing managers and production managers has long been accepted from the period of *Adam Smith, F. W. Taylor* and others. One modern writer who does not agree entirely with this approach however is *Peter ducker* who feels that specialization can be carried too far. Certainly, he maintains, if taken to the point where a worker carries out a specific operations which is repetitive, their may be monotony of work which may in turn lead to workers stress and frustration.

(e) *Autocratic and total control of the means and ways of producing and selling the products.* This is an extreme system but it may operate quite successfully. Although, apparently opposed to modern ideas on participation, the approach is not as unusual as might be supposed. Many production control systems rely upon strict planning and control without which a high degree of success may not be achieved.

3.10   LINE AND STAFF ORGANIZATIONS

Line and staff style of organization is the mechanism involving division of work and labor and also specialization in such a way that there are line managers and staff managers. The line managers, in this case, have direct executive power, responsibility and authority to make sure that the right decisions are made at the right time and place. On the other hand, the staff managers necessarily provide specialized supporting or advisory services to the line managers in order to help them in the process of implementing their line decisions. This is the main reason while staff officers are said to be in an advisory and supportive positions in the contemporary organizations.

However, the basic line of demarcation between line and staff officers in an organization hinges on the decision making powers and authorities associated with their positions and roles. Hence, the line managers normally have the final executive power to make decisions but the power and authority of the staff line managers is limited to advisory status and subordinate to and also stem from that of the line managers. For illustration although it is the duty and responsibility of the production manager to determine the choice of machine, material and men combinations, the human resource manager may advise him probably on the psychological aspect of such combinations.

From this analysis it would be observed that line authority makes a manager to instruct subordinates on what to do. Here, authority flows vertically down through the structure. This is said to be a direct relationship between superior and subordinate officers, and also each subordinate is made responsible to only one person (i.e. unity of command). Again, a staff relationship subsists from the appointment of personal aids to senior members of staff. Such category of staff, however, usually have little or no direct authority in their own right except as an extension of their superior. This implies that except in situations where there is delegated authority and assignment of responsibility for some specific functions, there naturally exist no formal relationship between the personal assistant or aid and other staff members.

Other concepts that are related to the concepts of line and staff organizations are functional and lateral relationships. Functional relationships refer to relationship which subsists between people in advisory or specialist positions and between the managers and their subordinates. The specialist renders a common service to all divisions of the firm but has no direct authority over the people making use of the services. The specialist, however, has a line relationship with his own superior as well as the subordinate staff working with him.

Meanwhile, lateral relationships are the ones which subsist between people on the same level along the ladder of responsibility in the hierarchical structure of the enterprise but in different divisions or departments. Although such relationships may be formally defined in practice, they are of the informal type which are usually based on contact and consultation, and are necessary for the maintenance of coordination control and effective corporate performance in the organization.

Despite the fact that the above dichotomous concepts of modern organizations exist in reality and they are practical, they are closely knitted that their difference might not be easily identified by the laymen in organizational analysis and management. However, there are certain benefits to be derived from the knowledge of line and staff organizational analysis. These include the fact that;

(a)   Line and staff officers are able to direct and focus their attention jealously and judiciously to important and perhaps more strategic problems or decisions of management of the organization,

(b)   Line and staff officers are able to practice division of labor and specialization in which case experts and specialist staffs are encouraged, to handle the jobs which they can do better. This is somehow impossible in either strictly line or strictly staff organizations,

(c)   Line and staff style of organization relieves management of managerial overload for certain categories of duties and responsibilities which might otherwise be impossible to delegate to line subordinates at lower management levels within the hierarchical structure,

(d)   Line and staff style of organization brings about economies of scale into managerial mechanism. This is because the staff departments such as personnel or purchasing divisions make possible the concentration and centralization of supportive services that are, required by different sections and departments of the enterprise.

On the other hand, line and staff dichotomy in modern organizations has some shortcomings including the following;

(a)   The system allows employees to receive specialist and expert information in the form of directives, instructions and advise through the line managers. This may however lead to the employees, misunderstanding or misinterpreting such information,

(b)   Line-staff dichotomy may lead to conflicts, friction and eventually confusion in an organization. This situation may in turn lead to instability, disunity, rivalry, unhealthily, competition and even disorderliness in the organization. This is because the goals of the line managers and staff managers are always different. Even where they succeed in establishing the same or similar goals, each of the officers may want to use different approaches or strategies to accomplish the goals. Line managers are often bitter staff personnel that meddle in their business. On the other hand, staffs personnel often complain that line managers do not accept their advice. There may even be some line managers who do not perform any definite function in an organization.

(c)   Line and staff dichotomy my split an operations or responsibility in such a way that it may becomes difficult do determine who should be praised or punished for good or bad performance, and

(d)   Line and staff dichotomy may lead to monopoly and arrogance among membership of the organization in which case one set of staff look down upon other category of staff. This may however lead to delay in operations and actions. For instance, the staff managers may delay or reschedule the performance of activities to suit its own convenience rather than the needs of the customer.

However, in the contemporary organizations, the conflict, friction and unhealthy competition that often erupt between line managers and their staff counterparts can be attributed to a number of factors including the following:

(a)   The staff managers usually consider themselves as experts and specialists and hence, they feel that their opinions and contributions must be accepted, respected and implemented by line managers. Line managers tend to jetsam the suggestions and advice from the staff manager even though such ideas might be very useful just because the staff mangers in most cases claim the superiority of knowledge and experts when compared to their line counterparts,

(b)   Sometimes, the line managers may claim that their staff counterparts contribute no value to their product, rather, they are considered as meddlesome individuals who are just interested in the responsibilities of the line mangers,

(c)   Line managers are usually people of some matured age with a lot of experience and expertise. Hence, they do not morally take to the advice and suggestions from the staff mangers who are usually of lower ages and perhaps experience apparently for the age differentials,

(d)   Line mangers and their staff counterparts usually compete among themselves to be rewarded for good performance and also to shift blame over one another for unacceptable performance. This always lead to friction and conflict among them.

In the meantime, it must be noted that most of these conflicts and friction can be ironed out among the line and staff managers if:

(a)   The duties, responsibilities and areas of possible jurisdiction are specified for each position holder.

(b)   Accountability and responsibility mechanisms are clearly established and specified,

(c)   Individuals and groups within the organization are made to be aware what is expected of them and what is expected of the others perhaps through appropriate program of education and training of employees,

(d)   Positions are rotated and/or shifted among the line and staff office holders,

(e)   Periodic meetings and consultative fora are Organized where line and staff managers jointly meet to iron out matters of common interests and areas of differences, and

(f)   A general overseer, liaison officer or simply a coordinator may be appointed to coordinate and integrate the operations and functions of both the line managers and those arts. This would serve to unify and harmonize the, whose effort off the organization at the end.

REVISION QUESTIONS

1.   Modern managers agree that there are two perspectives of the term "Organization", vividly discuss the two concepts with necessary examples and illustrations.

2.   Discuss your understanding of the terms *"Organizational Structure"*. What are the forms you think an organizational structure or chart can
take   and what are the conditions under which each of the forms you have mentioned may be adopted?

3.   Enumerate and discuss the merits and demerits of the various forms of organizational structure and organizational charts.

4. What is Organization? With necessary examples, in what ways would you like to classify modern organizations as corporate entities?

5. Distinguish between *"strictly formal organizations"*, *"spontaneous growth organizations"* and *"hybrid organizations"*. Which of the three styles of organizations would you prefer and why? Enumerate and discuss the various merits and demerits of each
of the organizational styles mentioned above..

6. What is organization structure? Enumerate and vividly discuss the major features of a good organization structure citing relevant examples. What are the major determinants of the choice of an appropriate organization structure in the modern industrial undertakings?

7. Write a short, but self explanatory, note on each of the followings:
   (a) Line and staff organization,
   (b) Matrix organization structure,
   (c) Organic organization,
   (d) Centralization and decentralization, and
   (e) Division of labor and specialization.

CHAPTER FOUR

SPECIALIZED MANAGEMENT TECHNIQUES

Things to consider:
* Authority.
* Responsibility
* Delegation.
* Decentralization.
* Communication as a Determinant of Decentralization.
* Decentralization of Managerial Authority.
* Decentralization and Physical Dispersion.
* Management by Objective
* Management by Exception

4.1 INTRODUCTION

This Chapter is primarily devoted to the discussion and explanation of the various specialized tools, techniques, principles, concepts or maxims of management. The common ones among these are the concepts of delegation, authority, Management By Objectives (MBO), Management By Exception (MBE), and decentralization. In dealing with delegation, authority and decentralization in an organization, there will be a need to look into the concept or nature, function and importance of each one of them and their relationship with one another within the organization in order to establish effectiveness and efficiency. Organization becomes vague and meaningless except in the context of responsibility, authority, accountability and delegation. However, before going into details of the relationship among the responsibility, authority and delegation within the organization or society, there is need to highlight some clear definition or explanation of all the above maintained terms.

4.2   AUTHORITY

Simply put it, authority is the right to make decisions, carry out actions and direct others in matters related to the duties and goals of a person. Max Weber made the classic analysis of authority. He saw it as the willing, unconditional compliance of people resting upon their belief that it is legitimate for them to refuse obedience. The key word in this statement is legitimate.

The extent to which people believe in the legitimacy of authority determines the amount of positive incentives or coercive measure a superior must employ to secure compliance to his aims. However, it should be pointed out that the very use of incentives or sanctions is evidence that authority is not accepted either altogether or in part. An interesting problem is what conditions are necessary to produce the perception of legitimate authority. According to Weber, there are three grounds for legitimating authority: tradition, charisma and legal (or rational). Each of these is explained in the following sub-sections.

4.2.1   Traditional Authority

Traditional authority rests in the perception that a certain person class, or caste is destined to rule by some preordained right. This perception may be found in the acceptance of a political system or it may be based on religious belief. Regardless, those who are in the ruling position obtain compliance by virtue of the fact that those who follow subscribe to the cultural values which support the ruling structure. A typical example is what obtains in the Yoruba traditional system of Administration

4.2.2   Charismatic Authority

Charisma is tied in with the notion of change usually brought about by an individual who has the personal ability to enlist the support of followers who believe in his goals. Change may be directed against the established traditional system of authority. Charismatic authority is legitimate in the sense that the followers make it so. The property of Charisma is thought to be a configuration of personality of his followers because they believe that the goals he seeks ought to be goals they should strive for as well. Charisma is grounded in the personal magnetism of the leader.

4.2.3   Legal /Rational Authority

Rational authority also involves change. But the change evolved by this process is not in response to a particular person. Rather it is change based on the emerging needs of an organization. People possessing national legitimate authority secure compliance to their goals because they are technically (functionally) equipped to spell out what sort of ends are necessary to be pursued for the good of the system. Followers accept these prescriptions because of the acknowledged expertise of the decision maker who is selected for his ability, in the sense of being technically qualified, to perform those functions required to further the rational progress of the organization.

4.3   RESPONSIBILITY

Responsibility is the obligation of an individual to perform assigned duties. It can be defined as the obligation to carry out duties and achieve goals related to a position. It can also be defined as the obligation to perform a task; it can be looked into as the task itself. Thus, it implies that a man who accepts a task can and should be held to discount for the performance of the task; he must 'make a reply' either in the form of successful performance or with reasons why success was not achieved. The second definition seems to derive its validity from the common practice of referring to the tasks a man should perform as his responsibility.

Responsibility arises from a superior–subordinate relationship; that is, superior (manager) has authority to require specific services from a subordinate. Authority flows from the superior to the subordinate when duties are assigned, and, at the same time, responsibility is the obligation of subordinate to accomplish those duties. Whether responsibility is continuous or is discharged by a single action, the source of delegation in an organization is by holding a subordinate responsible. However, the superior does not relieve himself of any portion of the original responsibility as he still needs to provide the subordinate with a close supervision..

The following example shows how responsibility flows through the entire organization. Suppose the board of directors of organizations holds the managing directors responsible for total operational performance. The managing director, in turn, holds the various general managers in turn, responsible for marketing manufacturing, and finance functions. They repeat the process, resulting in a series of obligations to be performed at various organization levels. At the lowest levels, supervisors hold operational personnel, such as machine operators and office clerks, responsible for their own activities. If the assigned undertaking fails at the lowest level, the superior answers for the actions of his or her subordinates to the next supervisory level and so on up the ladder. Hence, although responsibilities extend to the lowest organization levels, this does not relieve those at the higher levels of responsibility for the final results.

Having said as much, the next point to consider, and which is very important in modern management is known as responsibility segmentation. Segmentation of responsibility simply implies that if divisions of responsibilities can be assigned, the work load must be divided among the available personnel. Individuals' jobs, based on units of responsibility, are specified by grouping similar functions into individual work assignments. The basic principle used in this process is referred to as *functional similarity*. Such an approach makes. It is easier to find an individual who has the skilled and abilities necessary to undertake a specific job, since the job is composed of similar functions. This principle is also used in creating departments, work centers, sections, division and organizations units.

Responsibility can also be segmented or divided into overlapping responsibility, caps of responsibility, delegation of responsibility for functions that do not contribute to organization objectives. Having said as much, the next concept is that of overlapping responsibility which occurs when two or more individuals are made responsible for the same function. This unfortunate condition is caused by unclear specifications of responsibility limits or unrecognized duplicated of work in other parts of an organization.

Closely related to the above concept is that of gaps of responsibility. A gap responsibility occurs when all responsibilities for performing work have not been clearly foreseen. The net result is that a specific function must be performed, although it has not been assigned. However, Delegation of responsibility that does not contribute to organization objectives is the result of unclear or changed objectives. A specific function that was necessary for certain stated objective can become superfluous for changed objectives. To sheer size of a business firm, a government branch, or an educational institution can lead to performance of work that is unnecessary as well as to gaps and overlaps in responsibility.

4.4   DELEGATION

Having explained the concept of authority, we then turn to the concept of delegation in the next few sections. Delegation may be defined as the assignment of part of manager's work to others, along with both the responsibility and the authority necessary to achieve expected results. Delegation involves transferring to others the formal right to perform certain tasks, and the attempt to create an obligation on the part of the person receiving that right to perform the task to a certain standard. To do this, the man must also have the qualities of intelligence, moral worth, knowledge, experience, etc. Such that his subordinate will worth, acknowledge, experience, etc. such that his subordinate will accept his leadership without question.

Delegation can be viewed both as a defence mechanism to alleviate pressure on overburden top management, and as an aggressive move to secure the benefit of direct and immediate decision–making. Greatest advantage can be gained by delegating as far as the competence of subordinate the information available and the scope of impact of decisions will allow. Fear of delegation is caused by the fact that the Officer who delegates the work is still ultimately responsible. The following are generally accepted principles of delegation:

(a)   *Principle of Correspondence*: There must be party between authority and responsibility. A mismatch between delegated authority and responsibility could take one of three different forms,

(b)   *Principles of Absoluteness of Responsibility*: The responsibility may exceed authority or there may be mismatch in that authority is delegated in certain areas but responsibility is quite different activities,

(c)   *Scalar Principle*: This is another of principle of delegation which state that for delegation to work effectively, members of the organization should know where they stand in the chain of command. The scalar principle suggests that there must be a clear line of authority running step by step from the highest to lowest level of the organization. The clear line of authority will make it easier for organization members to understand to whom they can delegate, who can delegate to them and to whom they are accountable

(d)   *Unity of Command:* The unity of command principle states that each person in the organization should report to only one superior. Reporting to more than one superior makes it difficult for an individual to know to whom he or she is accountable and institutions he or she must follow.

(e)   *Maintain Open Lines of Communication*: This principle states that a free flow of information between the superior and subordinate should provide the subordinate with appropriate information with which to make decisions and properly interpret the authority delegated and facilitate feedback on the performance of the subordinate, and

(f)   *Establish Proper Controls Principle*: This principle went further to state that delegation must be accompanies by feedback processes to make sure that authority is properly used. Such controls need to be based on the goals, policies plans and standards built into the original definitions of assignments and results expected so that performance assessment and control is seen as valid and appropriate.

Finally, proper understanding of the relationship that exists among the concepts of delegation, responsibility, accountability and authority within the society and organization will ensure harmony, effectiveness and efficiency in the predetermined goals and objectives achievement in the organization and the society. The following illustration can be used to describe the above mentioned elements clearly using a restaurant as the case study. Suppose that you have just become the manager of a restaurant that is a part of a chain and that you are one of the ten restaurant managers who report to a district manager. When you take over as restaurant manager, you probably expect to be assigned a responsibility, the obligation of the assignment is to carry out the duties and achieve the goals that are related to your position as the restaurant manager!

More so, you might have the responsibility of keeping the restaurant open during certain hours, seeing that food is served, making sure the customers are satisfied, and achieving a certain profit margin. You probably also expect to be assigned responsibility, the obligation to carry out duties and achieve goals related to a position. For example, as the restaurant manager, you might expect to have the authority to hire employees, assign work, and order the food and supplies necessary to keep things running smoothly. You would also expect the position to involve accountability, the requirement to provide satisfactory reasons for significant deviations from duties are expected results.

Carrying out the story a step further, suppose you soon found that when you attempted to make decisions such as hiring a new worker, the district manager tended to interfere and even frequently reverse your decision. Yet, when the end of the month came and you had not achieve your expected profit margin largely because of interference from the district manager, the district manager still held you accountable for your short fall on results. Under this sets of circumstances, you might correctly conclude that you had been given the responsibility but not the authority needed to do your job.

In this situation, the district manager failed to ensure adequate delegation for the assignment of the restaurant manager's work; managers have to be accorded with both the responsibility and the authority necessary to achieve expected result in any modern management situation! Then delegating managers are still ultimately responsible for achieving the result and will be held accountable by their own bosses. In addition delegation facilitates developing subordinates to fill future managerial positions, thus strengthening prospects for adequate vertical co-ordination the future.

In conclusion, the above story gives clearly description about how delegation, responsibility authority and accountability relates with one another in an organization or society. It is not possible for someone maintaining delegation without responsibility and once this comes in accountability must also follow, because there is needs for the subordinate to give account of the task delegated on to him.

However, at times authority and authoritarianism are confused. Authoritarianism is a leadership style, a personal way of implementing power, which has acquired a negative commutation largely because it is through less able to achieve organizational goals and to produce human satisfaction than other leadership forms. In our analysis authoritarianism is more closely associated with power than with authority.

We must remember that power is connected with such practices as the use of incentives or coercion to secure action toward goals. The more a superior is required to use incentives or coercion the less his subordinates have accepted the legitimacy of his authority. Naturally, the most efficient and economical way of gaining compliance is by voluntary, willing submission to super–ordination.

Coercion and incentive programs are always more costly than if people are spontaneously motivated to achieve goals which they perceive as created by legitimate authority. According to *Chester Bernard*, the main vehicle for legitimating authority in organizations is communication. If people think that messages they receive are legitimate, they will accept the source which issues them as a legitimate authority and act accordingly to pursue goals which will satisfy their needs and the organizational needs concurrently.

Meanwhile, delegation in decentralized organization implies primary delegation of formal authority; that is. the pushing of decision making down the chain of command. In this situation, the district manager failed to engage in adequate delegation, the assignment of part of the manager's work to others, along with both the responsibility and authority necessary to achieve expected results. Delegation is important to vertical coordination because it allows the hierarchy to be both more efficient and more effective by enabling work to be done at the honest level possible.

In addition, delegation facilitates development of subordinates to fill future managerial positions, these strengthening prospects for adequate vertical coordination in the future. Generally, more delegating is done in a decentralized structure than in a centralized one. Even within a centralized structure, though, top managers must do some delegating because they cannot perform all the tasks available to them all above. Some tasks, however, cannot be decentralized or delegate, such tasks is that a division of a company cannot be allowed to make decisions on the wages and conditions of employment which may affect the whole company. Such decisions are normally reserved for a centralized negotiating body. Also, the function of acquiring finance cannot be delegated.

Delegation can be viewed as a defense mechanism to alleviate pressure on overburdened top management primarily because:
(a)   Delegation contributes to the improvement of performance of managers,
(b)   Delegation of authority assists managers to achieve greater flexibility and become more trustful,

(c)   Delegation is important for vertical coordination because it allows the hierarchy to be both more efficient and more effective by enabling work to be done at the honest level possible,

(d)   Delegation facilities development of the subordinates to fill future managerial position, thus strengthening prospects for adequate vertical coordination in the future,

(e)   Delegation also enriches the jobs of lower-level employees by offering workers the challenge associated with making significant decisions that affect their work,

(f)   Delegation often leads to the establishment of relatively independent units, such as divisions, whose output is easier to measure than that of units in a functional design,

(g)   Delegation helps in identifying talents. It enables the manager to assess the suitability of his subordinates for promotion by actually giving them some higher level duties to perform. With delegation, it is easy to evaluate subordinates and pin point those who are most likely to do well if promoted to a higher position,

(h)   Delegation builds a spirit of teamwork at all levels by giving others an opportunity to make decision,

(i)   Delegation enables subordinates to solve their own problems without excessive reference to the superior office,

(j)   Delegation motivates staff to want to learn. Thus it is the most effective and practical method of training and developing subordinates for higher responsibilities,

(k)   It prevents top–management overload; by delegating some tasks to lower level managers, top management would be free to concentrate on corporate priorities instead of focusing its attention on all issues, and

(1)   Development of skills and competence; the delegation of authority is essential to the development of technical, operational, administrative skills and competencies. Whether in accountancy, engineering, sales or any other occupation. It is of course, absolutely fundamental to realistic management development.

Managers must develop capacities and competencies in an atmosphere of trust, and tolerance of mistakes as a fruitful source of learning and experience. However, despite the aforementioned usefulness of delegation principles in the today's global managerial world, the inexperienced supervisors may be unwilling to delegate sufficient authority because of the following reasons.

(a)   The risk of losing control,

(b)   Real or presumed unavailability of qualified subordinates to carry out the assigned work,

(c)   The fear of possible threats from promising subordinates,

(d)   Enhancement of one's indispensability to the organization, and

(e)   Lack of delegating skill.

However, those reasons enumerated do not constitute legitimate grounds for refusal to delegate the proper amount of authority. An effective manager is willing to delegate authority needed to accomplish desire organization objectives. In order to enjoy the fruit of the modern management practice, the following guidelines will help you be an effective manager who is always ready and willing to delegate his authority to his subordinates for better effectiveness and efficiency:

(a)   The secrete of delegating is determining what each member of a work unit can do. Carefully choose the subordinate who should take on the project. Usually it is someone immediately below you in the corporate hierarchy. If you want to slip down tow ranks, work through that person's supervisor,

(b) Next, decide whether you want the subordinate to pinpoint the problem or propose a solution,

(c) Once you define your goals, consider whether the person you have chosen can handle the responsibility. Will the subordinates get frustrated? The art of managing is to figure what each person is capable of, and create assignments that are within their or slightly above, so they can learn," according to one expert,

(d) Do not make the mistake of spelling out in detail how the subordinate should approach the task. Be clear in your objectives, though, because some people fear that will appear ignorant if they ask questions. Encouragement question. To give a sense of purpose, explain why the task is important. If it is something that seems menial or insignificant, role that it is a preclude to more meaningful, assignment later on,

(e) Make sure that the subordinate has the time, budget, and data or equipment needed to get the job done- on a deadline. If someone needs training to accomplish the task, be prepared to make the investment. Yes, you could do the job yourself in the time it takes to train someone else, but the hours spent on training the individual will be recouped many times over in future,

(f) Unless the project is relatively simple, set up specific check- points to review progress so that both you and your subordinate can be sure that is progressing as planned. That way you can provide additional help, if needed, before the project is in serious trouble. If things are going well, you can let the subordinate know that you appreciate good work, and

(g)   Be prepared, too to live with a less than perfect
       result. Let subordinates know that you will support
       the outcome of their efforts, good or bad. Take
       responsibility for an occasional for an occasional
       blooper, says expert, and you will have loyal
       followers for life.

It must however be made crystal clear at this juncture
that it is not all operations that can be delegated in the
contemporary management practice. Most professional
management practitioners would naturally want to delegate:

(a)   Responsibilities that subordinates with special
       knowledge and more experience in certain tasks can
       perform better than a superior,

(b)   Things that could be done at less expense by
       subordinates who are paid less than the superior,

(c)   Responsibilities for which immediate action is
       needed and on which subordinate who are on the spot
       can act more rapidly than the superior,

(d)   Normal routine of subordinates such as the
       supervision of their own juniors, and

(e)   Those responsibilities that require subordinate to
       train and develop themselves in order to qualify for
       promotion such as technical and professional works.

The control function of the manager cannot be
delegated. It is an assigned duty the delegation of which
amounts to a state of abdication and contrary to the principle
of delegation. It means the manager or superior has
abandoned his authority and responsibility to see that the
right thing is done delegation, authority and accountability
go together. In the mean time, some employees today are
reluctant to accept the practice of delegation even where their
superior officers want to delegate to them with
commensurate authority mainly for the following reasons:

(a)   *Insecurity:* This can be a sort of obstacle to the
       subordinate in accepting delegation. More so while
       some subordinates was to avoid responsibility and

risks and so would like their bosses to make all the decisions.

(b) Some subordinate also find it difficult when it comes to acceptance of delegation because of the fear of criticism or dismissal for mistakes,

(c) Another common for reluctance is that subordinates may not be given sufficient incentive for assuming extra responsibility. Accepting delegation frequently means they will have to work harder under a greater pressure. Without appropriate compensation subordinates may be unwilling to do so,

(d) Lack of ability and necessary training to perform the tasks delegated to him by the superior, and

(e) Subordinates suffering from work overload may be incapable of accomplishing additional task delegated, and consequently feel reluctant in accepting a delegated task.

4.5   DECENTRALIZATION

Decentralization involves the division of organization into autonomous or semi-autonomous decision units where performance responsibilities and control are vested in subordinate organizational units. In human terms, true decentralization maximizes the amount of individual judgmental discretion exercised by an administrator. Meanwhile, traditionally, organizations have decentralized for one or more of the following reasons:

(a) *Cost*: The cost factor is operative when the size of an operation becomes uneconomical. Economists refer to this as diseconomies of scale,

(b) *Product Line:* This factor is operative when management considers that it is more efficient to manufacture and market a product through autonomous or semiautonomous product divisions.

(c)   *Market Area*: At times management considers it advisable to manufacture and market through regional divisions geographically decentralized, and

(d)   *Important use of Human Resources*: the opinion has long been held in participatory management theory that higher morale, greater job satisfaction, and better decisions result when people have more, rather than less, freedom to exercise independent judgment in important task decisions.

4.6   COMMUNICATIONS AS A DETERMINANT OF DECENTRALIZATION

Communication as a decentralization determinant is the consequence of organizational size and complexity. The larger an organization becomes the greater is the strain that is placed on its communication network. Communication as the traditional determinant still significantly affects managerial decisions to decentralize; the communication determinant, however, is a growing factor in decentralization decisions in practically every modern organizations.

4.7   DECENTRALIZATION OF MANAGERIAL AUTHORITY

A broader span of management occurs when a manager decentralized authority. Decentralization is to subordinates at lower levels in the organization. The degree of decentralization in an organization is not measured by the quantity of decisions that are passed down the managerial hierarchy, but rather by the importance and scope of the decisions and their impact on the entire organization. However, decentralization effects faster decision making and action *on the spot* without consulting higher levels. From Behavioral view point, decentralization creates a tendency toward greater interest and enthusiasm on the part of subordinates, since they have a greater share in management decision making.

4.8   DECENTRALIZATION AND PHYSICAL DISPERSION

The position is sometimes taken that a firm is decentralized when its management is physically dispersed. Physical dispersion, or physical decentralization, occurs when central managers are geographically separated from division or branch managers. Likewise, centralized management occurs when a central manager is heavily involved in the decisions that are made in distant divisions. Although, decentralization of decision–making authority, or decentralized management, usually goes hand in hand with physical dispersion, one does not necessarily lead to the other. Care should be taken, therefore, to distinguish between the two concepts. However, there is no simple formula to indicate the extent to which authority should be decentralized although the following factors are often considered whenever such precious modern management decisions are to be made:

(a)   Are the persons at the lower levels capable of making sound decision?

(b)   Which person down the line has the necessary facts to make a given type of decision?

(c)   Will flexible decisions be made at local level?

(d)   How important is the decision in terms of naira its impact on other decisions in the organization, and the morale of the managers down the line?

4.9 MANAGEMENT BY OBJECTIVE

Management by objective (MBO) may be defined as a systematically formalized procedure for formulating and clarifying, in broad terms, the objectives to be achieved by each worker or each division in an enterprise within a specified period of time so that the plans can be directly related to the ability and performance of individual members and groups within the system. MBO technique is usually a form of participative management approach whereby both the superior and subordinate officers jointly agree on what to do but the actual performance; that is, the methods or strategy to be used is left to the discretion of the subordinate officer. In this case, the subordinate has absolute control on the choice of the method and actual operation.

The superior officer or manager only needs to evaluate or assess the end-result of the process after the plan execution and upon the report of accomplishment by the subordinate. Consequent MBO approach to modern management involves the setting up of target or goals after a thorough negotiation between the manager and his subordinate, the specification of divisional goals, objectives, and short term performance target as well as specification of checks and balances to measure periodic performance. Hence, MBO as a management technique encourages joints participation in an organization.

MBO is used in modern management as a control mechanism because it measures the actual performance against verifiable predetermined standard jointly set by an individual and his manager. The concepts, therefore, emphasizes the pivotal function of goals and objectives setting in organizational performance. The process of MBO in modern organizations may be clearly itemized as follow:

(a)   An analysis of the broad organizational mission, vision, goals and objectives to identify the duties for the individual worker and also to spotlight the responsibility of the managers or supervisor,

(b)   The development of divisional or departmental objectives based on the corporate goals of the enterprise,

(c)   An analysis of the job description or job specification so as to establish the effort of the individual required; as well as his schedule of duties and responsibilities to be sure that these are all that are necessary towards goals accomplishment,

(d)   Pinpointing periodic. Performance targets; requirement and priorities for each worker in consonant with his superior officer,

(e)   Statement of individual workers performance standard and clear-cut objectives,

(f)   Specification of performance evaluation mechanism that will reveal the degree of successes or failures together with methods adopted to the worker,

(g)   Statement of the frequency and periodicity of meetings between the worker and his manager to evaluate the workers' performance,

(h)   End-of-the process review and discussion of the end-results by the worker and his manager,

(i)   Determination of mechanism for adjusting or modification of target or plans in response to actual performance, and

(j)   Appreciation and reward of the subordinate's efforts if satisfactory results are achieved.

Modern managers and administrators, however, agree that a lot of benefits may be derived from the practice of the principles of MBO in the contemporary organizations. For instance, the following points stand clear:

(a)   The practice of MBO allows the subordinate an opportunity to be self motivated as he also takes part in determining his own objectives or goals,

(b)   MBO encourages fairness, justice and objectivity in employees' treatment as it directly relates compensation or reward to actual performance of individual worker,

(c)   MBO assists in predetermining and developing the anticipate performance of each worker by the manager on the basis of targets jointly agreed upon by both parties: that is, the worker and his superior officer,

(d)   MBO is a useful method or technique of comparison between workers performance and their individual goal targets,

(e)   It assists in classifying and defining the job to be done by organizational members by encouraging the coming together to determine what the worker should do. This coming together allows the worker to have a clear idea or picture of what he is trying to achieve and how to make it practicable,

(f)   MBO encourages and facilitates effective commutation thereby promoting good relationship among all cadres of employees or organizational members whether subordinates or superiors by bringing them together to determine goals and evaluate performance,

(g)   MBO assists in highlighting the actual and potential sources of poor performance and specific areas requiring improvement for the manager and the subordinate through the frequent problem solving discussions thereby increasing the overall effectiveness and efficiency in the enterprise.

(h)   MBO allows for innovation and management development while young officers are encouraged to put their ideals and initiatives into use for the benefits of their organizations. This is ensured through their participation in the decision making process.

(i)   MBO encourages self-control and it is also a device for easy organizational integration. By participating in determining clear and verifiable objectives for himself, the individual has an opportunity to control his own performance without unnecessary need for supervision by any higher authority,

(j)   The principles of MBO integrate expectation and efforts of individuals in an enterprise into the corporate goals or perspectives of the organization. Each member individually and collectively is primarily concerned with his contribution to the overall organizational achievement,

(k)   MBO fosters the skills and personal development of all categories of staff and it brings about realistic goal targets as each individual member participates in determining his own objectives as well as his time limit to achieve it, and

(l)   MBO provides an unbiased criterion for performance appraisal by measuring actual performance and comparing it with established or predetermined performance standards. This drastically reduces the inherent subjectivity in employees' performance appraisal.

However, despite all the aforementioned benefits arising from the practice of MBO as a technique of management, the managerial approach still suffer from some shortcomings. According to *Oyedijo (1995: P. 140-142)*, not all goals can be quantified and verified, and hence, MBO has a limited application and utility in organizations. He agreed that increase in sales volume, for instance, is quantifiable and measurable, whereas improving administrative efficiency and staff morale is not. The emphasis on the quantifiable aspect of a man's job tends to neglect the qualitative aspects of the job.

As it is always the case in many contemporary establishments, the MBO system is really self-defeating and merely serves to mount pressure on the employees for higher productivity. This usually leads to its criticism by trade unions and workers' associations that it is mainly concerned with how to increase output and less concerned with the welfare of the operatives. Again, the concept of MBO places more emphasis on short-term objectives to the detriment of long-term goals by emphasizing what a worker is capable of achieving presently while neglecting the aspects concerning the long-term corporate goals

From experience, wrong approaches may be adopted by subordinate workers just to meet the predetermined target to which they are committed themselves before their superiors. The practice of MBO is directed or channeled towards the final outcome such as output level, product quality, profits figure, scrap or loss, etc. However, the choice of the methods and techniques is totally neglected. A machine operator may, in an attempt to meet the predestined goal, overwork the machine until it is damaged. Consequently, *the end may*, in this case, *not justify the means*,

Again, it always takes a long period of time to set attainable goals in modern organizations at all levels in an enterprise and put an MBO program in place. Implementation of an MBO program is usually costly, time-consuming and sometimes clumsy. It is usually introduced by consultants, who are in most cases outsider to the firm, and working to a fixed timetable. This means that, apart from the fact that the program may face serious antagonisms of the internal staff and their resistance, adequate time may not be given for the principles and techniques involved to be fully consolidated and assimilated before the consultants disengage themselves. Once this is done, the MBO system may suffer a setback and hence become another formality that would end up rotting inside a file cabinet!

The objectives talked about in the MBO program is rarely actually the objective of the organization. In practice, many MBO programs are imposed by operating managers and or personnel departments without much joint diagnosis to test its immediate relevance and the readiness of employees for such a program. This breeds, perpetuates and intensifies hostility, resentment and distrust between a manager and his subordinates.

MBO programs focus exclusively on individual subordinate job targets and do not give adequate recognition to workers' interdependency. This does not encourage team spirit at work, and also, the program reduces the validity of performance appraisals as it fails to consider the relationship of a subordinate's job to those of the others; that is, whether it is one of co-operation and complimentary or otherwise.

Arising from the above is the fact that in practice, MBO programs are usually introduced and implemented by consultants who are usually considered by the internal staff as outsiders. This may lead to serious antagonisms, rejection or even resistance from the internal staff as they tend to take the end-results as a kind of imposition that does not emanate from the firm. Again, the program should be handled by consultants who must be acceptable, intelligent, technically competent, modest, understanding, willing and ready to allow others to claim credit for their ideas and innovations. Such consultants are not easy to find in the industry today!

Finally, MBO programs do not give adequate wither to the areas of potential discretion open to an employee but not included in his job description; the employee tends to work to the letter of his job description or job specification to save time and other resources!   Despite the above criticisms, however modern management experts, both scientists and practitioners, have agreed on certain steps that should be taken to make the principles of MBO to be practicable in the contemporary organizations. These include:

(a)   MBO techniques should consider both the individuals and their organizations as complementary working partners that should exert mutual influence on one another. This means that each party should feel satisfied by the procedure adopted,

(b) The technique should allow for full participation of the subordinate in goals setting without being put under duress (undue influence). The procedure adopted in goal formulation should not be autocratic in anyway, and goals should not be externally imposed on the workers,

(c) The MBO techniques should normally afford the subordinate also to evaluate his superior officer; MBO does not imply a one-way approach where only the subordinate is evaluated always. This is particularly important especially with respect to the relationship which subsists between the two parties; the subordinate would want to determine how well his manager assisted him and allowed a conducive environment of work for him to perform,

(d) Other categories of workers should be allowed to participate in goals settings and strategy development as the way other people work may affect job performance by a worker. Personal jobs and group jobs should be delineated and given appropriate treatment,

(e) Both the long-term and short-term objectives for individuals and goals should be specified,

(f) Adequate necessary resources in the form of raw material, money, machines and time, etc., should be provided to the subordinate to carry out his assignment,

(g) Subordinate must be given adequate and reasonable supervision and authority to perform rather than allowing him to swim or sink to be praised or punished at the end, and

(h) Subordinate must be given commensurate compensation upon his satisfactory performance.

4.10   MANAGEMENT BY EXCEPTION

Management By Exception (MBE) is another important managerial technique which is especially applied in a situation where an executive officer (a manager or administrator) wishes to reduce the burden of coordination and control efforts on himself as part of modern management practices. The technique is actually a modification of the MBO, which was introduced into the management and administrative literature by F. W Taylor during the *taylorism* era. This technique of modern management implies that control information and reports from the organizational operation should usually be based on the principle that *only significant or extraneous deviation from acceptable predetermined standard set for subordinate officers demand the control action of the superior officer.*

By implication, when operations are still in line with the planed target, the subordinate should not bother his superior. It is only the abnormal situations outside the established range that are reported to the manager for control information and action. For instance, suppose the plan for monthly expenses of a department in an organization is within the range N10,000 and N20,000. Then, any expenses incurred within this range are allowed and should not be reported to the manager by the subordinate. However, a figure of, say, N5,000 or N23,000 that is outside this *domain* requires the attention of the manager.

Consequently, MBE implies that if the method and strategy being used as well as the expected outcomes still comply with the predetermined specification, there should be no reporting as things are working as planned. Otherwise, the attention of the manager should be invited for possible remedial action. From this discussion, therefore, for a smooth running of operations and in particular, the MBE techniques, a proper delegation of authority and assignment of responsibility together with provision of commensurate resources should be assumed. Also, an effective and efficient mechanism for regular reporting and accountability for performance should be put in place. Again, a precise definition of operational limits as well as the expected results becomes highly imperative. Finally, a clear statement of the approach or strategy to be adopted to accomplish the objectives being sought should be put in place

REVISION QUESTIONS

1. What do you understand by the terms *Management by Objective* and *Management by Exception?* Which of the two terms do you think is more practicable and more productive and why? Highlight and discuss the main merits and demerits of the terms based on your knowledge and experience of their applications in the industry.

2. With examples where necessary, explain the meanings and applications of the following terms as they are used in modern management:
   (a) Authority, (b) Responsibility,
   (c) Delegation, (d) Centralization, and
   (e) Decentralization.

3. Enumerate and discuss the fundamental principles upon which each of the following terms is based:
   (a) Authority, (b) Responsibility,
   (c) Delegation, (d) Centralization, and
   (e) Decentralization.
   Vividly discuss the merits and demerits of the above modern management terms based on your knowledge of their applications in the modern industrial organizations

4. Some amateur managers and even people in the administrative positions usually feel either reluctant or deliberate to delegate work to their subordinates. Why do

you think they do so and what is the consequence of the action?

CHAPTER FIVE

CONTROL IN MODERN MANAGEMENT

Things to consider:
* Nature of Control.
* Characteristics of Control Systems.
* Elements of a Control Mechanism
* Control Feedback Loop.
* Control Mechanisms in Practice

5.1   NATURE OF CONTROL

Control basically implies comparing actual performance with the established or predetermined standard, and reporting the various discrepancies observed to management for necessary actions. *Weihrich and Koontz (195, P. 578)* opined that the measurement and correction of performance in order to make sure that enterprises objectives and the plan desired to attain them are being accomplished. Hence, controlling function involves measurement and appraisal of work performed against the predetermined standards and the taken of appropriate steps to iron out discrepancies with due regard to the exception principle.

Control operations in modern management involve establishment of a clear cut goals performance rate, schedules and time specification, cross checking the performance or productivity rate, criteria for measuring the result and the identification of discrepancies as well as taking managerial steps to effect control. *Henri Fayol (1949, P.107)* asserted that control consist of verifying whether everything occurs in conformity with the plan adopted, the instructions issued and principles established. It has for its objectives to points out weaknesses and error in order to rectify them and prevent reoccurrence. Every organization must be controlled to keep it steady or to enable it change safely to adjust to the dynamic nature of its environment.

Control is required because unpredictable disturbances may arise and enter the system so that actual result (i.e. output of the system) deviate from expected result or goal. Examples of such disturbances in an organization would be the entry of a new powerful competitor to the market and unexpected rise in labor cost or unions demand, the failure of a supplier to deliver promised and relied-upon raw materials, workers stopping work to wonder and talk about, etc.

A control system must be initiated and the manager or administrator must be sure that the organization is capable of surviving these unexpected or unanticipated disturbances by dealing with them in appropriate manner. Control makes it possible to steer a system or organizational system to survive changes in the environment. For illustration, without a proper and appropriate means of control, an organization will be likened to a ship that sets sail in Nigeria, aiming at going to Ghana, but eventually find itself in Saudi Arabia!

Control is dependent on the receipt and processing of information. This information may be received from:
(a) Formal sources within the organization designed by the managers or administrators of the organization such as vouchers, various forms, computer printouts, etc.
(b) Informal sources from within the organization especially the work or pressure groups and other unauthorized information carriers.
(c) Formal sources outside the organization such as those obtained from macro-environment, telephone messages, etc.

(d) Informal sources from outside the organization (i.e. from the environmental source external to the organization) such as quantities of goods and cost of goods of competitors in the industry.

Control might be exercised to ensure conformity to plans and standards. It is, however, meaningless to consider control system without having an idea of what is to be achieved. That is, controlling of the laid-down and popularized systems. However, control can only be exercised through the use of information.

5.2 CHARACTERISTICS OF CONTROL SYSTEMS

Reliable and effective control systems have certain characteristics in common. The relative importance of these characteristics varies with individual circumstances, but most control systems are strengthened by their presence. Such characteristics include the following:

(a) *Accuracy:* Information on performance must be accurate. Inaccurate data from a control system can cause the organization to take action that with either fail to correct a problem or create a problem where none is in existence. Evaluating the accuracy of the information they receive is one of the most important control task managers face..

(b) and *Timeliness:* Information must be collected, routed evaluated quickly if action is to be taken in time to produce improvement.

(c) *Objectivity and Comprehensiveness:* The information in a control system should be understandable and be seen as objective by the individuals who use it. The less subjective or ambiguous the control system, will cause unnecessary mistakes and confusion or frustration among employees.

(d)   *Focused and Strategic Control Points:* The control system should be focused on those areas where deviations from the standards are most likely observable or where deviations would lead to the greatest harm. The system should also be focused on those points where corrective action can be most effectively applied. For instance, it would do little good to control parts quality after the parts have already been shipped to customers' parts quality is most logically checked immediately after the parts

are   out of the assembly line.

(e)   *Realism:* The cost of implementing a control system should be less, or at most, equal to the benefits derived from the control system. The best way to minimize waste or unnecessary expenditure in a control system is to do the minimum amount necessary to ensure that the monitored activity will reach the desired goals. For example, in most situations, it would be wasteful for a sales manager to receive daily sales reports. Weekly or monthly sales report is usually sufficient.

        Again, the control system has to be compatible with organizational realities. For example,

individuals   have to be able to see a relationship between performance levels they are asked to achieve and rewards that will follow. Furthermore, all standards for performance must be realistic.

(f)   *Flexibility:* Few organizations today are in such a stable environment that they do not worry about the possibility of change. For almost all organizations, control must have flexibility built into them so that the organizations can react quickly to overcome since adverse changes or take advantages of new opportunities.

(g)   *Prescriptive and Operational:* Effective control systems ought to indicate upon the detection of a deviation from standards, what corrective action should be taken? The information should be in a useable form when it reaches the person responsible for taking the necessary action.

(i)   *Authority for Setting Standards:* Consideration must be given to the need to involve those whose activities are to be controlled when setting the standards to make the control system   effective. When standards are set unilaterally by upper level managers, there is a danger that employees   will regard that standard as unreasonable and unrealistic.

(j)   *Direction of Feedback:* Feedback control information should direct to the individual or group performing the control activity and not only to the superior. This will ensure that those individuals or groups are able to take whatever corrective action as may be is necessary and would not view the control system as punitive.

(k)   *Tailored to Positions:* For instance, a control that will be suitable for a production manager will certainly not be applicable to the factory supervisor. Furthermore, controls for the sales department will differ from those for finance department.

(l)   *Tailored to Individual Managers and their Personalities:* For control information to be relevant it must be capable of being understood easily by the recipient. This is likely to be so tailored to the individual personalities of the recipient. For instance, some people such as the accountants and statisticians like their information in form of complex tables or data or voluminous computer printouts. Others people like theirs in terms of charts, while scientists prefer such information in mathematical models.

5.3   ELEMENTS OF A CONTROL MECHANISM

Remember that we have said that control is the activity, which measures deviations from planned or expected performance or result, and trigger or initiate corrective or remedial action. However, the basic elements of control systems are:

(a)   A standard specifying expected or anticipated performance. This can be a budget or plan on operation procedure or decision rules.
(b)   A measurement of actual performance or achievement;
(c)   Comparison of standard with actual performance or achievement.
(d)   Report of deviation or variation to a control unit perhaps by a manager, administrator or controller;
(e)   A set of corrective or remedial actions which the control unit can take to effect the change of performance if at present it were unfavorable; and
(f)   In the event of failure of the control units, action producing the required correct performance, there may be a procedure for higher level action. For instance, by changing the control unit or revising performance standards or even introducing more or improved resources or other input factors.

5.4   CONTROL FEEDBACK LOOP

Control is exercised in organizational systems by information feedback loops. Feedback is the return of part of the output of a system to the input unit as a means towards improved quality or correction of errors. For examples, the feedback to the Managing Director of PZ Industries, Lever Brothers Group, or UAC of Nigeria Plc on the progress on a capital investment programs, feedback to works manager in a manufacturing company on current production level, and at the operational levels, feedback to a shop-floor foreman or supervisor on rate of defective products or scraps being generated in the factory.

A feedback loop is, therefore, a close loop system. However, an open loop system is a control system without any feedback subsystem. A business organization, for instance, uses feedback for control purposes and, therefore, has a close loop control system. However, external influences must not be ignored. A good management information system must be designed to provide proper feedback as well as environmental information to optimize the organizational control system. A very useful concept in managerial control is that of double loop control feedback which is also referred to as Higher Level Control Feedback, HLCF and it uses the control information transmitted to the higher level in the organizational system. In big or giant organizations like multinationals, higher level feedback is reported to the most senior level of management.

Where as Single Loop Control Feedback, SLCF is concerned with the control of task (a special job), HLCF is concerned with multiple or overall control of the organization. The term double loop feedback indicates that information is reported to indicate both divergences between the standard and actual result where control action might be required and also the need for adjustment of the plan, strategy, and policy and programs themselves. The scale or scope of control action at higher level will be wider when compared with the one at the level of single loop feedback.

There will be larger variations (variances) or deviations requiring control actions or measures at the higher levels. Again, Higher Level Control Feedback consists of information gathered from measuring outputs, results or performance of an organizational system, and also the one from environmental sources. Another important concept as far as managerial control analysis is concerned is that of negative control feedback. This relates to information, which indicates that the system is deviating from its planned or prescribed course, and that some re-adjustment becomes highly imperative to bring it back on course. This feedback is called negative control feedback because control action would seek to reverse the direction or movement of the system back toward its planned course.

For illustration, if the budgeted sales of Odua Group of Companies for, say, the months of May and June 1999 were N200,000 each month whereas the report of actual sales in May shows that only N190,000 has been realized, this negative feedback would indicate that control action was necessary to raise sales for the month of June in the company to N210,000 in order to get back on the planned course. The negative feedback in this case would necessitate the June sales exceeding the budget by N10,000 because the May sales fell short of the budget by N10,000.

This is followed by the concept of positive control feedback. The positive control feedback normally resorts to control actions, which cause actual performance to be maintained or to increase the organization path of deviation from planned or predetermined result. For example, in business organizations where advertising budget is linked to sales, as sales increased beyond the original destined target, positive control feedback information would cause advertising budget to be increased.

However, many systems in practice are oscillating systems. This implies that the level of activities fluctuates and that this fluctuation is part of the plan. Typical examples are the cases of seasonal variations like products which are sold more particularly during *Id-El-Kabir* (a prominent Muslims festival called Ileya in Yoruba language) rush for clothing and some household materials.

The problems associated with the positive control feedback in oscillating systems are:

(a)   When to carry out the corrective process when actual performance diverges from plan; and

(b)   When to chat up the corrective process. However, if there were delay in applying control, the effect of corrective action might be to increase the size of the divergence from plan rather than to reduce it and in oscillating systems, delay action might increase the size of the error more and more until the system goes out of control.

Next are the concepts of open and close loop control systems. An *open loop* control system is the one where control is exercised, regardless of output or performance standard, by the organization. By this control system, there is no feedback loop and control is external to the system, and it is not an integral part of the organization. The control action is not automatic and may be made without monitoring the output of the system.

For example, consider a water heater without an automatic thermostat to control it, The system can be externally controlled by switching it off and on at appropriate time. Some of the *disadvantages* of the open loop control system might be the breakdown of communication system; in a production control system whereby measurement of output were not communicated in time to make the necessary adjustment to products input. Also, a department without a budgetary control system lacks the essential element of a feedback control loop and control may have to be exercised from outside the department such as reduction of staff or expenditure.

On the other hand, a *close loop* control system is the one where parts of the output are fed back to the input unit so that the output can initiate or trigger control action to change either the activities of the system or the systems input. Many mechanical systems like engines, thermostat in heating systems, etc are *close loop systems*. For example, in a stock control system with planned level of stock, the actual level of stock is measured and compared with the plan, while adjustment is made to the stock replenishment order quantity in order to bring the stock level in line with the plan or budget.

Complex systems such as giant organizations, whether in private sector like multi-products, multi-locations and multi-departments like the UAC, Peugeot Automobile Nigeria Plc, Kingsway Supermarkets, etc, or in the public sector like the multi-national and transitional organizations contain a large number of elements or components and pursue a wide range of objectives or goals.

The law of requisite varieties propounded by Ross Ashby states that complete control of a system can only be obtained when the control mechanism possesses varieties at least equal to the system being controlled. The effect of this is that relatively simple control system such as a departmental budgetary control cannot be expected to control the multipurpose activities of a complex organization. At best, such control or mechanism may only control a narrow aspect of the organization's operations. On the other hand, the varieties within a system or organization must be at least as great as the environmental varieties against which they are attempting to regulate themselves.

If there is a variety in environmental influence in the system, then the system influence must be suitably varied and sufficiently variable to adapt itself successfully to its environment. If a system does not have sufficient variety, it will be unable to adapt to changes and will eventually die or be replaced. For example, some political systems that could not adapt to social, economic or political changes are always overthrown. The law of requisite varieties applies to self-regulating systems in general but one application of the law relates to control systems. A control system, which is a subsystem of larger system, must be sufficiently flexible to be able to deal with the varieties occurring naturally in the system that it is attempting to control.

Control must not, therefore, be too rigid. Rigidity of any institutional structure must eventually lead to dissolution of the society by way of internal upheaval or ineffectiveness against external challenges. However, there are several ways of reducing rigidity and introducing the needed varieties into organizational systems control; the outstanding ones are discussed in the following paragraphs. An organization may allow a controller some discretion to judge what control is needed. In a business system, for instance, managers should not be instructed that a problem must be handled in a particular way especially when the problem involves labor relations, disciplinary procedures, and motivation of the work force or any other Behavioral matters. The response of individuals to control action by managers and administrators would vary because people are different, and even a person's moods change from time-to-time.

The next approach to solving the same problem is by introducing tolerance or allowable limits. When actual performance differs from planned results, control action should only be applied when variance becomes excessive and exceeds allowable tolerance limits. Tolerance limit recognizes that plans are based on an average or what is normal or what is expected to happen and so variation around this average will be due to natural causes for which there should be no reason for getting worried. Finally, there must be as many variables in the control system as there are variables in the system it is controlling. This implies that control should be fairly complex rather than simplistic since most social and management systems themselves are complex structures and organizations.

If the management of an organization attempts to control the organization by means of quantitative budgets or plans, this would appear too narrow-minded an action because it would exclude many factors in the organization's operations such as break downs, strikes, insufficient or inadequate supply of materials, etc. However, the attitudes and Behavior of the individuals and groups of individuals being controlled in an organization are of paramount importance to the success of any organizational control system.

Higher level of management may obtain feedback information as they attempt to alter operations to conform to the plan. However, it is the individual staff members who actually exercise control by accepting or rejecting standards, by exercising or not exercising care or by any other similar Behavior. Control system must therefore be designed with regards to human factors. However, various Behavioral guidelines have been recommended. For instance, the standards or targets must be accepted as being correct.

The method by which the standards are derived must be clearly understood by those affected and the standards must reflect realistically the capability of the section or department. Also, standards must be set so that occasional lapses, mistakes or errors are not unduly reprimanded. Individuals must be made not to belief that they are being unduly blamed for matters outside their control or area of competence. Again, there must be full participation by the individual and groups within the organization, in the setting of his/their performance target(s) and the acceptance of the target finally established by all.

Finally, feedback must be in two ways. It is not only that the information should flow upwards to the controller; it must also be provided for those being controlled. This feedback of information on performances and standards provides and promotes motivation for individuals as individuals and members of work groups, and provision of such information should be designed into the control system.

Meanwhile, for an organizational control mechanism to be effective, the following requirements must be met:

(a) The objective of the organization must be clearly, simply and rationally identified and specified. For instance, managers and administrators in organizations should not be misled or misdirected because of ambiguities and fallacies in organizational system objectives.

(b) Such an organizational objective must be relevant and congruent, and must focus towards its attainment.

(c) Such a organizational objective, procedure and technique must be economical, and the objectives must be few and realizable. The information gathering on performance, measurement yardstick must also involve minimum effort and time.

(d) The organizational objective and procedure for achieving it must be meaningful, realistic and priorities of the organizational system control should be based on the definition of organizational operations.

(e) The overall result of the control system itself must be operational. That is, the control system must be capable of practical application.

(f) The control system must be forward looking; it must be useful today as well as in the future in the organization.

(g) The control system must be reliable, consistent; adequate, appropriate and valid in all ramifications within the specific area of application within the organization; and

(h) The control system must provide expected or anticipated information as feedback for appropriate decision-making within the organization.

The major rationale behind system control in organizations whether in the public or in the private sector is to allow managers and administrators to direct, coordinate and harmonize better the operations of their organizations. Other concomitant reasons include:

(a) To improve quality standards and quantities of organizational products and thereby increase the net return on input factors.

(b) To design and implement an appropriate system of control and information feedback required to check performance progress and exert influence on the operations of the organization.

(c)   To maintain self-control, self-discipline and motivation on the part of both the workers and the management in the organization. When both the subordinate and his superior officer know what is expected of them individually or collectively, there may be possible adjustment in order to meet the required standard of performance or productivity.

(d)   To alleviate managerial burden on the key executives in the organization and facilitate more delegation of duties to subordinates. This helps to develop more executive talent within the organization and hence ensures continuity of organizational management.

(e)   To clarify, specify and delineate desired operation results accurately and in accordance with established plans, standards and results.

(f)   To identify, forecast and plan for the major anticipated trends, threats, opportunities, weaknesses and problems that may come up in the organization, and to develop appropriate strategies, policies and programs to handle them in advance; and

(g)   To measure both the standard and performance of a system or organization, and identify variations where they exist and the sources so that timely remedial steps can be taken before the whole effort of the organization is sunk.

Various managerial control systems especially budgetary control indicates from research that they are not as effective as the top management and management specialist would like to believe. Many managers and administrators do not consider that control systems are effective and some even ignore the various reports and statements since the information they contain is of little use to them because:

(a)   Sometimes the subject covered was outside the manager or administrator's control.

(b) Sometimes, the information arrived too late for effective action to be taken.

(c) Sometimes, insufficient details were provided.

(d) Sometimes the information supplied was thought by the manger or administrator to be inaccurate; and

(e) Sometimes, information is supplied in such a way that it could not be understood.

However, despite all these imperfections, the technique of control is still considered by the modern day administrators and management experts, practitioners and consultant as being associated with planning as part of scientific management. As with organizational planning, so in organizational control, there is no attempt to create a super-authority nor to create an extra, over-riding command; control is effected through the organization structure. It must always be remembered that the act of control is concerned with seeing that everything is carried out in its predestined order. It is a continuous process of measuring actual results of the operations of an organization, in comparison with the standard laid down as a guide.

It is however, important to bear in mind that as far as control in organizational management is concerned in its association with organizational planning, mainly with the provision of *information*, there is a distinction between *fact-control* with which we are now concerned and *man-control* which entails motivation or command and which is a different element of management entirely. What is sought after an organizational control technique is *information for management* on the progress of events, with no attempt to influence those events as an initial part of the system. The information discerned from its checks is fed to those with the responsibility for affairs so that their attention is directed to important factors, the alteration of which would lead to an improvement in overall performance.

Also, there is an advantage in making some of the necessary control information available for other purposes, notably for financial and cost accounting records. When financial standards are employed, it is possible to provide control information on income and expenditure so that the important features of surety of income at a sufficiently high level can be frequently checked. The financial information available from the figures of cost compiled at the various operations and processes of the organization can also be processed to provide a different type of control information which is of paramount use in showing the merits and demerits of alternative course of action.

Finally, significant numerals of dates or time periods are also a commonly used form of expressing of the standard from which the appropriate control information is expected to be provided. Whatever the form of expression used, the information provided is always to be made available by comparison of the results of working with the predetermined plans.

5.5   CONTROL MECHANISMS IN PRACTICE

In practice, if the process of organizational control is studied in detail, whether in private or public sector, the characteristics of it become clear. Fundamentally, there is always a process which is being worked out by operators through tools, machines or other forms, on the material of manufacture. The fundamental process is as true of the office as of the factory and will apply whether the objective is the manufacturing of goods for sale or the provision of a service. For purpose of analysis, it does not matter whether the materials are metal, chemical substances or paper work forms; nor whether they are purchased by the company carrying out the work or sent to it by customers to whom the services are provide.

Plans will have been formulated for the optimum employment of the available resources in line with the policies laid down.   These will have been transmitted through the line of authority as clear directives with adequate explanations, so that everyone concerned with any part of the process may know of the contribution he or she is expected to make. Therefore, *we have as preliminary to control "a process of the operation for which plans are laid down and the personnel is briefed."* As the process is carried out, errors may be caused by the activities of workers or by the inadequacies of machinery, power suppliers or material availability. In fact, there are innumerable opportunities, during the various sequences of activities which make up the manufacturing cycle for the work done and the movements leading to deviation from the plans laid down, to guide the process. If the plans are realistic, reliable and basically sound, deviations are serious as they interfere with the achievement of the aims if they were allowed to continue.

It is therefore necessary to recognize the character, likewise the extent reached by the deviations as soon as possible after they have occurred, so that their seriousness can be assessed. Any necessary corrective action should then be taken in time to influence events before they become too seriously disturbing. The object of the process of control is to reveal these deviation and their causes by a feedback of information which can be used to initiate appropriate correction. When the comparisons are made continuously and information about them is available immediately, the process is said to be in a *state of control.*

The action required from a management control is similar to that of a governor fitted to an engine as a speed control device. One of the earliest governors was of the ball type which allowed the position of balls rotating around a vertical spindle at a speed proportional to that of the engine, to alter the opening of ports to allow the steam or gas-air mixture to enter the cylinder. When the engine speed was high, the port was closed, when low, it was opened up to allow more steam to enter. In this way, the *fly ball governor*, as it was called, kept the engine running between determined limits of speed by a self-regulating feedback process.

It will be observed, however, that particularly all control systems have the attributes of comparison of plan and performance, as well as those of identification of deviations reported by feedback, so that their seriousness can be assessed and corrective actions specified. These are examples of cybernetic systems of control in which a governing or monitor action is built-in so that corrections are made whenever deviations become apparent. They are examples of *close loop systems.* However, management control in organizations are typical examples of *open loop systems* in which the information on deviation is fed out for corrective action to be specified by a person called the organizational or system controller with the title of manager or administrator. The methods of sensing the information in organizational management are in the simpler examples, manual in type and involve the institution of perhaps clerical procedures by which frequent comparison can be made between plan and performance.

The application of managerial control should be fairly widespread throughout the organization if maximum advantage were to be gained from the availability of information about deviations from plans. The different groups of activities, which are subjected to control, by comparison of plan with performance, are the concern of separate independent specialists. In some cases, their job title reflects this by containing the word *controller* as production controller, financial controller, or material controller. Each controller then specializes in the organization and employment of the procedures necessary for information to be provided about the variables with which his technique is concerned. Basic requirements which must be considered by all controllers are the methods of formulation of the plan in specific terms; the methods of checking for comparison with the plan; and documentary procedures to be used for reporting deviations.

The actual planning is not always the controller's responsibility and it is usually better that it is not, since it is not possible to view this more objectively when making the subsequent comparison. The deviations revealed might be just as much a criticism of the plan as of the performance as what has happened is real and what was expected is hypothetical. The variables with high degree of susceptibility to control are the output of parts and products from operations and processes against plans which have been laid down in respect of both quantity and quality; the timing of that output in relation to the calendar; the level of stocks held throughout the factory which allows the work to proceed without interruptions; the idle time of machines spent on repairs or breakdowns; and the cost of output, not only in total but broken down into each constituent item of expenditure.

The systems control techniques associated with each of the above mentioned variables will be briefly considered in turns to shows the scope and extent of control systems and the methods by which they are put into practice particularly in the modern industrial organizations:

(a) *Quality Control:* This involves the system or technique of checking or verifying the items in stock to discover how many parts are produced to the required quality standard. It may be done by simple inspection devices to expose defective products and also reveal the reasons for them so that corrective actions can be taken. Also, the timing of the output in relation to the calendar has been stated to be susceptive to control the pre-requisite for this is the data plan or schedule, which determines the order of priority in which the various items being manufactured at the same time must be tackled.

(b) *Process Control:* This is concerned with ensuring that the sequence in which the parts are loaded onto machine or any conversion process is in accordance with schedules of work. This control system or technique can best be instituted by clerical procedures operated in a central chart room adjacent to the factory floor.

(c) *Stock Control:* This is one of the voluminous clerical procedures of a control system since records must be kept of all materials stocked. On each individual record card, fluctuations in stock are recorded. So, it is necessary to enter every withdrawal from stock by a requisition being presented to stores, as well as every occasion on which replenishment stocks have been received.

In this way, the record should always carry a balance figure, which agrees with the quantity physically held in store. Reservations of stocks for a particular purpose are also shown so that, of the balance in stock, the *free* stock not allocated for any particular use will always be known. All these must be properly done and checked if work were to be allowed to proceed according to plan, with no hold-up of production for awaited materials.

(d) *Maintenance Control:* To keep plant and machinery in continuous system, there should be a form of maintenance control work or system which is necessary to be transformed from a series of emergency operations to continuous program of work. The appropriate plan for guidance of this work will include two constituent parts. One is concerned with the maintenance to be carried out by different tradesmen at stated intervals while the other specifies the date and time of availability of each machine for maintenance.

One of the objectives of maintenance control is to keep production costs to a minimum. This being the case, it is obviously not practical to make arrangements of such length and complexity that could make the cost of the maintenance to exceed the cost of the breakdown it is endeavoring to obviate.

(e) *Cost Control:* This entails control of cost of production which requires establishment of a standard or expected cost which, having been predetermined, can be used as a base for comparison with actual cost incurred. A particular level of plan efficiency is assumed from past records and the output of the factor is budgeted and the cost of this output calculated from this assumption.

The use of standard costs by which to judge the historical or factual cost focuses attention on the cost variances which demand action if high efficiency were to continue. When standards are used for the control of expenditure in this way, there is a greater assurance that a particular profit margin will result from this practice.

(f) *Budgeting and Budgetary:* This is a control system which covers the organization rather than a department of it. When resources are utilized in standardized manner, the actual financial implications are measured and compared with the budget figures for control of operations.

(g) *Management Audit/Internal Audit:* Management audit implies a comprehensive appraisal and review of an organizational management process including the extent of effectiveness of the system of delegation, adequacy of the method of planning and control, skills in supplying management information as a guide to action, its use of human and physical facilities and in general the competence of supervisory and specialist teams. On the other hand, internal audit implies auditing of account operations of an organization to identify where lapses are likely to occur, and where remedial action will have to be taken.

Conclusively, in the management and administration of the modern day organizations, irrespective of their scope or size, orientation and ownership the significance of control mechanism cannot be under-estimated. Practically in every aspect of human endeavors, control must be applied in its totality; that is its process, methods or techniques.

As part of the general planning process, control systems or mechanisms should be made in an attempt:
(a)   To minimize wastages.
(b)   To sustain proper maintenance.
(c)   To eradicate sub-optimality; and
(d)   To institute an appropriate form of built-in-checks and balances into the organizational operations system.

Consequently, excessive deviation from plans can be dealt with appropriately before the whole organizational effort is sunk for lack of foresight. Hence, it may be rightly asserted that *the pivot element upon which the principles of scientific management in organizations is based on control mechanism.* From the discussion in this section we will agree that controlling is one of the most important functions in modern corporate management and administration.

REVIEW QUESTIONS
1.   What do you understand by the term: System Control? "Control is dependent on information within an organization." Do you agree? Elucidate.
2.   With practical examples from what obtains in the contemporary organizations, discuss vividly the various control elements with which you are familiar.
3.   (a)   With illustrations from practice, explain your understanding of the term: *feedback control loops."*
     (b)   Write short, but self-explanatory note on each of the following: (i) double loop Control Feedback,

(ii) Negative Control Feedback, (iii) Positive Control Feedback; and (iv) Open and close loop control feedback.

4. Using your knowledge and experience of the happenings in the modern day organizations, elucidate the concept of the *Law of Requisite Varieties* citing an example from both the private and public sectors.

5. What can you say about the Behavioral aspect of systems control? Discuss fully the way the managers and administrators go about controlling their organizational activities in practice.

6. Outline and discuss the major control techniques with which you are familiar in the modern day public and private organizations.

7. How would you determine the effectiveness and efficiency of the various control mechanisms in a named organization with which you are familiar in your locality?

8. There have been remarkable works done on the concept, principles and practice of systems control by organizational theorists and management scientists; what do you think are the factors responsible for this phenomenon?

CHAPTER SIX

CORPORATE POLICY

Things to consider:

- Nature of Policy.
- Characteristics and Benefits of Policy.
- Sources of Organizational Policy.
- Policy Formulation Models.
- Policy Process.
- Policy Formulation.
- Policy Implementation.
- Policy Evaluation.
- Management Guidance

6.1   NATURE OF POLICY

Many notable writers had contributed and are still contributing to the field of policy and strategy analysis most especially in the area of description and application. In the most general form, policy may be best described rather than to offer a single not so much popular definition to the concept. This is mainly because the place or scope of policy and strategy extends to analysis of those facts or factors extraneous to the particular organization. The variables in this respect affect and are affected by the progress and evolution of a company's long range plans and strategy choices in terms of survival, growth, entry into and exist from markets as well as competitive Behavior.

The externalities in this case include legal, economic, political, social, cultural and technological phenomena and they may affect corporate activities and consequently affect the firms' strategic plans. Organizational policy is the study of the finance and responsibilities of top level general management and the problems which affect the success and survival of the corporate entity of the company. The problem of policy in an enterprise has to do with the choice of purposes, the unification of organizational features, the identification, statement and definition of organizational problems in terms of what needs to be done, how to go about doing it and when, and the mobilization of available resources for the achievement of goals, aims and objectives at the corporate level despite the constraints imposed by surrounding circumstances which are in most cases unfavorable or uncompromising in nature.

However, policy has been defined by *Ladipo Adamolekun* as a course setting involving decisions of the widest ramifications and longest time perspective in the life of an organization. At once, this definition introduces us to the concept of *decision*, which is often used interchangeably with the term policy. The point of difference that deserves mentioning in this definition is that *policy* usually has wider ramifications and a longer time perspective than a *decision*. Policy is a standing guide for making administrative decisions as it relates to a single objective. E. F. L. Brech in his book, *Management; Its Nature and Significance*, Page 75 described policy as *a pattern of direction for the guidance of those who carry responsibility for the management of the affairs of an enterprise.* It is a corporate normative guide for making and implementing decisions for management thinking and actions. Alternatively, corporate policy is nothing but internal administrative law which guides the thanking and action of managers. Each time a question about a particular matter arises, the manager would just turn to the policy manual for the established solution. For example, what discount to give to what category of orders?

Policy is an established way of doing business and directing actions in a specified area of management. It is an internal administrative law governing executive actions in an organization. It is also a statement of principles indicating the general pattern of Behavior to be followed to secure implementation and achievement of organizational objectives. It is the expression of the operational implication of strategy in detail. This implies that the full implication of strategy is amplified and clarified by thinking through the more detailed policy that guides the execution of strategy.

Other terms commonly found in the modern management literature in association with the concept of policy and decision analysis, according to Adamolehun, include policy science, policy development, policy making, policy and decision, policy formulation, policy implementation, policy evaluation, policy impact, policy maker, decision making, decision maker and decision theory. Although we shall not attempt to define each term in turn in this book, the specific meaning attached to each one will be made clear at the first mention whenever it it becomes necessary.

Organizational policy investigates and examines the functions and responsibilities of the top level management in selecting the direction of the corporate organization and in establishing qualities and benchmarks for monitoring and controlling organizational performance. Organizational policy specifies the organizational product-marketing decisions, the way and the direction in which the firm seeks to grow and change, the competitive tools, techniques and methods it would employ, the means by which it would enter a new market, the manner by which it will configure its resources, the strength it will seek to exploit, the weakness and threat it will seek to avoid or minimize, and so on.

Corporate policy is a concept of the corporate organization which provides a unifying theme for all its activities. Each of the main functional areas in an enterprise has its own related policy. For instance, we speak of marketing policy, finance policy like dividend policy and capital structure policy, personnel policy like *grow your own* policy and *recruit the readymade* policy, and production policy and decisions just to mention but a few. Each of these functional policies is interrelated and they combine to form what is known as the corporate policy as we have corporate planning and corporate strategy in the same logical reasoning.

In a small firm, all these functional policies are the responsibilities of one man; that is, the owner and hence coordination is not difficult. In large corporation, however, as in the case of the multinational, transnational or multi-products firms, these functional decisions and policies are separated and put in charge of different persons. Consequently, formal coordination becomes imperative. The hierarchical structure is used to achieve this purpose. Higher officers' policy however may over-rule that of the lower cadres; the latter having been integrated level of authority, decision making is a long term, strategic and concerned with the entire organization as a whole. This is a distinguishing feature of the corporate policy from departmental operational policies, the routine or day-to-day corporate arrangements.

However, the public sector approach to the study of modern management and administration focuses attention on the policy process as an important characteristic of public sector analysis. This approach began as an important dimension in modern management literature during the first three decades of the 19th Century. The approach is even regarded by the contemporary students of public administration as an emerging applied discipline in the social science family. Prominent among the believers of this school of thought usually refer to this specialized field of knowledge as *policy science*. Meanwhile, it must be stated here that the overall emphasis so far in the various discussions of the public policy approach to modern management is on the improvement of the public sector policy process.

Having provided some operational definitions of the term *policy,* we must now define the latter. A useful definition states that a decision is a conscious choice between two or more choices. This definition is particularly helpful because it is appropriate for both the simple decisions we make in daily domestic life and the more wide-ranging decisions that the government of a nation state makes in its external relations. For example, when a person takes a decision on the choice of what to wear each morning, he will be making a conscious choice between two or more sets of clothes. In the same vein, during the month of September 1975, Nigeria had to take a decision on the Angolan question. She had to make a conscious choice between a set of alternatives.

6.2   CHARACTERISTICS AND BENEFITS OF POLICY

It should be noted that policy is not an order or command. Neither is it a procedure, a system or a method as such. The main features of a good organizational policy are that it must be:

(a)   Simple and relevant to the organizational operations. It should not be two complex for human understanding,

(b)   Flexible, adjustable and adaptable enough to be able to respond to environmental changes such as responsiveness to social, economic and technological phenomena in the environment,

(c)   Adequate and up to date to be relevant at all time to matters at hand or matters of the moment,

(d)   Consistent and not conflicting; it should allow and accommodate equal opportunity or treatment to like issues and situations,

(e)   Definite, clear and reduced to written to prevent operatives from formulating their own personal opinions on different kinds of matters and develop their knowledge of what they suppose to do or how they are required to act in certain ways,

(f)   Planned and systematically developed in line with corporate culture and acceptable pattern of Behavior in the organization,

(g)   Easy to implement within the limit of the organizational resources,

(h)   Consistent with, or conform to, ethical standard. That is, it should not be in conflicting with moral values of the society where it is to be used,

(i)   Able to lead to development of a clear-cut corporate image or personality for the company, and

(j)   Broad enough to give or allow room for discretion within a tolerant or allowable limit where this becomes imperative.

In the mean time, there are many advantages of formulating a sound policy and these include the fact that policy:

(a)   Provides consistency of action and ensures fairness and a normal predictable pattern of action,

(b)   Guides the thought and actions of managers and simplifies the process of decision making by management,

(c)   Minimizes management problems as it helps to clarify management's view points and philosophy within designated areas of operation,

(d)   It helps to define procedures and systematically Organize efforts to achieve corporate purposes,

(e)   Policy offers an important avenue for correlating many facets of the enterprise with strategy and for relating activities and decisions directly to specific objective,

(f)   It provides purpose and coordination throughout the organization and hence creates the framework within which each function is carried out,

(g)   It facilitates delegation of authority and assignment of responsibility and thereby permits the establishment of relatively autonomous decisions while ensuring that overall control is retained,

(h)   It helps to anticipate and prepare for future conditions and resolve as to how they will be dealt with in advance, and

(i)   It serves to maintain favorable management climate by producing test of confidence in making administrative decisions.

6.3   SOURCES OF ORGANIZATIONAL POLICY

Although there are various approaches to the understanding of the concepts of policy, modern management philosophers have agreed that corporate policy may be classified into originated policy, appealed policy, imposed policy, and implied policy. *Originated policy* is derived from the jobs or functions of an organization as started in the memorandum of association. They are usually laid down by the board. This category of policies is usually formulated by top-management, Board of Directors or the Managing Director, and spread across and downward the lines in the organization. Such a policy aims to guide subordinate managers in their operational activities.

It flows logically from the goals and objectives of the company. The Board of Directors will first observe the goals and objectives before organizational policies are set. However, policy is also said to be originated if those who are responsible for its implementation are below the Board in hierarchy. *Appealed policy* is the one that arises as a result of different appeals of subordinates to their superior officer in the hierarchy of managerial authority. For instance, a manager that is not sure of his authority on how one particular matter should be handled may consult his superior officer. A decision in this case on a regular basis turns to become an unwritten policy. Appeals are taken upwards and decisions are made on them and hence, a kind of common law is established. Precedent develops and becomes guide for future managerial action.

The shortcomings of appealed policies however are:

(a)   They are often inconsistent, incomplete, uncoordinated, un-integrated and decisions based on them may not properly or perfectly guide the thought and action of subordinates as really desired by top management,

(b)   They may bring about formulation of policies not immediately known to top management, and

(c)   Sometimes, appealed policies may be in conflict with originated policies.

Imposed policy is the one which arises as a result of external factors like the government and suppliers or customers. It usually occurs when there are internal deficiencies. It is also imposed by external bodies like the trade unions through negotiations on the company. It may be from the pressure groups as well or economic group of nations as the case of the United States and Allied Forces on Iraq during the Gulf war which eventually led to the dethronement of *Sadam Hosanne* in 2004.

The emergence of an externally imposed policy signifies that the internal or originated policy is deficient, inconsistent, unrealistic or weak such as deficiencies of originated policies in Nigeria as an example of the third world countries have led to externally imposed policies like Governments interests and intervention is sustenance of economic planning, growth and development in the economy. Hence, government has legislated that a company cannot declare dividend unless it makes an after-tax profit. Another example is that a company that has the usual practices of paying its suppliers late may be forced to adopt *cash with order* policy by its supplier or else there will be no supplies.

Finally, the *implied policy* is the one that arises from the actions of managers: that is, by implication. When an action is just unconsciously taken and nothing dangerous is noticed traceable to the adoption of the policy, and if the manager is allowed to follow suit in future, it becomes an *acceptable policy* since it has been done and therefore *no rejection implies acceptance*. Such policies arise from the initiatives of the managers.

6.4   POLICY FORMULATION MODELS

In the quest for knowledge about how decisions or policies are made (or formulated) within modern organizations (both public and private), modern management philosophers have developed a number of models. The most common of these models are *rational comprehensive model*, *satisficing model, incrementally-disjointed model*, and muddling through model. Since a model is an abstract representation of the real would, there is no suggestion here that any one model represents the real-life situations. However, each model can be assessed in terms of its descriptive, prescriptive and research values.

A model's descriptive value will be scored high if actual decisions follow the lines that it predicts. The score for prescriptive value will be high if the model is one that practitioners can adopt with maximum advantage. On the final analysis, however, the extent of a model's usefulness and validity as a tool in modern management research studies will dictate its research value.

6.4.1   Rational-Comprehensive Model

Any discussion of models of policy formulation usually starts with what is called the rationalism or rational-comprehensive model *(RCM)*. The model implies that operations, actions or activities should take place after all necessary variables have been thoroughly considered and decision has been taken in the light of the best available information. Economic rationality is the overall guiding principle in the model. The model encourages objectivity and it leads to rational decisions and Behavior

The main aim of this model is to establish the extent to which a policy decision can be rational; implying that the decision is based on a clarification of all objectives, a survey of alternative means of reaching the objectives, identification of all possible consequences (including costs and benefits) of each alternative and an evaluation of each set of consequences in the light of the objectives, and finally the choice of the 'best' alternative.

Generally, the 'best' decision is also considered as the most rational within the context in which the decision is made. As a description of what modern managers or administrators do in practice, the rational-comprehensive model is commonly scored very low. This is because in real life, no policy maker ever has the time to carry out the necessary survey of every possible choice and to identify all possible consequences. Time and other resources constraints are always present and at the end, one cannot really talk of the *best policy decision*.

However, as a prescription of what policy makers ought to do, it is widely recognized that the rational comprehensive model has much to recommend it. It has even been described by *Ladipo Adamolekun* as *a prescriptive model par excellence*. The model is widely used in research studies on policy and decision making in modern organizations. In actual facts, other policy formulation models have been developed essentially in reaction to the existence of the rational-comprehensive model.

6.4.2 'Satisficing' Model

In response to the rational-comprehensive model of policy formulation, *Herbert Simon* postulated that the manager as a policy maker is often contented with a course of action that is satisfactory. He then classified managers into two: that is, *the rational economic man and the administrative or social man.* According to him, while the rational economic man endeavors to maximize, the *administrative man* satisfies.

To arrive at a decision that is satisfactory, the social man does not examine every possible alternative; he limits himself to a selected sample of possible alternatives taking into account time and other resources constraints. He does not attempt to carry out an exhaustive analysis of every alternative and he takes a policy decision after considering those factors that he considers the most critical. Simon further claimed that the individual policy maker operates within certain limits determined by his unconscious skills, habits and reflexes; his values and conceptions of purpose, and the extent of his knowledge and information available. This is sometimes referred to as the concept of *bounded rationality.*

Apparently, Simon's main interest was to provide a descriptive explanation of how modern administrators formulate policies or make decisions. Meanwhile, the model has been criticized for focusing almost exclusively on policies considered satisfactory to the top management at the apex of their organizations; little account is taken of the other staff within the organizations and the contributions of outside factors are excluded to a large extent. However, there is abundant evidence that Simon' descriptive explanation of policy formulation is rated very highly by both practitioners and students of Modern Management and Administration.

6.4.3   Incrementally-Disjointed Model

The next popular policy formulation model is called Incrementally-Disjointed Model (*IDM*) or Incrementalist Theory. This model can be summed up by the hypothesis that managerial decision making usually takes place on continuous basis in response to the ever changing, dynamic and turbulent modern operational environment. By Implication, incrementally-disjointed model, sometimes called *incrementalism* is the opposite of the *RCM*. *IDM* implies acting on the basis of available information at a particular time. The decision taken at this time may be varied later on depending on circumstances. The strategic approach is tantamount to the *"wait and see"* strategy because every event is treated equally with the others. IDM however may be subjective and it encourages inconsistence managerial operations.

This hypothesis assumes that rational policy making is impossible in the modern society in which organizations find themselves. According to the American scholar, *Charles Lindblom*, who has written most extensively about incrementalism, policy makers tend to take one small step at a time, and new policies therefore tend to bear a close resemblance to their predecessors. He has also referred to this step by step approach to policy making as *successive limited comparison*. Having developed his theory within the American context, *Lindblom* had to take account of the role of pressure groups or lobbyists in the policy making process. Consequently, he argued that policies are not based on a rational analysis of the various views and he therefore described this road to policy making as *partisan mutual adjustment*.

According to *Ladipo Adamolekun*, the incrementalist theory of policy making process has two major advantages; first, because only small (incremental) changes are planned for, it allows for a new policy decision to be tested and abandoned if found undesirable before much damage is done. Second, incremental policy decisions are not so difficult to execute. This is because they follow past precedents as closely as possible, and once the machinery does not resist the change, it means that smooth implementation is assured.

However, the critics of incrementalism argue that it cannot explain or account for spontaneous (or sudden) changes in operating environment. This position applies in particular to developing countries like Nigeria, where some policy decisions cannot really be explained as a modification of some past ones. For example, as Adamolekun put it, the decision to include a special chapter in Nigeria's 1979 constitution on the fundamental objectives and directive principles of state policy is a radical change in the country's constitution-making tradition. It cannot be described as an incremental decision. This is because several aspects of the contents of the chapter will, of course, qualify to be called incremental decisions.

A second major shortcoming of the incrementalism is that it prescribes a conservative attitude to policy formulation because of its use of the close comparison with past experiences and practices which are presumed to be generally satisfactory and in need of only small changes. Thirdly, in an institutional framework different from that of America, policies could be quite distinct from the sum of pressures being exerted by pressured groups. Finally, it can be argued that the anti-rational position of incrementalism leaves no room for the development and application of rational analysis, especially with contributions from modern analytical tools and techniques that seem more practical and factual.

However, on the evidence of leading scholars and practitioners, the concrete experiences in the public bureaucracies of the United States and Britain suggest that this model must be scored high in respect of both its descriptive and prescriptive values. The descriptive value is likely to have been enhanced by the fact that one man's incremental decision could be another man's radical change. And in practice, a fundamental decision opens the way to several incremental decisions just as incremental decisions prepare the way for a fundamental decision.

Again, the evidence in modern management and administration literature also suggests that the research value of this model must be scored high if not very high. A good measure of its influence in research studies in modern management and administration is the fact that there is hardly any serious study on policy and decision making produced during the recent past years that does not refer in one way or the other to the incrementalist model of policy making whether directly or otherwise.

6.4.4 Muddling Through Model

Amitai Etzioni in his reaction to both the rationalism and incrementalism, proposed what he called a *'muddling through model'*. This approach to policy formulation is also known as *mixed scanning strategy or mixed-scanning model*. Muddling through model (*MTM*) combines the main features of *RCM* and *IDM*. This implies that the drum will dictate how the administrator/manager will dance at any particular time. Hence, MTM is partly objective or rational and partly subjective.

The purpose of this approach or technique is to allow the concurrent application of the rational comprehensive strategy and incrementally-disjointed strategy in different circumstances. Whilst in some environments, incrementalism will be adequate, in others, the rational comprehensive model will be most suitable, and in others, the satisficing technique may be the one that is needed. The situation may arise especially in making fundamental decisions; for instance, the declaration of war, which can also provide the context for a series of incremental decisions.

Considered critically, the mixed-scanning technique appears to seek to provide an answer to a major weakness of incrementalism; that is, its inability to explain radical social innovations and fundamental decisions. The model also accommodates the differing capacities of modern managers and administrators as decision makers, some of whom could be incrementalists while others are rationalists. On the negative side, however, the basis for the compromise implied in the mixed-scanning strategy is difficult to determine. And more importantly, it is not clear how practising managers and administrators are supposed to apply the mixed-scanning model.

In all, then, this approach deserves to be scored below average in respect of each of our three criteria: that is descriptive, predictive and research values. However, it must be made clear here that *a strategic manager has no one best approach. This is because he makes use of the best alternative strategy on the basis of the nature and character of the managerial/administrative phenomenon.*

6.5   POLICY PROCESS

The models of policy formulation summarized in the previous four sections relate to the activities commonly involved in the policy formulation stage of the policy process in contemporary organizations. However, regardless of whichever model is adopted, the following four steps are involved at this stage: problem identification, development of alternatives, analysis of alternatives, and selection of the one alternative that seems the most promising. Existing studies of the policy formulation stage by management philosophers suggest that two issues deserve attention: that is, the modern manager as the policy maker on the one hand and his operating environment, and the technique and tools available to him on the other.

Until the last two decades or so, the emphasis in the management and administration literature on policy studies was on the policy formulation stage of the policy process. Of course, it was recognized that policies have to be executed, but the implementation stage was simply taken for granted. Some of us now know better! The implementation of established policies is not an automatic affair. It is a vital stage in the policy process that deserves systematic study and analysis in its own right.

Almost at the same time as policy implementation was beginning to receive attention, some students of the policy process and strategic management started to draw attention to the evaluation of policies including the actual policy outputs and their overall impact on different target groups within the modern organizations. Consequently, we are now clear that the policy process in any enterprise consists of three major stages: these are policy formulation, policy implementation and policy evaluation; all of which will be thoroughly discussed as we go on in this chapter.

6.6. POLICY FORMULATION

As an extension of our attempt to explain the term policy, we have discussed the four major models or strategy of policy formulation. What remains in respect of this stage is a consideration of the modern manager as the policy maker and his operating environment as well as the techniques and tool that are available to him. In the first instance, who is the policy maker? In answering this question, we should observe that anybody in administrative or managerial position at whatever level is a policy maker. Such a person may be in the private sector or he may be in the public sector.

In a parliamentary governmental system such as the one which exists in Britain, governmental policy decision making is considered the responsibility of the political executive. The political executive in turn is responsible for its actions before the parliament which exercises sovereignty on behalf of the masses. Within the political executive, however, there is an unresolved debate over the respective roles of the political functionaries and career officials in policy making.

The traditional view, according to which policy making is the responsibility of political functionaries whilst career officials are mere policy executors, is widely accepted as totally unrealistic. The permanence of career officials and their expert knowledge of, and skills in, modern management and administration combine to put them in an advantageous position in their relationship with the political functionaries. The result of all this is that in the determination of governmental policies, the career administrators play an important role.

Although a presidential governmental system, like the case in Nigeria, differs in some significant respects from a parliamentary system, the respective roles of the temporary political functionaries and the career officials are also a subject of controversy within this system of government. In the American model of administration, the scope of operations of the career officials is reduced through the appointment of numerous political appointees who are expected to provide support for the political executive office holders. This implies that in the American governmental system, career officers play a significant role in policy formulation.

Very few students of modern management and administration would today limit a consideration of those who make policies to the debate over the respective roles of political executives and the career officials. Existing studies of the policy process in several countries show that policy making is a complex exercise which involves a large number of actors. For instance, in countries that have adopted the Western democratic system in which the legislature and the judiciary are formally recognized as sharing power with the executive, these two other arms make significant contributions to the policy-making process. Indeed, no serious study of policy making in American government can fail to assign an important role to the Congress. Also, the American judiciary in general and the Supreme Court in particular, are widely acknowledged as making significant inputs into policy formation.

During the short period that Nigeria has been operating the American style of presidential system of administration, the manner in which both the National Assembly and the courts can contribute to policy making has become obvious to observers of the system. It is in reference to this diverse number of actors involved in policy formulation in modern management and administration that some contemporary philosophers have developed a *pluralist theory of policy formulation*. Others argue that rather than speaking of *pluralism* in policy formulation, the dominant actors in the policy making process are representatives of the elite within each society; the elite refers to those who are regarded as superior social elements by their status, knowledge and wealth either in the society or in their respective organizations. Hence, the balancing of the various views presented by the different actors in the policy process within the context of a *pluralist* or *elite* framework is what *Lindblom* called *partisan mutual adjustment*.

Meanwhile, in the context of the contemporary public sector management and administration, the *pluralist and elite theories* are usually associated with countries that are styled as western liberal society democratizes. The socialist states formally reject *pluralism* since the party ideology is expected to determine all policies. In practice, however, there is evidence of both *pluralism* and *elitism* in the socialist states. For example, those who dominate the policy formulation process within the party constitute a kind of *elite* even if their *elitism* is solely a function of their *commitment to the party ideology*. Essentially, whatever

251

strategy or model is adapted for policy formulation in an economy or an enterprise, the circumstances of modern management and administration demand that attention should be paid to the availability of relevant information and the nature and extent of workers (in the case of the private sector policies) or public (in the case of the governmental policies) involvement in the policy formulation process.

In the opinion of some modern philosophers on modern management and administration, internationalized research in the form of a *think tank* is the form of gathering information for policy makers especially in the public sector. Commissions and advisory bodies are sometimes used as instruments for generating information. For instance, the *think tank* approach is widely used in the United States where independent or private policy analysis institutions play a significant role in the planning and development of governmental policies determination. It should be observed that these private institutions sometimes carry out studies at the request of government agencies or the government agencies take advantage of the policy studies carried out by the institutions on their own initiative. The leading policy analyzes institutions in the United States, for instance, include the *Rand Corporation, the Hudson Institute, the Brookings institution and the Urban Institute.*

In Britain, the government *think tank* is called the *central policy review staff* and several departments have established functioning Research and Planning Units. Commissions and advisory bodies are also used extensively. In France and West Germany, it is in respect of economic planning that elaborate information gathering takes place. The *Commissariat for Planning* established in France in 1946 bears the responsibility for this function while in Germany, it is the *Council of Economic Experts* that performs a similar function. In Nigeria a *think tank* called the *National Policy Development Center* was in existence between 1976 and 1979. The current practice, however, consists of reliance on *ad hoc commissions* and *advisory bodies* and on *special advisers to the President and the governors.*

The most common objective in expanding the scope of consultation and participation in policy formulation as a sub-process in the policy process is to facilitate compliance. All modern governments have acknowledged the need for this emphasis, although the concrete steps taken towards its achievement have not been impressive. However, it is still a widely-acknowledged hypothesis that different forms of coercion are still used and the implementation gap; that is, meeting the inability to implement a given policy fully, in many cases, is traceable to inadequate consultation and participation at the policy formulation stage.

Recall that there are four distinct steps or stages in policy formulation; that is, *problem identification, development of alternatives, analysis of alternatives, and selection of one alternative that seems promising.* It is in respect of the second and third stages that a range of techniques and tools have been developed over the past few decades to assist the modern manager as the policy maker. A group of these techniques comes under the umbrella term of *operation research* and it includes specific techniques such as *linear programming, game theory, queuing theory, probability theory and network flow analysis.* What is important to note here is the fact that these techniques, which are based largely on mathematics, computer science and statistics, help immensely to widen the range of choice to be considered by the contemporary policy makers in organizations.

Meanwhile, be informed that with specific reference to the assessment and ranking of choices, the techniques that have been developed include cost effectiveness analysis, cost-benefit analysis, the idea of opportunity cost and the construction and use of models. Cost effectiveness analysis helps to determine which alternative is the most efficient for achieving the given objective. On the other hand, cost-benefit analysis helps to determine whether an efficient alternative is in fact worth its cost. Adamolekun has allowed us to know and understand that the idea of opportunity cost refers to the cost of what will be given up by choosing a given alternative. The opportunity cost represents what we are not able to do by virtue of choosing to do something else. Of these techniques, the most widely used is cost-benefit analysis (*CBA*).

The objective of the *CBA* as we have been told in most current literature on Financial Management is to identify and weigh the costs and benefits of various policy options such that the policy maker is in a good position to know the balance of cost against benefits to be derived from the specific option that he chooses. The usefulness of the techniques to the decision maker include the fact that in cost-benefits study, objectives or goals of expenditure are made explicit, alternative ways of achieving these objectives are explored and the results of the analysis are available for all to inspect. The cost-benefit approach aims to provide the decision maker with a selection procedure called the cost-benefit criterion.

Contrarily, despite the usefulness of the CBA in the private sector, the major problem with the technique is the difficulty of measuring precisely the costs and benefit of social goods and services in the public sector! A good illustration of this problem cited by Adamolekun was the attempt in the late 1960s to determine the location of a third airport for London by the use of CBA. The best CBA experts were employed and adequate financial and other resources were put at their disposal. The CBA experts subjected three possible sites to detailed analysis, attempting to measure and weigh the costs and benefits of every conceivable factor including pollution, noise and so on. At the end, the political office holders decided to reject the recommendation of the *CBA* experts.

Their decision was based on political values and judgment, and the final decision had still not been taken in 1982. It can also be made clear that *CBA* is itself a supporting tool for Public Policy and Budgeting System (*PPBS*) which is widely acknowledged as the major techniques for policy making in the public sector. Experience about the use of the technique however obviously shows that it can assist the policy maker in respect of each of the four steps in policy formulation.

Another technique that is worth discussing briefly is the construction and use of models. Model can be used to compare the performance of options and to discover the relative effectiveness of them. Our mathematical experience should tell us that we can manipulate the variables and other factors that constitute an alternative in such a way as to predict what will happen in the real world if that alternative were adopted. Observe that in this case, we are referring to models as being both qualitative and quantitative. A qualitative model can be transformed into a quantitative model through the symbolic language of mathematics.

A quantitative model is essentially a mathematical expression in which a particular problem is represented by a set of equations and numerical values are assigned to the variables in order to develop alternative courses of action. The problem of applying mathematical model in public administration, for instance, is the fact that the awkwardness of administrative reality is not easily subject to the quantification that is essential to the construction of mathematical models. A special form of model is the scenario in which people attempt to forecast the nature of the environment in which a given set of options might have to be operationalized in the future. Scenarios are used mostly in the field of foreign policy analysis.

Meanwhile, it is important to stress that the tools and techniques of policy analysis mentioned above are intended to assist the policy maker. They cannot replace him. In the final analysis, it is the quality of the policy maker's judgment that will determine whether or not he makes a good choice after all the analysis has been completed. The critical role of judgment also comes into play during the first step of problem identification or objective setting. And whoever conducts the analysis, whatever its degree of sophistication, invariably influence the quality of the policy that comes out of the exercise.

Hence, modern managers have to continuously examine their judgment as they proceed with their work along the policy formulation process as failure to recognize this fact could lead to a situation in which the expert analyst mar the efforts of the manager as the policy maker; a very perceptive used by a student of the policy process with considerable practical experience in the subject, *Geoffrey Vickers of Britain*, when he decided to underscore the crucial role of judgment in decision making by giving the title *The Art of Judgment* to his book on the subject.

With specific reference to the breadth and depth of analysis that experts have carried out, the following warning about limitations of the perspective deserves attention: that analysis is always incomplete, that we always operate under constraints, that many significant aspects of many problems cannot be satisfactorily quantified, that there is a danger that analysts and/or customers of analysts will rely too heavily on quantification, that political considerations are sometimes paramount, that not everyone at every time has to ration his resources, that one can always use more time to do more analysis, and one never have enough facts.

The final word on the effort being made to strengthen and improve the policy process at all levels must be on the way in which politics and other subjective considerations intrude at practically every stage and at times in the most unexpected ways. This is perhaps the strongest support for those who claim that the administration of public affairs in particular is an integral part of the political process. And the major lesson that flow from this is that for as long as the political process is most often dominated by non-rational factors, the relevance of rational analysis to the policy process must not be exaggerated.

Now that policy has been identified by its nature, characteristics, scope or coverage and significance as a directive to management both in the public and the private sectors, it is possible to turn to the group of people whose deliberation result in policies that express the objectives and purposes of the enterprise, usually the Board of Directors as they are often called in the private sector. As you would observe, attention so far in our discussion of policy formulation has been devoted more to the public sector. Although most of the techniques discussed here are equally applicable in both sectors, further discussions in the rest of this section will be central on the situations in the private sector. However, whatever presentation therein will also be applicable with little modifications in the public sector as will be observed.

It has become the commonplace that the board is usually appointed by the owners, the shareholders, to represent them in governing the company's affairs. It is usually required of a director of a company that he has an investment in the company so that its success will, to that extent, be linked with his own. It is not common, however, for all the directors to have a substantial stake in the business they control, and articles of association generally require them to have only a nominal shareholding.

Every company must maintain a Register of Directors' shareholdings which must be available for inspection by members at the Annual General Meeting, (*AGM*), and for some days before and after. Shareholders are therefore able to see to what extent their directors have sufficient faith in the company to entrust a portion of their own savings to it and when they buy or sell shares, and at what price. With the disappearance on a broad scale of the old type of entrepreneurial industrialists, and the advent of the professional manager, directors tend more and more nowadays to be skilled practitioners of the industrial arts.

It must be borne in mind that not all directors are expected to be equally skilful in all aspects of their company's affairs. Some are appointed because they can on certain occasions bring a particular skill or experience to board deliberations or have personal contacts that can be useful to the company. Therefore, retired politicians and service chiefs are not infrequently men of sound judgment and integrity and with a wide experience of people and the world outside the industry who make valuable contributions to the deliberation of the board.

Similarly, men skilled in particular types of business activity, often holding directorships in a number of other companies can be useful when problems in their specialist fields are under discussion. Meanwhile, it is not necessary for every director to attend all board meetings. In fact, a director appointed because of his specialized knowledge may attend only when he can contribute his experience to the problem under discussion although all directors have a legal right to attend all meetings of the board and are jointly responsible for the conduct of all the company's affairs.

It should however be noted that the average director is not an elderly buffoon who lives well but spends little time on the company's premises as he is often caricatured. In a report published in 1959 titled "A Survey of Larger Companies" by *R. Harris* and *M. Solly* in the Institute of Economic Affairs, London, it was shown that of the directors in 148 large companies, 70% were full-time officials of their companies and nearly all had worked for their companies for at least five years before they were appointed to the board. In the same year, at the Institute of Directors Affairs, a survey of its membership revealed that the majority of its members were under 55 years of age and that only 900 were over 70 years of age. These figures suggest that the elderly director is the exception and that the younger executives have been getting onto the board of their companies to help to shape its future policies.

6.6.1 Composition of the Board

Normally, the board is composed of a number of persons of different ages and professions, possessing one common interest; that is, the prosperity of the organization. It should be a balanced group of individuals who can get on well with one another, but are nevertheless able to talk freely and frankly on all important organizational matters they discuss. To maintain a balance, it is necessary for there to be a chairman of strong character, able to summarize the views of his colleagues without endeavoring to impose his own will upon them too frequently.

Since the deliberations of the board should be based on facts, it may be necessary to provide the directors with a secretariat for the preparation of material to be submitted for board's deliberations. Although, propositions will often be put into report form by subordinate organizational executives, an independent line of research may also be followed up by the board's own research offices. The variety of members needed to contribute their knowledge and experience to deliberations varies according to the type of organization and the sort of problems it faces. The managing director provides an essential link between the formation of policy and its execution by the managers, but he may be closely associated with several executive directors so that the board will fully represent the various divisions of internal management. Apart from full-time members on the board, there are often several directors who have specialized interests such as law, science, finance, engineering or economics. These tend to offset the rather myopic attitude of a board composed entirely of executive directors who work full-time in the organization and may know little beyond its own practices.

To provide breadth of experience and bring worldly wisdom into the board room, it has been common in the past to appoint pears and their sons. The breadth of vision of the directors is essential to board's deliberations because they may be asked to consider the future of the organization for many years ahead and to make due provision for it. This function calls for a well-developed sense of prediction, forecasting and planning based on a broad knowledge of the past and of present changes that have made the prevailing situations possible.

6.6.2 Board Duties

There is no doubt about the division of responsibilities between the board, where one is established, and the executive management. The routine or operative management that proceeds continuously and is so essential for the success of a company's operation is an executive task for which the Managing Director of the company's affairs is peculiar to the board. In addition to these matters, there are duties connected with the revision, where necessary, of the objectives and purposes of the undertaking in the light of changing conditions. Some of the many and varied types of purpose and even through the graduation of importance among them, all must be reviewed by the board intermittently as occasions demand.

As representatives of the shareholders, directors have the role of fulfilling the statutory obligations imposed upon them by the company's act and these must at all times be faithfully discharged. For this reason, the board must check the performance of their chief executive whom they have made responsible for putting their directives into effect or action. They need to be assured that the results continually being achieved are in accord with the long term objectives laid down.

For this purpose, they will institute a proper system of appraisal by means of which they can keep in close touch with the conduct of the company's business. Since the financial affairs of the organization reflect all the acts undertaken, it is possible to gain a reasonably succinct assessment of achievement by reference to reliably prepared financial statements. The profit and loss account and balance sheet of a company are not sufficient for this purpose since they are normally prepared only at yearly internals and then mainly to satisfy the shareholders and the Registrar of companies. A great deal of data available within the company can be processed for reporting to the board but this task must be done systematically. The higher control method developed by *T. G. Rose* exemplifies a method by which the trends of organizational affairs can be followed at top level by the submission and consideration of monthly reports.

With their unified duties and commensurate responsibilities, it would be expected that the board of any but the smallest organization would be fully occupied. The peculiarity is that boards of directors seldom meet more than once a mouth and then only for a short period of time. Even on the day of a board meeting, many hours may be spent in touring the factory and in having a meal, in addition to the central deliberations necessary for the making of decisions upon the items included in the agenda for the meeting. It follows that the directives of the board cannot be made in anything but general terms. The work of determining means and methods to be used in following the course of action outlined in policy is left to the executive management. The major areas of board duties in modern management and administration however are formulation of policy, strategic decision and policy, change of policy, marketing strategy and policy, and prudent financing and policy,

The formulation of the policies necessary for the direction of the course of action to be pursued in achieving the organizational objectives must be carried out by taking into account all the relevant factors. These will relate to both the internal and external affairs of the company. That is partly why external or part-time directors are appointed to offset the executive director's concentration of attention on internal affairs. In the course of deliberations to determine policy, their must often be an evaluation of the facts involved in any decision that will ultimately need to be made on that policy. The managing director is the specialist in this as it affects his own staff. It may be necessary to consider imponderables like human relations and morale that will be affected by any policy decision taken. Hence, when a policy to "*get tough*" and insist upon management right to manage is being discussed, the possible effect upon trade union opinion of an intransigent attitude on the part of the management is an imponderable factor, yet it must be fully evaluated if the policy to be adopted is to be appropriate.

Also, when decision on policy is being made, due regard must be given to previous experiences in similar circumstances. It is not possible, however, to rely only upon experience, as "*flair*" is of great value when a final judgment had to be made as to which of several alternatives is to be preferred. It is often possible to defer a firm statement of policy until definite data is made available by experimentation directed by the board. Such a procedure is not predetermination but a practical means of finding the best basis for a firm decision. It is more disadvantageous for an organization to have its policies continually revised because they have not been deliberated carefully enough in the light of all the circumstances than to delay a final decisions until sufficient data are made available.

However, when arriving at decisions on future courses of action for the basis of policy, it is important that the board adopts strategic decisions rather than merely decisions. There is an element of competition in most industrial activity and it is therefore, desirable that adopted policies should be likely to lead to plans that gain competitive advantages. The stratagems used in warfare to deceive the economy in order to gain an advantage may not be necessary in industry and certainly deceit and trickery should be avoided. Adopt strategic plans that are better than those of its industrial *'enemy'*. For this to be possible, the identification of policy must be clarified by strategic decisions of the board.

In considering the dependency of an organization upon a single product or range of products, it may be necessary to postulate the future position in order to make plans to assure the organization's success. This may lead the directors to consider the possibility of diversification of activities in order to avoid complete dependence upon a single line of product. The need for diversification may be enhanced by a contingent occurrence associated with a current development. For instance, if extensive research into the causes of cancer of the lungs revealed an apparent connection between cigarette smoking and the incidence of lung cancer, the directors of organizations concerned with the production for sale of smokers' requisites would need to consider their strategy in the light of the widely publicized new development.

To go on as before, without taking any notice of the research would hide for the time being any embarrassment the new information may cause, but it would merely defer a decision until a later date when the advantage of time in which to take action would have been lost. It is necessary in such circumstances for the board to deliberate upon the evidence report to weigh this in relation to its effect on the long-term prosperity of the organization, and to develop a strategy appropriate to the maintenance of a competitive base for the organization's business.

If it were considered by the board that the research findings were so significant that they would lead either to the public's revulsion from the habit of smoking or to some form of ban being imposed by legislation, it would be necessary to determine a complementary objective to which the organization could turn. For a company making cigarette lighter, any serious reduction of the smoking habit would be harmful, dangerous and might be disastrous. The organization's board would therefore have to decide quickly;

(a)   Whether an action for diversification of products was necessary,

(b)   The type of product to adopt as a complement to existing production, and

(c)   The speed with which the course of action should be pursed.

The cigarette lighter is machine-made metal product comprising a number of component parts that have to be assembled to make it complete. It is retailed through tobacconists, largely, to the adult male population. A complementary product would have to share as many as possible of these features. The new product chosen by the board might be a dry-shaving machine, which has similar attributes to the lighter except for the channel of distribution. The tragic element of foreseeable future problems must be turned to good account by the taking of steering action in sufficient time to avert the anticipated disaster, but not too soon. That is, the sale of lighters may not decline as rapidly as expected and both lighters and shavers cannot be produced in quantity simultaneously without other changes.

There comes a time in the affairs of many organizations when the wisdom of continued diversification of product lines has to be considered. This also sometimes happens in large groups of companies when the complex activities of subsidiaries render it difficult to coordinate them effectively by a central holding company. Although this is a feature that should continually be deliberated by the board, it is usually done intermittently and often as the result of a specific occurrence that draws attention to the embarrassment that can arise through having too large a group of activities. For example, consider an imaginary company originally formed to manufacture road trailers. It has now grown and diversified to the point where it has subsidiaries within the group in the vehicles, engines, plastics and chemical fields.   One of the products of the chemical division is a fuel additive, originally developed for use with its own engines and using by-products and spare capacity of the chemical division. It is now discovered that an increasing number of road accidents is being caused by sudden engine failure on overtaking or taken off (as it happened in the Nigerian Military plane that killed several young military officers in the ranks of majors in 1992) whenever the fuel additive is used in private cars using high-grade fuels. This additive was marketed for use in commercial vehicles using low-grade fuels and is a satisfactory and valuable product for that use. The board of the group is now faced with legal, moral and managerial problems requiring early decisions.

Leger advice will be taken on the responsibility for the accidents, but the moral problem is a vexed one; that is, the product was not sold for private cars but there was no warning of any possible dangers. The managerial problem relates to the revealed need for more intensive testing by appropriately qualified personnel. This would require very extensive laboratory and road testing facilities. The final decisions will be affected by the profitability of the fuel additive business and its share of the total profits of the group. It might well be decided that here is an instance of diversification leading a company, by apparently logical and obvious steps, into a field in which it has too little experience for proper control.

If the overall importance of the product to the group is small, it might well be decided to hive off the additive business by selling it to a company already in the motor fuel business and with the necessary facilities for thorough testing. On the other hand, if this product is important to the group and development is likely to lead to improved products with wider uses, the directors of the group might decide to install the necessary facilities, engage suitable managers and technicians and improve the board capabilities by appointing a director experienced in, and qualified for, the motor fuel industry.

This example illustrates too great a degree of diversification leading to embarrassment, even possible to tragedy, through lack of expertise in a new field. It is, of course, more common for the bad effects of over-diversification, without improving the quality of management and the board, to make themselves apparent only through the profit and loss account; that is, lack of experience in a new business field leading to poor profitability. Nor is lack of experience the only difficulty, diversification can cause embarrassment merely by the difficulty of controlling too wide spread and diverse an organization.

It cannot be assumed that marketing policy appropriate to past conditions will necessary be as effective in future circumstances. If tariff barriers were reduced by political action (as announced in the 1993 Nigerian national budget by the chairman of the Transitional Council, Chief Shonekan), what effect would this have on the marketing ability of the company? The board must deliberate this sort of question in sufficient time for any necessary action to be taken. Or the channels of distribution traditionally used for marketing the product may be subjected to criticism by the apparent success of rival companies using other methods.

When an established company producing consumer durable goods for use in the home finds that rival which started from small beginnings has mushroomed into a formidable competitor by the use of direct selling, this is a fact that must be critically considered by the board if the company's strategy policy is to be appropriate to the situation. If the directors consider that the existing channels represent their best method of marketing, they will market the company product using appropriate techniques in the form of publicity, sales promotion aids and competitive marketing prices. On the other hand, if the directors come to the conclusion that their existing channels are inflexible and give rise to a too rigid price structure for their products, a policy decision may well be taken to alter drastically the marketing methods of the company in an effort to retain its competitive position.

Directors may have to make provision to meet contingent occurrences and for this purpose, they watch for activity in the world around that may have some bearings on company practice. One of the aspects to be kept under constant review is the incidence of taxation. For example, a complicated tax situation arose around 1956 in Britain because some British companies sold technical expertise into other companies, mostly overseas. As this was not a sale that produced income in the normal way, it had formerly been usual to treat the receipts from the sale of "*know how*" as a capital gain and un-taxable. A later judicial decision however suggested that part or all of such receipts must in future be regarded as revenue and taxable. An appropriation to cover the maximum amount of tax that could be involved in such a transaction would therefore be laid down as policy of the company.

It would also be wise to ask the company's accountants and lawyers to work out a scheme leading to the minimum tax liability and an estimate of the liability, as it might well be decided that the net receipts from the transaction would be too low to justify a sale at all. The board has to be concerned with other matters of prudent financing too. It may be judged that a substantial proportion of the operating margin should be appropriated to general reserve. The directors of one company in Nigeria with a net after taxation of ₦16 millions set aside ₦4 millions in one year for this purpose recently. This poses a problem for smaller company since the inclusion of a large reserve fund in balance sheet figures may attract overtures from financiers for merger or an out-and-out takeover of the company.

In addition to building up reserves, the board will arrange for the financing or capital investment in additional machinery, and buildings as required. In relation to the figures quoted above, ₦10 million had been expected by the company during the year on plant and buildings. Also, all the net earnings of a company cannot be retained for internal finance. The directors have an obligation to give a fair return to the people who have invested money and made the activity of the company possible. They must therefore decide in what proportions the earnings are to be distributed to shareholders. And what this will mean in terms of rate of dividend. Dividend policy is, indeed, a difficult problem.

Technological innovations tend to make capital equipment consumption before it is worn out and new machines cost more because they are better. Highly mechanized production therefore requires considerable provision out of profits for its replacement if the company is not to be faced with the necessity of raising more capital, possibly when the investment marketing is depressed. Many shareholders, but certainly not all, have been more interested in the possibility of a long-term, tax free, capital gain by a steadily rising stock marketing quotation for their shares rather than higher, but taxed, divided income. In a situation where capital gains are also liable to tax, many shareholders would prefer the taxed "bird in the hand" of present dividend income rather than the "two birds in the bush" of possible future capital gains which would also be taxed.

6.6.3   Characteristics of Direction

By quoting examples of practical applications, an attempt has been made to illustrate the characteristic activity of directors in carrying out the duty of steering their company towards defined objectives. It is possible to summarize such acts of direction in a simple list that clearly indicates the characters of the directors' work as follows:

(a)   The determination of policies that reflect the objectives and purposes of the enterprise,

(b)   The relation of industrial activity to the total environment in which it occurs, by the consideration of external social, economic, and possibly political affairs when decisions are taken,

(c)   Calculation of risks of specific courses of action over long periods ahead; due consideration being given to any alternatives,

(d)   The application of the knowledge of a whole series of integrated facts of business life to every problem,

(e)   The taking of strategic decisions, and

(f)   The incorporation of adequate flexibility so that there can be a change of direction of activity if and when this becomes necessary.

6.7. POLICY IMPLEMENTATION

The implementation stage of the policy process is the stage that some interested groups and individuals usually become aware of the existence of a new policy and they normally try to push for either the modification of the policy or its total abandonment especially if they were not involved in its formulation or if they think that they are not going to be favored by the particular policy execution. This state of affairs, by implication, usually occurs particularly in situations where the consultations and participation at the policy formulation stage were hasty and inadequate.

A good illustration in Nigeria is the government policy on a unified grading and salary structure of the 1970s for the public service. This policy resulted from some of the recommendations made by the *Udoji Commission* that reviewed the public services between 1972 and 1974. A close study of the *Udoji Report* reveals that the consultations on which the Commission' recommendations were based were inadequate and incomplete. Indeed, the Commission disclosed this inadequacy in its report and suggested that additional consultations be carried out. The federal, government, however, adopted the policy recommended and, without any additional consultations, proceeded to implement it. As a result of the protests from two major groups; that is, the universities and public enterprises, that made cases for being excluded from the structure, further consultations were carried out in 1981 to further consider the salary structure. Having made this important point, let us now turn to an examination of the policy implementation process. At a policy implementation stage, the following subjects deserve attention. First, it is essential that the policy to be implemented is clear, direct and specific. Second, there is usually the question of the implementation organization. Third, there is the question of the target group to be affected by the new policy to be implemented. Fourth and finally, there is the operating environment within which the entire implementation process would take place.

The need for clarity and specificity in the policy to be implemented is an obvious prerequisite for effective policy implementation. With regard to the implementation organization, the critical questions to be considered include the structure of the organization and the quality of its human resource. Is it an institutionalized organization? Is it to be implemented among the political or administrative cadre? How qualified or unqualified are the personnel who are supposed to implement the policy? What is the nature of the leadership which subsists in the organization? And what is the capacity of the organization in relation to the nature and scope of the policy to be implemented? The answers to these questions have important consequences for the extent to which the settled policy is implemented.

In examining the target group to be affected by the new policy, the following questions deserve careful consideration. To what extent is the group Organized? Is it an institutionalized group? What kind of leadership has it got? Has the target group had previous experience of one or more new policies? The answers to these questions are likely to provide useful indication about the ease or difficulty with which the new policy will be implemented.

With reference to the operating environment within which a settled policy is to be implemented, the important point to make is that there are factors in the operating environment that will influence the way the policy is implemented as well as the way it will be influenced by the implementation of the policy. A good illustration of this point according to *Ladipo Adamolekun* is in the area of local self-government where the culture and social life-styles of the people at the grassroots are critical in terms of their impact on the policy that is to be implemented, just as the implementation of those policies affecting local government influences the cultural and social life of the people. The salient features of the policy implementation process reviewed here may be influenced by three key concepts; namely, tension, institutionalization and feedback.

Usually, the purpose of new policy is to bring about some kind of change in a given work situation. It is in the process of transforming an actual situation into a desired state of affairs; usually assumed to be somewhat qualitatively superior such that tensions may arise. This means, then, that the process of policy implementation generates tension. This tension will be noticeable both within and between the implementing organization, the target group in the organization and the operational environmental factors. For example, tension can arise within the administrative staff implementing the policy in the organization especially where the personnel available is inadequate for implementation of the policy. The manage-ment of this tension, whenever it occurs, determines to a great extent the success of policy implementation.

The second concept is that of institutionalization. Although the implementation of a new policy does not necessarily lead to the creation of new institutions, there is a strong tendency for the people to expect that this is the case. In general, it is when a policy to be implemented cannot be accommodated within the existing institutions that a new institution might be created. When this happens, the question arises as to the survival of the new institution. If the institution survives, it is said to have become institutionalized. However, it is important to emphasize that the time factor is crucial in the institutionalization process because a new institution cannot be judged over a period of one, two or even three years; it takes several years before a reasonable verdict can be reached.

The third and final concept is that of feedback. In the process of actually implementing a new policy, new tensions might be generated that could elate back or are fed back; and hence the term feedback, to the implementation process. Onetime in the course of policy implementation, new demands emerge that have to be transmitted to the policy-making machinery. Such demands are then processed and transformed into one or more policies that in turn have to be implemented. In other words, the formulation and implementation of policies are not completely distinct phases of activity; that is, there is no definite end to the policy implementation process.

To provide a practical dimension to the conceptual explanation of what takes place at the implementation stage of the policy process, it is instructive to consider briefly the different ways in which a random number of factors and institutions can affect policy implementation. According to *Ladipo Adamolekun*, when the Nigerian Supreme Court declared the 1981 revenue allocation act null and void, the court decision automatically nullified the implementation of the act. The 1982 presidential appropriation bill that was based on the nullified act could not be presented to the national Assembly.

On the other hand, the courts can facilitate the implementation process. The progress made in implementing policies relating to civil rights in the USA since the 1950s is usually attributed to the 1954 Supreme Court ruling on *Brown v. Board of Education*. The legislature too can hinder or facilitate the implementation process. By December 1981 several state assemblies in Nigeria had established implementation and monitoring committees to carry out legislative oversight of the implementation process.

Finally, implementation can be facilitated or hindered by political struggles over the questions "Who gets what?", "When?" and "How?". The struggles could be interministerial or intergovernmental. For example, between October 1979 and December 1981, intense struggles between federal and state governments in respect of *housing the masses* have significantly limited the concrete results achieved. Perhaps, the most important point to emphasize in respect of policy implementation is the extent to which success or failure in implementation depends on the activities already carried out at the policy formulation stage. For instance, if because of the sophisticated techniques adopted in the analysis of alternatives that emerged in a policy choice exercise of the implementation is taken for granted, a resounding failure might occur. So many assumptions and probabilities characterize these techniques and the best way out is to approach the implementation process with maximum flexibility and carefulness.

However, peculiar to the private sector is the fact that in carrying out the defined objectives and purposes of an enterprise, the action of the board of directors will be circumscribed by external factors. In addition to taking full account of all such external factors as bear upon their decisions, the board will need to consider the internal aspects of their policies before they finally determine the form of their directives. If a proposed policy is not practicable in the light of any restriction of financial resources, skill or time, it must not be adopted as policy. Accordingly, in the course of their deliberations, the board will be well advised to consult their managers and request their comments and constructive criticism on matters under consideration.

The managers' contribution will be made through the managing directors in his capacity as the link between direction and management. This not only ensures a greater degree of practicability of policy directives, but also has the advantage of contributing to the morale of all executives by given them a sense of participation in the direction of the company's affairs. The board is concerned only with policy-making and should any intervene in the work of the executives who are carrying out their defined jobs within the limits of the policies laid down. Similarly, management has to guide and supervise the execution of policy and should not become too closely identified with the determination of general or corporate policy.

The managing directors, is the key person in separating the two functions so that they do not overlap. At the same time, it may be vital for the directors to be assured that their policy is being implemented in the way they intended. Therefore, there is a need for a system whereby the success achieved in the implementation of policy is reported back to the board-room. This not only provides a check upon the practicability of the directives issued but also permits the board to discharge its responsibility for the ultimate command of their executives.

General policy directives laid down by the board are expressed in broad terms without full details of the method by which they are to be put into effect. Nevertheless, they provide a guide to the manner of carrying out the major objectives of the enterprise. It is necessary for general policy directives to be divided into sections so that their appropriateness to the different divisions or sections of the enterprise becomes clear. This does not affect company policy as determined by the directors; it is merely a division of the whole into complementary parts.

Having been given the broad general lines of policy, it is possible for management to fill in some of the details of how the various divisions of the company will play their respective parts in taking action. This policy enlargement is primarily the responsibility of the top executives in each major divisions of the undertaking. They interpret the policy as it affects them and determine the action they must take within their own sphere to implement it. To avoid duplication of efforts or interpretation alien to the intention of the policy, it is necessary for the chief executive to take command of the detailing of sectional policies that effective coordination is maintained.

The management meeting, a committee of top executives from each division of the company, is of some use for such coordination. Although contributing an individual interpretation of policy in the light of his own experience and anticipated needs, each members of the meeting contributes to a collective harmonization of the project by the specification of sectional policies in a coherent pattern. The section of the undertaking whose work is quickly reflected in the solvency of the company is that concerned with finance particularly in respect to its duty to seek for, and properly use, the capital needed to finance the enterprise. To amplify the policy on activity and solvency in terms of a financing sectional policy, there could be a determination that the company should operate within its own resources.

6.7.1   Personnel Policy

The sectional policies so far discussed show how general policy is broadened in scope or coverage and effect. It will be seen that the examples so far given do not specify the detailed procedure. They suggest only broad courses of action, but they are narrower in concept than the general policy from which they sprang, being concerned only with the application of the policy to the work of a single division or section. However, there is one sectional policy that differs in type from the others. This is personnel policy, the effect of which pervades every aspect within the undertaking. it is not possible to isolate the application of such policy to a single division or section as with finance, sales, etc. since responsibility for getting things done through people is the universal characteristic of management activity.

Although often thought of as a sectional policy because of its relations to the courses of action to be pursued in relation to only one of the factors of production, personnel policy is, in practice, of general application throughout an organization. In determining it, its effects throughout the undertaking must be considered. Having been adopted as policy of the entire company, it must be acted upon by every manager in every division. Personnel policy usually embraces employment, promotion, training, joint consultation, negotiation procedure and redundancy.

6.7.2   Marketing Policy

Marketing is the managerial process by which products are merged with market so that the transfer of ownership of goods and services from the producer to consumers is affected. The American Marketing Association, however, defined marketing as the performance of business activities that direct the flow of goods and services from the producer to consumers. Another way of defining marketing is through the system approach. Marketing may be defined as a system of interrelated activities designed to develop price as and services to a group of consumers. Marketing may also be defined as a managerial process which deals with the identification, anticipating and satisfying customer's needs through exchange

As far as marketing policy is concerned, majority of it pertains to pricing; that is, pricing policy. In this respect, the common marketing policy strategies are pricing relative to competition, cost, uniformity, differentiation, geographical location, leadership, product line, peak load, and promotion. Pricing relative to competition may take the form of pricing to meet competition; that is, make sure you don't price above marketing ruling price, pricing above competition; this is done to deceive consumer as to the quality of one product r just to make an abnormal profit, and pricing below competition; to penetrate marketing or to cover up one's in efficiency.

On the other hand, pricing relative to cost may take the form of mark up pricing: this is used by most profit oriented companies when they charge price above their cost of production under normal condition. It may also take the form of break-even pricing; this is common to non-profit marketing organizations or governmental organizations where their primary concern is to cover their expenses. Finally, Pricing relative to competition may take the form of mark-down pricing; this is done by cooperative societies or government by subsidizing the cost for the common people. Also when company wants to clear the store, it may offer goods for sale at a price below their cost pricing

In pricing elative to uniformity, there are two strategies i.e. price equality and price discrimination. Price dissemination is when companies charge different price to different customers taking into consideration their locations and cost of transportation while the otherwise is price equality where the same prices are charged regardless of the location and transportation to all customers, Also, pricing Relative to Price Differentiation. This has to do with given incentives, discounts, credit facilities, samples, etc., as relates to individual customers. Each customer is considered on the basis of circumscribing condition in terms of quantity purchased and frequency of purchase.

Again, in pricing relative to geographical location, companies charge prices peculiar to each location in consideration of geographical ones or environmental factors. This is followed by pricing relatives to prices leadership. This is when a company is No 1 in the industry and its own price dictate what of her organizations price would be. In pricing relative to product line, companies charge different prices for all products for the simple reason that different product has different cost elements and objectives. The pricing relative to peak load is used when there is a limit to amount of goods and services a company can provide and customers are rushing for the product and companies charge price that will reduce demand. Finally, pricing relative to promotion is applied occasionally as it often generates more sales.

6.7.3   Dissemination of Policy

Policy should not normally be regarded as a secret. In fact, it is a secret in which nothing is secret! It is an open secret. It is imperative that it is affected by its implementation. This is especially true of personnel policy on such matters as remuneration and redundancy, which have a general application to all workers but it may not be so easy to apply in the case of other policies imposed by external circumstances which it may not be in the interest of the company to announce publicly. There must be judicious dissemination in making policy generally known.

It is of little use to give information for information's sake. There will inevitably be certain aspects of policy that are without relevance to particular managers. For example, there is no need for the superintendent of a machine shop to be notified of, say, the details of policies that concern only the sales division. It is the duty of the chief executive to inform the executives under his command of the policies formulated by the board of directors. Since he took part in the deliberations which led to the policy coming into existence, the chief executive is able to pass over to his subordinates the underlying spirit as well as the working of the policy. The executives, in turn, can then amplify their sections of the policy to their own subordinates, to guide them in making their decisions.

If policy is to provide a coordination of activities by harmonizing the work undertaken, all decisions must be made after putting into account the full range of applicable policies. Knowledge of policy is fundamental to decision making. For the effective working of management without too much reference back along the line of command, full information on company policy should be provided to allow the appropriate decisions to be made at every level of responsibility. These calls for a well developed system of communication by which policies are amplified and relayed through the various levels of manager down to the workers who will be affected by their implementation.

The best medium for the communication of policies is the written word as this obviates the distortion liable to occur when reliance is placed upon the recollection of loosely worded spoken instructions. Also, a written statement of policy can be expressed in precise, unambiguous phrases that cannot be misunderstood, and a document is available for reference if details of the policy expressed are forgotten or disputed after an internal of time.

6.7.4   Pricing Strategy

Marketing policy cannot be discussed in isolation of pricing strategy. Hence, the need for this section. In other to appreciate what is meant by pricing strategy, we need to approach the concept from two difference angles; that is, penetration strategy and skinning strategy. The concept of skinning was propounded by *Joel Dean* in 1950 and it appears to be just as useful now as it was just introduced. The basic idea of skinning is to set a relatively high initial price for the product and then gradually reduces it over times. This strategy assumes that demand for the product is inelastic. The high initial price is designed to skim the segment of the market which is not sensitive to price while the subsequent price deduction broadening the marketing by tapping the more elastic sectors of the marketing. The major advantages of the approach are that:

(a)   It generates greater profit per unit than when lower price is charged,

(b)   It charges high initial price and gradually reduces; this allows the company to obtain maximum profit which each market segment can produce,

(c)   The extra fund generated can be used for expansion,

(d)   It helps to restrict sales at a time when the company is unable to meet demand,

(e)   It slowly lowers price to make it easier for the organization to produce more when demand increase, and

(f)   Skinning is a safe and conservative approach because if a company sets a high price, it can later be reduced while a low price initially may be difficult to raise.

On the other hand, the main demerits of the skimming Strategy include:

(a)   Short run profit is sacrificed for market share,
(b)   It is a high risk strategy that can lead to substantial losses if sales do not reach the predetermined target, and
(c)   The lower price suggests longer time to cover production and development expenses,

6.8 POLICY EVALUATION

As would be expected, three sets of activities are involved in the evaluation stage of the policy process which may also be referred to as the evaluation process; that is, measuring outputs or performance measurement, comparing output performance with the desired results, and correcting any deviations or inadequacies. These occur whether in case of public sector policies or those that belong to the private sector. A policy can be evaluated by any of the policy makers, those charged with implementing the policy, members of the public affected by the specific policy under consideration and outside experts or consultants.

However, outside experts only have a role if called upon by any of the other potential evaluators. The public's measurement of policy output is usually a subjective exercise; that is, a determination of the extent to which specific policy output fulfils the expectations of different groups of policy users. The comparison that one individual or group of individuals carries out will not necessarily be the same as that of another individual or group. This means that different and sometimes contradictory verdicts can result from the public evaluation of policies.

The remaining two groups of policy evaluators; that is, the policy makers and the policy executors are commonly grouped together as the government in the public sector. For example, in contrast to the two other groups of policy evaluators, it is only the government that can meaningfully engage in the third activity associated with policy evaluation;

that is, correcting inadequacies and deviations as far as the public sector public policy evaluation is concerned. However, a common practice in a country like the United States is for governments at the federal, states or local to sponsor evaluation exercises conducted by experts or consultants.

Invariably, in evaluating policy output, the overall emphasis is on the two enduring concerns in administration and management literature; that is efficiency and effectiveness. Efficiency in this case refers to the relationship between inputs and outputs and the ratios commonly used for this purpose include output generated divided by resources consumed, actual activities performed divided by resources expended, and objectives attained divided by activities performed. Each of these ratios however may be multiplied by 100 to obtain the required results in percentages.

Effectiveness refers to the degree to which a program attains its objectives and the ratios which apply include actual resources consumed divided by planned use of resources, actual program activities performed divided by planned activities, and attainment of objectives attributable to a program divided by attainment desired. These results may also be equally multiplied by 100. Hence, both the cost-benefit analysis and cost effectiveness analysis are techniques commonly used by policy evaluator. Because policy evaluation seeks to relate policy objectives to a policy program or project, modern managers and administrators must be quite familiar with the following evaluation techniques: management by objectives (MBO), planning programming and budgeting systems (PPBS) and zero-based budgeting (ZBB).

Given the role of the legislature in the budgetary process as is usually the case in the public sector, certain legislative activities can be described as contributing to policy evaluation. Two obvious examples are legislative hearings and investigations. In general, however, evaluation exercises must not be limited to quantifiable costs and benefit alone. The unquantifiable and intangible aspects as well must be taken into account. Again, policy evaluation must also be concerned with matters relating to the quantity and quality of goods and services provided and the timeliness or otherwise of their delivery most especially in the private sector where effectiveness and efficiency are usually the main order of the day.

It is these aspects of the evaluation process that have actual direct consequences for the ordinary citizen in an economy. For instance, a good score in terms of cost which fail in respect to timeliness is likely to leave the affected citizens or staff whichever is applicable dissatisfied. Consequently, the significance of evaluation process of any policy lies in the fact that it draws attention to critical factors which help to determine the citizens' attitude to the conduct of corporate governance and administration of the contemporary organizations.

6.9 MANAGEMENT GUIDANCE

Policy is the foundation for management activity. It is the firm basis on which alone sound superstructure of accomplishing a work can be built. Managers can instigate and supervise work only when they have definite knowledge of the aims of their undertaking, of the type of goods and services it intends to provide, of the size or scale of operations it expects to conduct and when they have a good general idea of the methods to be used to achieve their purpose.

Good management makes its most effective contribution to the success of an enterprise when its acts are based on clear policy directives, which both record the general aspects of the activity to be pursued in achievement of the objectives and also provide a measure of guidance about the means by which the aims can be achieved. Policy determines the course of action to be pursued and determines the boundaries within which the activity must take place. This is illustrated by an arrow showing the direction to be steered, and placed within a tube that represents the limits of permitted action in the diagram in Fig. 14.

With this slight derivation, a single general direction would be followed along the tube, which marks the overall trend of policy being pursued. Analogues to this, management has to proceed from a present, identifiable position, to a future, hypothetical one, by following the general direction of policy; that is, keeping "within the walls" in so doing. To do this, it is necessary to adopt practices normal to the activity being supervised and then to specify methods of adaptation as circumstances require. These practices and adaptation procedures can be specified in such a way that the general tendency is to follow the direction indicated by policy for the attainment of the defined or predetermined objectives.

Resent Position 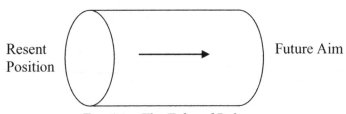 Future Aim

Fig. 14: The Tube of Policy

At the same times, there is scope for initiative since any appropriate activity is permissible within the defined limits. This permits the flexibility of action needed to allow adjustment to changing or unforeseeable conditions that may arise. By such means, policies are translated into practices for their implementation by being intelligently interpreted and applied with due regard to changing external conditions and to the peculiarities of every department and division of the undertaking.

REVISION QUESTIONS

1   What is policy? In your own opinion, from what sources do you think an organizational policy may be obtained?

2.   "An organizational policy may be considered as an internal administrative law which guides executive actions" Do you agree? Expatiate on your own opinion.

3   How would you recognize a good corporate policy in an enterprise? Vividly discuss the usefulness and shortcomings of formulating policies in the contemporary organizations especially in your country.

4.   In your own opinion, what are the factors you would like to considered when making decisions as to the nature of corporate policy in your company were you the Managing Director?

5.   How would you define a policy process? The policy process in your company may be broken into some stages. Discuss in details the activities involved at each of the stages of the policy process in any sector of your country's economy.

6   Three models of policy formulation may be identified   in the modern private and governmental organizations. Vividly discuss each of the models. Justify their relevance in the contemporary industrial organizations in your country. . .

7.   Of the all the stages of the policy process, which of them would you consider the most important and why? Enumerate the various interest groups that may wish to evaluate the corporate policy of an organization. Why do you think each of them is interested in such a somehow tedious exercise?

8.   An organization without a sound policy may be likened to a ship sailing on an uncharted course.

9. The Managing Director of an enterprise may be likened to a director of an orchestral who dictates the appropriateness of all the equipment as well as the melody for the overall success of the band. Discuss vividly your own view of this assertion drawing your instances from the contemporary organizations with which you are familiar in your locality.

CHAPTER SEVEN

CORPORATE STRATEGY

Things to consider:
* Nature of Strategy.
* Characteristics of Corporate Strategy.
* Strategy Development.
* Is Strategy Actually Necessary?
* The Process of Corporate Strategy.
* Determinants of a Good Corporate Strategy.
* Problems of Corporate Strategies Implementation.
* Chandler's Thesis.

7.1   NATURE OF STRATEGY

Complementary to the concept of policy is what is known as strategy. Strategy is the broad determination of the goals of an undertaking and the specification of the alternative courses of actions to be taken to achieve the predetermined goal of the undertaking. According to *Alfred D Chandler,* corporate strategy is the determination of the basic long term goals of an enterprise and the adoption of courses of action and the allocation of resources necessary to carry out the goals. Again, *Igor H Ansoff* is of the opinion that strategy provides a broad concept of the firms business, set forth specific guidelines by which the firm can conduct its search and subject the firm's selection to the most attractive opportunities

To *D. C. Rogers,* strategy is the mode of plan of action for allocating scarce resources to gain competitive advantage, achieve an objective and capitalize on a perceived opportunity at an acceptable level of risk. *James Brian Quinn* propounded that corporate strategy or plan is used to describe the whole future activities of a business. It is the plan that determines how an organization can best achieve its desired end in the light of the opposing pressures imposed by competition and limited resources, In the words of *Peter Drucker,* strategy is the company's basic approach towards achieving its overall objectives. It is a careful, deliberate and systematic approach to clarifying corporate objectives, making strategic decisions and checking progress toward the objective.

By this chain of definitions, it could be observed that strategy is the pattern of decisions in a company that determines and reviews its objectives, purposes, goals, produce the principal policies and plans for achieving these goals and defines the range of business which the company is to pursue, the kind of economic and human organization it is or intends to be and the nature of economic and non-economic contribution it intends to make to its beneficiaries.

Corporate objectives are those of a company as a whole but not that of parts sections, departments or elements of it. Strategy decisions are those that affect or intended to affect the organization as a whole over a long period of time. Medium term decisions are called tactical decisions while routine decisions are called operational or day-to-day decisions and concerned with the daily activities of the enterprise.

7.2 CHARACTERISTICS OF CORPORATE STRATEGY

In modern management, the main features of corporate strategy as being practiced in the contemporary industrial society include the following:

(a) Corporate strategy is anticipatory and its formulation involves a careful, systematic, deliberate and strategic planning,

(b) It is concerned with the business as a whole. Hence, production, marketing and financial strategies are not corporate strategies but functional ones as they all relate to just some sections or portions of the whole organizational entity,

(c)   Corporate strategy cuts across specialized areas of the corporation, and

(d)   It covers the time period that is long enough to provide management with an opportunity to anticipate future problems and hence, to have greater freedom of action. This implies to identify and prepare for opportunities in advance. It also allows for identification and fencing away threats and eradicates weaknesses.

Essentially, corporate strategy deals with product-market positioning; that is, how the firm will select marketing and products areas in which it will compete (i.e. choice of product marketing combination), the direction in which the firm will seek to grow and develop, the profit and growth objectives it seeks to achieve, the interaction within the firm and its external parameters (the world around or environmental domain), its internal adjustment policies and programs to changes in marketing places or other elements in its external environment; the competitive tool the company will employ such as price changes, offering quality discount to customers, introduction of new product lines, employment of consultancy services as well as the way in which the company will configure its resources.

However, one may ask "Why is it that corporate strategy has become a necessity in modern management"? The answer to this question is that it has become highly imperative for modern organizations to formulate policies and strategies due to the complex, nebulous, turbulent and oscillatory nature of the ever-changing environment of the work such as its uncertainty and even the risky realities surrounding the contemporary work environments

7.3 STRATEGY DEVELOPMENT

Strategy development as in the case of policy formulation can be viewed as a decision making process which is primarily concerned with the development of organizations objectives, the commitment of its resources and the environmental constraints. In formulating a strategy, the most basic steps to be taken would include the following though not strictly in the order of descending magnitude:

(a) *Identifying the Company's Mission:* That is, the long term objectives of the organization implied by the organization's mission. Remember that mission is broader than objective. The strategy to be formulated has to be directed towards the long-term objectives of the organization,

(b) *Corporate Analysis:* That is, capability analysis. These are analyzes of the company's weaknesses and strengths in terms of marketing capability, personnel capability, etc. these are mainly internal analysis, which seeks to establish the "how" of taking advantages of the opportunities available, and secondly to address how to overcome or correct the weaknesses manifested too.

(c) *Examining the value system of the company with reference to what and what the management cherished* That is,. Management preference. The value analysis helps up to know what we can really and reasonably achieve and commit ourselves to, and

(d) *Analysis of the Societal Values.* Since the organization operates within the society, after examining the values-system of the organization, emphasis should be shifted to the values of the society in general. Societal values to a greater extent influence the values of the organization. In contrast, the organization can influence societal values via corporate advertising.

The above sequence of approaches to strategy development can be reduced to a paradigm as illustrated in the following Fig.15. There are other relevant and complex models in modern management literature as well as portfolio matrices such as *Ansoff (1967)* and his companions. Although, the components of the model are dealt with individually, they are interconnected. While we discuss in sequential manner, this is not to indicate that this represents the way in which the process might work in practice. Formulation process is likely to be of an interactive nature, sometime perhaps, containing negotiation and compromise.

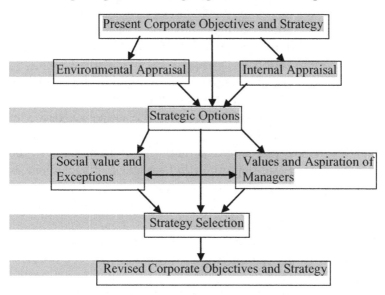

Fig.15. Strategy Development Model

7.4 THE NECESSITY OF A STRTEGY

To define strategy is not to prove that it is necessary for all firms. The question of its usefulness as a management tool must therefore be examined. This can be done by examining the alternative to strategy which is to have no strategy at all; that is, to have no rules beyond the simple decision to look for *profitable prospects*. Under this managerial approach to business, the firm does not select formal objectives, performs no internal and external appraisal of the *world* around, and formulates no search and evaluation criterion or rule. Instead, it would just inform the world of its interest in "*good*" profitable opportunities. It would evaluate each new opportunity on the merit of its individual profitability. The major merits of this managerial approach include:

(a)   Economy of money, time and executive talents required for thorough strategic analysis in the short-run. Such savings however varies considerably depending on the circumstances surrounding the organization,

(b)   The field of potential opportunities will be in no way restricted. Objectives and strategy or policy limit the field of company's search. Since strategy is based on uncertain and incomplete knowledge, there is a chance that some attractive opportunities will be missed. An opportunistic firm takes no such chances at all. Once there is no limitation, one can just spread or extend his tentacles to whichever place(s) opportunities are available,

(c)   The firm reaps the full advantage of the delay principle (complacency) by delaying commitment until there is an opportunity. It is able to act on the basis of the best possible information which reveals the true nature and character of such opportunities, and

(d)   By avoiding the formulation of an explicit strategy, the company does not play into the hands of its competitors. Corporate strategy is too important to be revealed to the entire organization and as a result passed on indirectly to company's competitors. It is therefore suggested that strategy should be private and be shared only by top management members or at best those who are to act on it.

The problem with this approach is that many of the key employees involved in the implementation of strategy will have no clear guidelines as to what contributions they are expected to make, and hence loosing the merits of using corporate strategy as a tool for focusing organizational efforts on well defined objectives. In respect of this point, it is important to state that major demerits of using corporate strategy is that the firm will not be taking up better opportunities as they arrive because of over- concentration on a specific strategy.

Here, the argument is that based on uncertainty of the environment and inability to obtain information about the future means that unforeseen opportunities will arise as time proceeds which may be by-passed because of the company's dedication to a strategic plan which was formalized and promulgated or decreed when less information was available. This means, in effect, that a good strategic plan should be flexible enough, where there is one, in order to accommodate these unforeseen opportunities. Indeed, a good strategic plan should be reviewed regularly as information about environmental changes becomes more readily available.

By implication, the major dements of having no strategy at all in modern management include the following:

(a) In the absence of strategy, there are no rules to guide research for new opportunities both internally and externally. Internally, R&D department has no guidelines for its contributions to diversification. The external acquisition department similarly lacks focus. Hence, the firm as a whole either passively waits for opportunities or pursue a *"buck-short-search"* technique (uncoordinated search)

(b) Project decisions will be of poorer quality than in firms using formalized strategy. Without a focus for its efforts, the staff will lack the depth of knowledge in any particular area needed for recognizing outstanding opportunities. As a result, managers acting in such cases will be forced into extreme forms of Behavior; conservatives will refuse to take order, better information might be reasonable risked while entrepreneur will be gambling without appreciation of potential costs and danger,

(c)   The firm would have no formal provision for partial ignorance. No yard stick will be available to judge whether a particular opportunity is the rare one or whether much better ones will still be coming to surface or emerge in the near future,

(d)   Without the benefit of periodic appraisal, the firms will have no assurance that its overall resources allocation pattern is efficient and that some product lines are not obsolete,

(e)   The firm will lack the internal ability to anticipate and prepare for change. Managers will either do nothing or risk the danger of acting at cross purposes, and

(f)   Through the process of formulating corporate policy and strategy, managers have an opportunity to come together to develop a shared perception or perspective of the mission of their business and how the enterprise should be run because they all get involved in goal-setting and strategy selection for the organization; hence, making it possible for them to pool and share their experiences, orientation, aspirations and resources. This brings about the much desired harmony of objectives and of actions.

The question is now is that having seen the usefulness and both sides of corporate strategy, do we then agree that all companies must operate with strategy? The answer to this pregnant question is not far fetched. This is because the type of firms that needs the most comprehensive strategy is a fully integrated operating and giant one. Since its product marketing decision is of a long lead time one, it needs guidance for Research and Development and it must be able to anticipate and prepare for change. Much of its investment is irreversible since it goes into R. & D. which cannot be recovered and physical assets that are not easy to dispose off at will. It will therefore minimize bad strategy and programs.

For companies that are operating in relatively dynamic or unstable environment, there is also a need for a comprehensive business strategy with which to guide their decisions and actions. However, for companies operating in predictable or stable environment, a comprehensive strategy may not be necessarily required because they do more of routine operations and maintenance work than a change oriented management that requires strategies for success, survival and growth.

7.5   THE PROCESS OF CORPORATE STRATEGY

Although the strategic development process in modern organizations differs depending on their peculiarities, the following steps seem the common general pattern:

(a)   The appraisal of the industry's strength and weaknesses as well as political, social, economic, ecological and technological changes,

(b)   Evaluation of the company's present situation and prospects as well as its strength and weaknesses,

(d)   Assessment of potential risks and opportunities,

(e)   Selection of quantified objectives among various competing alternatives,

(f)   Planning of the development of physical, human and capital resources,

(g)   Establishment of structural framework for implementing the plan and achieving satisfactory results, and

(h)   Sequencing of company activities necessary for attaining corporate growth; that is, preparing detailed plans and programs as well as schedules and assigning tasks to carry out the strategies or plans.

7.6.   DETERMINANTS OF A GOOD CORPORATE STRATEGY

The success or otherwise of an organization in modern time is largely dependent upon the policies, programs, procedures and strategies of the organization; and the soundness or otherwise of all these variables is further dependent upon numerous factors which include the following:

(a)   Availability of resources for its implementation,

(b)   Practicability of the strategy without legal constraints or unnecessary legal complications, etc,

(c)   Consistency with overall objective of the company and ethical issues of the society,

(d)   Guaranteeing adequate returns on investment,

(e)   Economy of natural resources usage,

(f)   Guaranteeing stability and security of employment of all workers,

(g)   Selected in accordance with problems and opportunities at hand or being anticipated,

(h)   Should increase the prestige of the company and its representatives,

(i)   Should contribute to corporate growth in terms of absolute value or as a percentage of the market positioning,

(j)   Contribute to social welfare in one or more forms or dimensions, and

(k)   If two or more strategies are pursued together, they must be compatible and be pursued together simultaneously.

7.7   PROBLEMS OF CORPORATE STRATEGIES IMPLEMENTATION

Naturally, there is no sudden change in administration or management style that would not be resisted by people upon whom it will first be practiced. Consequently, a change in organizational policy or strategy would not take place without creating some crises if care is not taken. Hence, some of the difficulties of implementing new policies and strategies in modern organizations are as follows:

(a)   Usual conflict of goals between organization objectives, departmental objectives and individual objectives,

(b)   Over concentration of executives on operational efficiency of the organization to the detriment of long-term goals,

(c)   Difficulty of improving administrative efficiency and effectiveness,

(d)   High intensity of rivalry, friction and unhealthy competition among the executives due to departmental part or portion of the strategy probably on what part to take in strategy implementation perhaps due to uncoordinated efforts, and

(e)   Problems of how to motivate key executive members.

Meanwhile, much of these bottlenecks can be removed through decentralization as this:

(a)   reduces over-emphasis on operating decision making,

(b)   minimizes goal conflicts,

(c)   increases or improves administrative efficiency, and

(d)   Enhances motivation of the organizational executive members.

However, the extent to which a company's strategy will be implemented successfully depends, to a large extent, upon the relationship between the organizational structure of the company and the strategy it has adopted. It cannot be considered an exaggeration that the organizational structure of the company must be designed to suit the particular needs of the strategy chosen. Once this is achieved, the major problems become those of motivation and commitment, and the design of incentive systems as well as information evaluation which are the main criteria to achieve this end result. Neglect of organizational structure aspect is likely to have adverse effect on whatever the strategy adopted by the organization.

7.8.CHANDLER'S THESIS

It is important that the administrative structure a company adopts be suitable for the business strategy which it has chosen. *Alfred D. Chandler (1962)* studied some American companies in 1962 and observed that since 1918, many of the companies had changed from functional to multi-divisional structures. In the functional structure. The organizations activities were divided into series of specialized functions such as marketing, finance, production and personnel. The coordination of such functional arrangement was undertaken by the general manager as the chief executive.

In contrast, a multidivisional structure is the one in which the activities of the organization are divided into a series of autonomous multi-functional divisions. These divisions are usually product divisions although divisions organized along geographical lines are also common. Despite the fact that the divisions in the *Chandler's* study were responsible for operations, broad strategic decisions were undertaken by a general office which monitored and coordinated the performance of the divisions. Hence in the multi-divisional structure, it is the product division rather than the functional divisions which are responsible for operating decisions.

Based on his study, *Chandler* observed that these administrative (structural) changes were mainly the result of changed strategies in the companies concerned. He therefore concluded that structure follows strategy and that the most complex type of administrative structure is the result of several basic strategies. In other words, a new strategy creates new structural or administrative demands since information through geographical dispersion; vertical integration and product diversification add new resources and new activities to the company. Although the old administrative set up could still be used to administer the new activities, it is likely to become increasingly inefficient as the company becomes more diversified and expanded.

However, it is important to note that there is no one administrative structure that is suitable for all organizations at all time. The organizational structure that is most suitable depends upon the corporate strategy that is chosen by an organization. According to *D. F. Charnon (1973)* in his contribution to the Journal of Business Policy, Vol. 3, No 1, 1973 titled *"Corporate Strategy and Organization Structure in British Industries"*, the British companies have tended to follow much the same course as their counterparts in the USA although in the United Kingdom, product diversification and structural changes were much more gradual and came very later than the situation in the USA. Structural changes after large scale product diversification was much closer in the UK and the changes from a functional to a multi-divisional structure was often achieved by a more gradual transition, first to a type of holding company structure, and eventually to the ultimate adoption of the multi-divisional system.

In order to overcome much of these multi-dimensional problems of division, regrouping and integration, it is important that the administrative structure of the organization be well suited to tackle them. In the *Concepts of Corporate Strategy* by *D. W. Jones (1971)*, edited by *Keneth Andrew,* Andrew illustrated that the nature of the corporate strategy must be made to dominate the design of the organizational structure and process, that is, the principal criterion for all decisions in organizational structure and Behavior should be that they are relevant to the achievement of organizational goals and objectives. This is why in both the *Chandler's and Charnon's* analyzes, it was the extreme changes in corporate strategy which promoted the ferocious changes in the administrative structure which eventually brought the replacement of the functional structure by the multi-divisional structure in highly diversified firms.

CASE STUDY
SOUTHWEST AIRLINES

For most of the last fifteen years, the U.S airline industry has been one of the least attractive to be in. between 1978 and 1993, when the industry was deregulated, twenty-nine new airlines entered it. This rapid increase in airline carrying capacity led to a situation of overcapacity. As more and more airlines chased passengers, they lowered fares to gain them, fares fell to levels barely sufficient to keep the airlines profitable. Since 1978 the industry has twice engaged in an intense price war: from 1981 the whole industry lost $700 million, and between 1990 and 1992 it lost a staggering $7.1 billion-more than it had made during its previous fifty years.

Yet despite the hostile environment, one company, southwest airlines, not only remained consistently profitable, but actually improved its performance while its competitors were wallowing in red ink. Southwest is a regional airline with a major presence in Texas. In 1992, when all the other major U.S. airlines lost money, southwest reported a sharp jump in its net profit to $105.5 million on revenues of $1.68 billion, up from $26.9 million on revenues of $1.31 billion in 1991.

Two factors have made southwest profitable: its low costs and the loyalty of its customers. Its low costs stem from a number of sources. Southwest offers a no-frills approach to customer service. No meals are served on board and there are no first class seats. Southwest does not subscribe to the big reservation computers used by travel against because it deems the booking fees too costly. The airline files only one type of aircraft, the fuel-efficient Boeing 737, which keeps training and maintenance costs down. A major assets, too, is its very productive work force. Southwest employees say that they are willing to work hard because they feel appreciated by the top management. As one flight attendant put it, You don't want to let Herb down. Herb Kelleher, the CEO, has been known to help flight attendants serve drinks and maintenance engineers service planes. In addition, southwest operates a generous stock option plan that extends to all employees. As a result, employees own about 10 percent of the airline's stock, which gives them a further incentive to work hard.

Southwest's customer loyalty also comes from a number of sources. Its low-cost structure lets Southwest offer its customer's low prices. This builds loyalty, which is further strengthened by the airline's reputation as the most reliable carrier in the industry. Southwest has the quickest turnaround time in the industry, its ground an incoming aircraft and prepare it for department, thus, helping keep flights on time. The company also has a well-earned reputation for listening to its customers. For example, when five Texas medical students who committed weekly to an out-of-state medical school complained that the flight got them to class fifteen minutes late, southwest moved the department time up fifteen minutes. Furthermore, Southwest's focused route structure it serves just fifteen states, mostly in the south-has helped it build a substantial regional presence and avoid some of the cutthroat competition that the nationwide airlines have had to grapple with.

Marks and Spencer (M&S) is a British retailing institution. Founded in 1884 by Michael Marks, a Polish Jew who had emigrated to England to England, the company has been a national chain since the early 1900s. By 1926 the company had a branch in every major town in the country and had become Britain's largest retailer, a position it still holds in 1994. Primarily a supplier of clothing and foodstuffs, M&S is one of the world's most profitable retailers. In 1992 M & S's 20 United Kingdom stores had sales of $7.5 Billion. M&S accounted for 15 percent of all retail clothing sales in the United Kingdom, and 4.6 percent of all food sales. According to the Guinness Book of Records, in 1991 the company's flagship store are Marble Arch London had a turnover of $3.700 per square foot more than any other department store in the world.

The secret of the company's success lies in the way if follows some key strategic principles, many of which wee already well established by the 1920s. M&S provides a selective range of clothing and food items aimed at rapid turnover. The firm sells all its products under its own St. Michael label. M&S offers high quality products at moderate rather tan low price. This combination of high quality and reasonable price encourages customers to associate M&S with value for money, and the firm's ability to deliver this combination consistently over the years has built up enormous customer goodwill I Britain. So strong is M & S's reputation among British consumes that the company does no advertising in that market-a major source of cost saving.

To achieve the combination of moderate prices and high quality, M&S works very closely with its supplies, many of whom have been selling a major portion of their output to M&S for generations. The focus on quality is reinforced by M & S's practice of having its technical people work closely with suppliers on product design. Suppliers are more than willing to respond to the firm's demands, for they know that M&S is loyal to it suppliers and as it grows so do they. The sales volume generated by M&S is strategy of providing only a selective range of clothing and food enables M & S's suppliers to realize substantial economies of scale from large production runs. These cost savings are then passed on to M&S in the form of lower prices. In turn, M&S passes on part of the saving to the consumer.

Crucial to M & S's effectiveness is a clear focus on the customer. The tone is set top management. Each senior manager makes a habit of wearing M&S clothes and eating M&S food. Thus managers develop an understanding of what it is that customer want and like about M&S products, by staying close to the customer they can improve the quality and design of the products they offer. The customer focus is reinforced at the store level by store managers who monitor sales volume and quickly identify lines that are selling and those that are not. The store manager can transmit this information to suppliers, which have the capacity to quickly modify their production, increasing the output of lines that are selling well and reducing the output of lines that are selling well and reducing the output of lines that are moving.

Another central feature of M&S is its pioneering approach to human relations. Long before it became fashionable to do so, M&S had developed a commitment to the well-being of its employees. M&S has always viewed itself as a family business with a broad responsibility for the welfare of its employees.

M&S offers employees medical and pension plans that provide benefits that are well above the industry average. The company pays its employees at a rate that is well above the industry average, and it makes a practice of promoting employees from within, rather than hiring from outside, furthermore, there are a series of in-store amenities for employees, including subsidized cafeterias, medical services, recreation rooms and hairdressing salons. The reward for M&S is the trust and loyalty of its employees and, ultimately, high employee productivity.

Also vital is the company's commitment to simplifying its operating structure and strategic control systems. M&S has a very flat hierarchy; there is little in the way of intervening management layers between store managers and top management. The firm utilize just two profit margins, one for foodstuff and one for clothing. This practice reduces bureaucracy and frees its store managers from worrying about pricing issues. Instead, they are encouraged to focus on maximizing sales volume. A store's performance is assessed by its sales volume. Control is achieved partly through formal budgetary procedures, and partly through an informed probing process, in which top management drops in unannounced at stores and quizzes managers there about the store. In a typical year, just about every store in Britain will receive at least one unannounced visit from top management. This keep store managers on their toes and constantly alert to the need to provide the kind of value-for-money products that customers have come to associate with M&S.

Required:
Critically analyze the issues and problems emanating from the above case and recommend appropriately.

REVISION QUESTIONS

1.   Many notable philosophers have contributed to the study of strategy and strategic management in modern management literature. What is Strategy? In your own opinion, what do you think should be the major features of a Corporate Strategy as it is commonly used in modern management and administration?

2.   In developing a strategy for use in an organization, what are the activities that must be undertaken? Illustrate appropriately the sequence of activities involved in the process of strategy development in modern organizations.

3.   Many textbooks, journal articles and other study materials on strategy and strategic management are flying about on the Internet and otherwise nowadays. This is in response to the need for dissemination of information about the necessity for a sound knowledge of the discipline now known as strategic studies/management. Enumerate and vividly discuss the relevance of Strategic Studies as a course of study to the practice of modern management and administration in your country.

4.   Enumerate and discuss the process of corporate strategy development in a company of your choice with which you are familiar. Is strategy actually necessary for growth and survival in all organizations? Justify your opinion.

5   Suppose you are the Executive Managing Director of XYZ Limited, a multi-product company in Lagos and you are interested in developing a corporate strategy for your company. What are the factors you would like to put into consideration?

6.   What do you understand by the terms *wait-and-see strategy* and *anticipatory Strategy*? Which of them

would you advocate for use in your company and why?

7. What do you understand by Chandler's Thesis? Is
this theory applicable in today's managerial world? Discuss in details the major problems of strategy implementation in the contemporary corporate organizations and the various ways of combating the phenomena.

CHAPTER EIGHT

OPERATIONAL ENVIRONMENT

Things to Consider:
- Nature of Business Environment.
- Placid, Randomized Environment.
- Placid Clustered Environment.
- Disturbed Reactions Environment.
- The Turbulent Field Environment.
- Methods of Collecting Environmental Data.
- Appraisal Environmental Data.
- Approaches to Organizational Strategy.
- Collection of Environmental Data.
- Strategies for Adapting to Environmental Changes.
- Other Strategic Alternatives.

8.1   NATURE OF BUSINESS ENVIRONMENT

The firms' needs for strategy, policy and planning become gloomier as the characteristics of opportunities and stress determined by its environment become more apparent. Therefore, the first task of a strategic planner is to perceive or conceive and to analyze the shape of the future well in advance. The broad panorama of economic, technology, social and politics trends will usually shape the world into the blend that will be adaptable to different circumstances. It is necessary therefore to study these trends in product, marketing, technology, consumers' wants and Behavior, competitive Behavior and the world politic so that the planner can use the knowledge of them to shape the strategy of the enterprise.

The environment of a firm in actual fact consists of all groups and institutions that have an actual or potential influence on the organization's decisions and ability to achieve its predestined targets. It is the sum total of physical and social forces and institutions that are relevant or potentially relevant to the organization's goal setting or goal achievement which are taken into account by the members of the organization when making decision and planning.

However, operational environment of an enterprise may be split into two: internal or micro-environment and external or macro- environment. Internal environment consists of relevant and potentially relevant physical and social factors and institutions within the boundary of an organization that are taken into account when making decision and plans. The factors here are directly under the control of the managers. The main components of this class of environment include the company itself, its employees and their local trade unions, the shareholders, the materials available, etc.

For illustration, the constraints of a business as a form of organizational environment restricting the achievement of profit maximization objective might be scarcity of key resources such as cash or skilled labor, increase in cost of production, technological and economic constraints limiting what goods and services that can be produced internally. Time might be another internal restriction because it may prevent a worker from doing his job properly as his work may be needed in a rush.

External environment, on the other hand consists of those relevant and potentially relevant physical and social factors as well as institutions outside the boundary of an organization whose actions can affect the achievement of the business, and whose impacts therefore influence, decisions and plans that are made by members of the organization. The elements of this class of business operational environment are said to be beyond the control of the managers.

The main components of the environment include the vendor or suppliers, the consumers; both the industrial and private buyers/users, the marketing intermediaries, the competitors, the natural and ecological environment; which determines the quality and quantity of finite and infinite materials available and the ease with which they exploit and are exploited, the technological environment, demographical environment, the economical and infrastructural environment, the political environment, the social-cultural environment, the local environment and the financial organizations, the media organization and possibly the interest and pressure groups.

For illustration, a business enterprise exist because of its interaction with its external environment which is the source of supply of raw materials and labor and which provides the marketing for the company's finished products (goods and services). While the environment is supporting the company in these ways, its influence also acts as constraint. Hence, in making plans and budget policy objectives, the effectiveness of external parameters/factors must be considered.

Taking the government as an example, successive government have in the past exercised control on trade and industry in a number of ways and among this are regulation of hours of work, minimum wages, control of the work environment, training and safety of workers, borrowing of finances from the banks, price control, etc. Also, the government levies taxes on profit and income tax on wages and salaries earned in employment. All these force companies to act in a manner which might not be an efficient way of working towards its predetermined objectives. The problem may arise by the company trying to minimize the amount of tax to be paid and its actual payment and acting as a collection agency for the government such as sales tax collection.

The law is also an example. The requirements of the law are charging day-in-day-out and it covers a wide area of company's activities such as commercial, industrial and mercantile including the company's acts. Another example is the competition; unless a company enjoys a monopoly, the activities of its competitors are of extreme importance since severe competition will create rivalry and the marketing wars among the company's. Also, by companies negotiating with members of the trade unions or with people who are not employees of the company may have dysfunctional effect on the activities of the company, if it result in, say, strike action which will disrupt the operations of the firm. The attitude of the employees towards the company may also have adverse effect as well as regards their affiliation to the outside trade associations.

Another approach to analyzing operational environment of a modern organization is through its characterization based on its causal texture, and this approach was championed by *Peter Drucker*. He was of the opinion that the main problem in the study of organizational changes is that the environmental context in which organizations exist are themselves changing at an increasing rate and towards increasing complexity. Consequently, to promote our understanding of the changes taking place, it is necessary to study the characteristics of organizational environment, and hence, he identified four types of business environment. These are *placid, randomized environment, placid clustered environment, disturbed reactions environment, and turbulent field Environment.* These are explain in the following four sections

8.2   PLACID, RANDOMISED ENVIRONMENT

In this type of environment, goals as well as goods and bad opportunities and problems are relatively going on changing in themselves and are randomly distributed. It corresponds to *Herbert Simon's* idea of a surface over which an organism can *locomote*. Most of this surface is beard but at isolate widely scattered points. In the context of industries, it means that there are no connections among the companies. No division of labor and each company work alone and do not depend on any other for its survival. A critical property of organizational response under *placid random condition* is that there is no distinction between tactics and strategies. The optimal strategy is just the simple tactics of attempting to do one's best on a purely local basis.

More so, the best tactics can be learned only by *trial and error* and only for a particular class of local environmental variances while organization can exist adaptively as single and indeed quite a small unit. This becomes progressively more difficult under the other types of environment where an element of uncertainty is introduced.

8.3.PLACID CLUSTERED ENVIRONMENT

This is more complicated but still a placid environment. It is characterized by clustering. Goals as well as good and bad opportunities are not randomly distributed but *hanged* together in certain ways. It corresponds to the *economists' imperfect competition*. The clustering enables some parts to take on roles as the other parts or become main objective with respect to approaching or avoiding the others. By implication, some forms of organizations begin to arise. The environmental parts begin to develop collections among themselves especially between suppliers and users.

The new feature of organizational response to this kind of environment is the *emergence of strategy as distinct from tactics*. Survival becomes critically milked with what an organization knows of its environment. If an organization attempts to deal tactically with its environmental variances, as it occurs, it has to know its environment very well as to pursue a goal under its nose may lead it into the part of the field that is full of danger while avoidance of an immediate difficult thing may lead it away from potentially rewarding areas. In the clustered environment, the relevant objective is that of optimal location as some positions are desirable as potentially richer and rewarding than others.

To reach these locations requires concentration of resource, subordination to the main plans and development of a distinctive competence in reaching the strategic objective. Organizations under this condition, therefore, tend to grow in size and also to become non-tactical with tendency towards centralized control and condition.

8.4. DISTURBED REACTIONS ENVIRONMENT

This may be compared to the *economist' oligopolistic market* in which there are more than one organization of the same kind. It is dynamic rather than static. The existence of a number of similar organizations has become the dominant characteristic of the environment. Each organization does not only take account of the others when they meet at random but also has to consider that what it knows can also be known to the others. The part of the environment to which it wishes to move itself in the long run is also the part to which the others seek to move. Knowing this, each organization will wish to improve its own chances by hindering one another and each knowing that the others must not only wish to do likewise but also knows that each of them knows this.

The presence of the similar others creates an enunciation of some of the causal factors in the environment. Hence, competitors seek to improve their chances by hindering one another each knowing that the others are playing the same game. It now becomes necessary to define objective in terms not so much of location but also as of power or capacity to move more or less at will; that is to be able to meet competitive challenges. To achieve flexibility, control and coordination are decentralized and premium is placed on quality and speed of decisions at various peripheral points.

8.5   THE TURBULENT FIELD ENVIRONMENT

This operational environment is more complex than the others. The dynamic processes which create significant variances for the component organizations arise from the field itself. That is, the dynamic properties arise not only from the interaction and interrelationship of the component organizations but also from the field of operation itself .

8.6   METHODS OF COLLECTING ENVIRONMENTAL DATA

Corporate environmental data may be collected for thorough managerial analysis using series of methods and techniques. One of these approaches is called *QUEST* which is an acronym for Quick Environmental Scanning Techniques. It becomes necessary because structural differences have introduced differences of decisions among managers concerning goals and time perspectives and relationships. The managers look at problems and opportunities as well as strength and weaknesses from their own departmental point of views. *QUEST* is therefore a technique of collecting information whereby managers are brought together and list all the changes which they perceive in their operating environment.

The common stages of QUEST, however, are:

(a)   *Preparatory Stage* where printed questionnaires are circulated to relevant senior level managers reports are received based on information from their analysis of strength and weaknesses,

(b)   *Development Planning Stage* where   executives'

brain-storming is used to define the organizational mission together. The purpose here is to define their common purpose,

(c) *Scenario Development Stage* where managers will conducts an informal debate among themselves and the debate is based on the scenario suggestion by the report in the brain-storming section. Time factor or *fun time event* are arranged in their emerging sequence such as price of raw materials to fall, employment opportunity to open, etc. This may be stated for five years or more in order of sequence; probably chronologically, and

(d) *Strategic Option Identification Stage* where decisions are made for dealing with the expected threats and opportunities.

However, the major advantages of using the *QUEST* to collect environmental data include the following:

(a) It develops a sense of shared and collective understanding among managers,

(b) It promotes a coordinated view of problems and opportunities,

(c) It builds up a sense of commitment to strategic planning,

(d) It emphasizes team approach in solving managerial problems,

(e) it focuses managers' attention on strategic areas, and

(e) Finally, it is systematic, inexpensive and good for obtaining qualitative information.

Other common techniques of collecting environmental data for managerial analysis are:

(a) *Delphi Techniques:* This is just a method of collecting information from different managers without them meeting one another face-to-face,

(b) *Outside Experts:* These include consultants, marketing researchers, trained experts, trade associations and research institutions

(c)   *Deliberate opportunity identification.*

8.7.APPRAISAL ENVIRONMENTAL DATA

Whatever strategy employed by an organization should be based on information available about the environment of the organization. Before strategy can be built or developed, one must have obtained information from both internal and external sources through internal and external appraisal of the operating environments. Internal appraisal involves trying to assess the strength and weaknesses within the firm. Here, one is trying to obtain relevant information of particular relevance to the management, employees, etc.

External appraisal relates to assessment of opportunities that can be taken advantage of. For instance, What are the qualities of our management teams? Our workers? Our techno-structure? Our financial capacity? Our marketing effort? Research and Development? And so on. All these relate to internal appraisal or evaluation in terms of readiness and willingness as compared to other companies around. What qualification, past achievement, ages, exposure, heath, etc do we have? Each of these attributes will be scored and analyzed to rate the corporate performance among the companies or organizations around. For instance, the younger the ages, the better. Also managers of old ages, say 65 years, will not produce dynamic administration.

Employees' appraisal involves how many employees do we have? Their experience? Ages? And so on. How does the position of the company in the industries look like "are we the market leader? Are we just beginning? Are we at the market peak? How well is our products being accepted at the market places? And so on. What is the size of our business and what is our reputation in the mark place? And so on.

What about our state of finance? Do we have credit line or credit advantage? What is the ratio of our loan capital to equity capital? Does our company facing low cash flow situation? Do we have tax advantage? What productive facilities are available to us? What type of equity do we have? Are they belonging to the old-brigade type? How often can we replenish them? Are they modern, old or deteriorating? And so on.

We need to assign values to each or groups of any combinations of these variables which shall add up to 100 and the result so obtained will be used to measure the capacity of the corporate entity of the company. Marketing and distribution of the company will also be assessed. Does the company have too many customers? And or too low customers?. On account of transportation, too many customers may not be advantageous. One needs to buy more vehicles for the field workers, and so on. The product suitability and R. & D. situations also need to be investigated thoroughly. For example, is the R. & D. procedure sound enough and can innovation prospects be revealed? Do we have talented R. & D. experts or do we just imitate others? All these are forms of internal appraisal.

On the other hand, the external appraisal involves such information like "How many competitors do we have? What is the size of each competitor? What price do they charge? Are they marketing oriented? Which of them has the best product? Does it sell at a low price? Does it sell at local or foreign marketing? Does it have better reputation than us? And so on. Economic, technological and even the social environment also needs to be thoroughly studied because that strategies should be based on them is generally recognized. This should also be based on opportunities.

However, there are more cases where strategies are designed to assess weaknesses than opportunities. Five areas however exist where the search for strengths and weaknesses as well as opportunities has to be carried out. These are:

(a) *Competitors* which are necessary to determine the effects of competitors on national, local and international scene on the company's competitors, its research, its suppliers and its position in the industries can be assessed. However, all competitors cannot be studied. They have to be classified with attention focused on the most important one;

(b) The company should determine whether any *political change* at the local, national and foreign scenes will affect its business. Some of these are anti-pollution and trade union laws, rising nationalism especially in developing nations, taxations, anti-trust legislation, safety legislation, tariff and total agreement, economics federation of nations, government sponsored research, nationalization of industries at the local scene, changes that may be significant include parking regulations, opening hours for shops, construction of roads and buildings etc, it should be noted that only political changes of strategies importance needs be considered.

(c) The changes in *economic environment* include changes in the fiscal and monetary measures of the government like taxation, import and excise duties, wages and incomes, interest rates, cash ratio, liquidity ratio, cash receipts and special deposits.

(d) Changes in *social environment* such as attitudes, Behavior and competition are critically important to the design of strategies. Attitudes to work are declining and thus must be considered when designing organizational elements of strategies. Society is applying increasing pressure on all companies in respect of pollution and environmental aesthetic so that the equipment, product etc must take this into account. Changes in education, wealth and life styles also affect product designs and advertising

317

(e) *Customers* can also be found in external environment. We need to know where, when, why and how they buy products and even which product do they buy and in what quantity and on what condition. The internal appraisal should tell what kind of business the company is in while the external appraisal should tell what opportunity and strength are available so that we have what is known as cruciform chart as follows:

Strengths	Opportunity
Threats	Weaknesses

8.8. APPROACHES TO ORGANIZATIONAL STRATEGY

There are two main approaches to the study of organizational strategies. These are *"wait and see"* approach and *"anticipatory"* approach. The merit of the *wait and see* approach is that the *true character* of opportunities and problems are available while the *anticipatory* approach does not allow this. The major disadvantage of the *wait and see* strategy however is that one has to wait for the event to happen first which may be hazardous or disastrous. It may be too late and the company may be *applying medicine after death*! For example, government may pronounce placing embargo on importation of some key articles. This has to be anticipated and planned for.

There are specific strategies for specific events depending on characteristics of such events. For instance, there are strategy of diversification, the strategy of acquisition, the strategy of coalition, the strategy of postponement, strategy of internal regulations, risk mitigation strategy, bargaining strategy and contingency strategy. All these deal with evaluation of the various phenomena in the society. For illustration, instead of sticking to the existing product line that is facing difficulties, the company may decide to diversify to make use of the existing heaps of opportunities elsewhere. This involves leaving the production of traditional product to that where new opportunities exist.

There are four types of diversification. These are *horizontal diversification* where the company changes from production of one product to that of the other while dealing with the range of products that have similar nature or features. It is actually widening of one's presence in the same market. *Vertical diversification* is what we call *forward integration* where one goes deeper in the same line of marketing and also another form of vertical diversification is the *backward integration* where one tries to withdraw his tentacles to some extent from the market.

Having read this chapter, the question is that assuming you are the Managing Director of XYZ Limited-a company that intends to take-over another smaller company ABC Limited. Which areas of your company will you assess? Again, suppose you are to produce the necessary guideline to follow in the process. Then, the main questions to ask about this include who owns the company?

To do this, the major shareholders must be identified, their needs determined, their addresses and ages must be known and their family connections, if any, must be established. Does a bank or financial institution hold shares in the company? If so, how much? Are the owners reputable in the society? Do they have any experience? Are they young or old? If they are young, they may go and set up a better company somewhere to compete with the existing business. If banks and financial institution hold share in the business, there may be no problem of finance. Are trusts involved in the shareholding? If yes, this may create some legal problems. What is the share structure? What is the ratio of loan capital to equity capital? What are the voting rights of the shareholders etc? All these questions so far relate to the *ownership* and *capital structure* of the business

The next step relate to an objective analysis of the *management of the company*. Make a complete list of the top managers. Analyze them by age, educational qualification and length of service. Examine their contract of employment or contract for employment. Examine their background and relate all available information to the past performance of the company. Compare this with the present and then project for the future. Decide whether or not they are worth of employment.

After this, examine critically the *finance and profitability of the company*. Examine their financial statements for the past years to forecast for the future only to the extend that the past may be an indicator of the future. Examine the promptness in rendition of accounts. Observe any sign of problems. Regular lateness in rendering accounts may be an indicator of poor management. Examine the projected operating and financial statements to see what the future holds for the company. Examine the statements for profitability. Relate past forecast and projection to actual results! Examine the balance sheet to establish the value of stocks, intangible assets, contingent liabilities, tax liabilities, dates of maturity of loans, obtain information on fixed assets covering property both freehold or leasehold, age and condition of buildings, machines; whether old or modern and the state of performance.

The next thing to do is to consider the *types of Activities or operations of the company*. Find out whether it is in a growing or declining stage. Can your own company manage the new company's business? Is the required expertise available in your own company? And so on. You also need to evaluate the position of *competition* in the industry. How much competitors are there and what is the intensity of the competition in the market? Is the company that is being taken-over taking advantage of all opportunities? What advantage will the acquisition or take over bring to your own company inform of service or integration? There is no end to this search! The required presentation is actually dependent on the experience of the analyst or researcher.

8.9. COLLECTION OF ENVIRONMENTAL DATA

Strategic decision is based on data relating to internal strengths and weaknesses of a particular undertaken and it must reflect data about environment, threats and opportunities of the business. Hence, for strategic decision to be a desirable one, the organization has to carry out environmental appraisal both internally and externally. Internal appraisal contains searching for information on management of the company such as organization structure, the quality of planning and decision making, the data handling and information retrieval system, the business acumen and flair of the company, the system effectiveness and cost control, the method and speed of opportunity identification, the skill of personnel and the management of human resource as well as industrial relations.

The position of the company in industry also has to be appraised. This relates to the strengths and weakness of the firm in terms of size and bargaining power with customers, suppliers and employees, the company reputation, flexibility and adaptability. Data have to be obtained on the finance of the company in terms of whether the company profit is fluctuating or not, the ratio of the company's loan capital to equity, the cash flow, tax advantages and disadvantages, Production facilities in terms of equity, location of the company office and factory plants, production technology, how liberal the transport services is etc,

Again, the marketing and distribution systems of the company have to be exploited for possible data. This consists of marketing capability such as whether the company has many or few customers, the loyalty of distributors to the company, the effectiveness of the companies advertising and promotion programs, the effectiveness of the sales force, the efficiency of good and service delivering systems and information, the suitability of the company's products, etc. These help to determine whether the product line is too wide or too narrow and to know whether the company's product is compared favorably or otherwise with the competitors' own. Finally, the effectiveness and strategies of distribution channels need to be considered.

The company should know the weakness and strengths of its employees or workforce, their number and quality in terms of experience, education and practical exposure, development, satisfaction, motivation, etc. R. &. D. activities like identifying prospect for innovation and development, and so on. External appraisal has to be done with a thorough analysis of the competitors, the government and political actions and policies, economic situation in the country, the social system, technological system, the consumers, ecological system, the financial institutions, media organizations and the suppliers for collection of appropriate data and information.

8.10. STRATEGIES FOR ADAPTING TO ENVIRONMENTAL CHANGES

There are several alternative strategies that an organization can adopt to deal with changes in its operating environment. However, as already explained in section 8.8, the common ones are *wait and see* strategy where the company waits until changes occur and then react in the most appropriate manner. The main advantage of this is that the

322

nature of the problem or the true character of opportunities presented by the change will be known. Also the decision taken under such condition is less risky. The only demerit or danger of this approach is that action may be too late to have a meaningful impact.

An alternative to this strategy is known as *anticipatory* approach where the company anticipates and prepare for changes before they occur. This approach is planning oriented and hence very practicable. The only danger of the approach however is that experience, judgment, intuition, and other subjective variables may be relied upon to a significant extent which may serve somehow to jeopardize the company's interest. Again, there is more less certainty that expected change will actually occur!

8.11. OTHER STRATEGIC ALTERNATIVES

Whatever situation an organization finds itself, there will always be a strategy to cope with it. In this vein, organizations in modern industrial society have specific strategy for reducing risk, exploiting opportunities or overcoming threats as in the following subsections

8.11.1. Prevention, Postponement and Modification Strategies

Where a company has political influence, it may prevent or modify legislations that may affect its business interests. This can be done through intensive lobbying. Where a company fears before price war among its competitors, it may propose cartel and thereby preventing the war. Where a company depends on a customer or supplier, it may reduce its price for that customer or allow the supplier to raise the price to certain agreeable limit. Where the company is facing a threat from an overseas competitor, it may dump goods in the competitors market as a warning.

8.11.2 Risk Mitigation Strategies

The most popular of these strategic alternatives is diversification. To mitigate implies to make things less severe or less painful. If the threat comes from a change in marketing environment, the company may seek new marketing condition. If the threat is to the company's product, it may seek different lines of products especially if it has been depending on a single line of products. If from suppliers in one nation or states, the company may seek suppliers in different nations or states. If the threat is from economic cycle, the company may seek a new business that is counter-cyclical, that is, non- seasonal.

8.11.3 Contingency Strategies

This is used when the occurrence of events is thought to be probable and that it must be provided for using different alternative approaches

8.11.4. Acquisition Strategy

This is where the acquiring company is larger and the acquired company is central to the bid. There is no obvious advantage to the acquired. Many acquisitions occur apparently:

(a) because one or both companies wish to diversify,
(b) to allow acquirer to grow in size,
(c) to reduce the dependence of one product by the acquirer,
(d) to obtain greater business stability,
(e) to obtain needed technical techniques,
(f) to cut cost due to economics of large scale,
(g) to break into new market,

(h) to acquire write-off,
(i) to enable owners of the acquired company to retire,
(j) to let acquired get more cash,
(k) to reduce competition facing the acquired larger company, and
(l) to reorganize a fragmented industry.

An acquisition strategy should however be adopted if the cost of buying new business area is less than developing into it, if the acquisition is considered urgent for the survival of the acquirer, if the risk of developing into new area is greater than buying it and if the company to be acquired is not in the state of collapse.

8.11.5. Merger's Strategy

Here, the companies concerned are of more or less equal sizes and there are obvious mutual advantages to both of them. Many mergers occur to make stronger the partners in their existing business areas. Other reasons for adopting merger's strategy by modern organizations are those listed under acquisition.

8.11.6 Coalition Strategy

This involves companies coming together to form trade associations to provide facilities and deal with common problems and threats in their operating environment. For instance, manufacturers' associations whose main aim is to help in forming economic and political policies of the government especially as regards the possibility of government making policies and legislations that can affect the performance of the concerned organizations adversely.

8.11.7. Bargaining and Negotiation Strategy

The companies adopting this strategy may attempt to reduce competition within the industry and make the marketing more stable by negotiating among themselves. In this way, an accurate prediction of the competitors' moves is made possible.

8.11.8.Internal Regulation Strategy

This refers to a kind of structural adjustment, reengineering or re-organization which is aimed at producing a disciplined and unified system that can move quickly and effectively to certain environmental threats challenges and opportunities. In essence, internal planning, establishment of programs, standard procedures and decision rules are all attempts to stabilize the internal environment of contemporary organizations.

CASE STUDY

OKITIPUPA OIL CORPORATION

One of the most significant changes in the environment of business in the recent past has been the Oil crisis of the recent past. Starting with the first oil embargo by the OPEC countries in 1999, Ayetoro oil companies began a frantic search for more domestic oil. To serve the oil companies, a large number of oil-field suppliers sprang up. These suppliers manufactured oil-well pipe, steam generators, derricks, oil pumps, oil-transport pipeline, and countless other Kinds of oil-field equipment. The richest of these companies went into the risky business of manufacturing offshore oil rigs. One such company was Okitipupa Corporation popularly known as OKITI-OIL CORPORATION or simply "Okiti-Oil". Okiti-Oil grew very rapidly through the first few years of the oil shortages in 2000's and started a N12 billion expansion program. Also, it decided to buy 24 jack-up rigs or offshore rigs when settled on the ocean floor in shallow areas. These rigs were designed particularly for the Gulf of Jalingo in Taraba State cost N40 million a piece.

Just as the company stared to sign contracts to have these rigs built, Ayetoro Oil Companies began experiencing an oversupply of oil. Unable to sell enough oil and forced to purchase large quantities of oil under contract from various foreign countries, the last thing they wanted to do was to sponsor more and more oil well exploration in Ghana. Okiti-Oil was hard-hit. It now has 16 rigs that it is obligated to buy at a cost of about N1 billion while having drilling contracts for only three of the company's drilling rigs to be in use. The outlook is about the same in many companies up to the early part of 2004. In particular, however, Okiti-Oil is hurt by its collection of jack-up rigs as are some other firms in the industry. Consequently, even when oil companies start leasing oil rigs again, they will be able to bargain for very low prices. Hence, profit for oil rig companies in Ayetoro will be depressed or nonexistent in the next foreseeable future.

Meanwhile, Okiti-Oil has N562 million in long-term debts and is worth only a bit over N400 million on papers. Recently, Oil-field suppliers have laid-off workers by the thousands. Research and development has come to a halt, and many are failing going out of business. Okiti-Oil is a little better off than others, but it, too, is feeling the pinch.

Required
(a) Identify the major problems in the above case.
(b) Even though energy suppliers are in constant demand, why have the Oil-field suppliers such as Okiti-Oil been so dramatically affected by their environment?
(c) Explain how you would analyze the energy demand and supply were you an executive Officer at the Okiti-Oil in order to predict the changes in Oil Company demand for offshore oil rigs.
(d) In the light of the current attitudes the world over towards nuclear generation of energy, how do you think oil-field suppliers now see their future?

REVISION QUESTIONS

1. What is Business Environment? Enumerate and explain the main components of Business environment in your country.

2 Based on your knowledge and experience of what obtains in your country, how would you classify operational environment of modern industrial undertakings? Explain fully the Behavior of each alternative classification you have mentioned.

3. Make a list of environmental data which may be of interest to each participant in the modern industrial enterprises. How do you think such a set of data you have listed may be obtained from the environment optimally?

4. Most firms usually analyze and appraise their environment for effective and efficient decision making. Why do you think this is so? Enumerate and vividly discuss the various ways of appraising environmental data in the contemporary industrial organizations.

5. What do you understand by the term *Diversification?* Write short, but self-explanatory, note on each of the following:
    (a) Vertical Diversification,
    (b) Horizontal Diversification,
    (c) Forward Integration, and
    (d) Backward Integration.
6. What do you understand by the term *Cartel?* Discuss the contributions of Cartel formation to the development of your country's economy
7. Differentiate between merger and acquisition strategies. Assuming you are the Managing Director of XYZ Company Limited, an Ayetoro-based larger company that intends to acquire ABC Company Limited, a smaller business venture in Lagos. What aspects of the two companies would you want to consider thoroughly before taking the final decision and why?
8   Organizations in the contemporary industrial settings have various strategies for reducing risk, exploiting opportunities and overcoming threats. Enumerate and discuss in details these strategies.
9.. The major objective of globalization drive in modern business is to extend the scope of the market for various products, increase competitiveness among various firms, and the instrument for this is information technology. Enumerate and explain the various strategies which a company that is entering into an international market may adopt. Which of the strategic options you have mentioned do you prefer and why?
10. In other to be socially responsible, modern organizations should reciprocate the contributions of their operating environments by performing some duties. However, there are various schools of thought on this issue. Vividly explain the position of

each school indicating your own preference. What
are the main responsibilities of corporate organizations
to each of the interested parties from the economists'
point of view?

CHAPTER NINE

CORPORATE OBJECTIVE

Things to Consider:

9.1   NATURE OF CORPORATE OBJECTIVES

A firm is a purposive organization whose Behavior is directed towards identifiable ends, objectives or goals. When made explicit within the firm, objectives becomes tools of many uses in appraising performance, control, coordination and all facets of decision making process. One of these uses is the role which objective plays in strategic decisions making. Corporate objectives may be imposed on an organization by top management or it may be generated or developed through a synthesis of lower level objectives or arrived at through a bargaining process among participants in the firm. Regardless of the process by which it was formulated, however, objectives are determined by business, economic, social and technological as well as ecological variables.

Objectives are decision rules which enable management to guide and measure the firms' performance towards its purpose. It is a measure of efficiencies of the process. An objective involves three elements. These are the particular attribute chosen as a measure of efficiency, the yard stick or scale by which the attribute is measured and the goal; that is, the particular value on the scale which the firm seeks to attain. The central question to address before specific values are assigned is *"What kind of objective should the firm seek to achieve?* Should it be maximum profit? Maximum value of stockholders' equity? Or a balanced satisfaction of its stakeholders (Stakeholder theory and satisficing theory of the firm)?

One way to answer this question is through philosophical approach which is the study of the aesthetic, ethical and economic values within the firms as well as socio-economic and political environment. The answer will be a statement of what the firms' roles and objectives should be in the modern society. Several philosophically different approaches however exist. While each has apparent merits, none appears to have clear advantage over the others.

Another way to answer the question is through historical analysis of business objectives used and how it has evolved. Since explicit use of objectives is a relatively recent management technique, this approach is difficult as little appears to have been done in this field of analysis. The third approach is to construct a practical system of objectives which is consistent and usable on the one hand, and can be related to current business practice in modern management on the other. This is the approach commonly employed in the contemporary industrial society. Starting with the assumption that long term profitability is the central objectives of any reasonable and rational economic enterprise, one can construct a system of objective which can be individually related to performance yard stick commonly used in business and management practices.

9.2. CURRENT PHILOSOPHY OF CORPORATE OBJECTIVE

At sight the question of objective of a business firm would appear to be non-controversial and crystal clear, however, traditionally or historically, a business firm is regarded as an economics institution with economics interest or mission, it has developed a measure of efficiency (profit) common and unique to all business organizations. The society emphasizes business efficiency very highly because of the economic importance of large corporations. Profit is therefore seen (by business executives) as the main measure of efficiency; that is, the measure of business success and survival or failure remains traditionally the profit and loss account. It seems therefore that profit maximization or profit seeking would be the natural single business objective.

In actual fact however, objectives are currently one of the most controversial, ambiguous and not easily delineable issues of business ethic. Distinguished writers and philosophers, however, have sought to remove profit from its position as the central motive in business and replace it with doctrines such as equal responsibility to stakeholders, long term survival or a negotiated consensus among various participants in the firm. Some have even branded it morally and socially objectionable. Several reasons have been postulated, propounded or put forward for this confused state of affairs.

The first is the growing conflict between long and short terms demand and for the firm resources. During the 18th and 19th centuries, the first technological innovation made necessary long-term product research and long-term anticipation of capital equipments needs; hence it seemed appropriate to use long-term profitability as a yard stick of the firm's success. Increasingly, in this 20th century, the influx capital equipment need have forced concerned with

333

long-term problems. If short term profitability were to remain the principal performance yard stick, investment in project with long-term maturity would naturally be neglected. The result would be a severe treat to the survival of the business in the long-run. Therefore, to ensure survival, the concept of the firms' objective must be expanded to cover the long term horizon.

The micro-economic theory of the firm (a major body of theories which gave rise to the 19th century theory of profit maximization) could not accommodate this expansion for two reasons which are:

(a) Because it is basically a steady state theory concerned with successive dynamic equilibrium condition and hence not capable of dealing with decision between long and short range horizon and

(b) It does not recognize the exchange between investment for current profit and those for current returns.

In recent years, however, a number of economic and business writers have offered alternatives to short term profit maximization such as maximization of company's net present worth, maximization of market values/shares or growth. Each of these taken by itself is logically persuasive but none appears superior on philosophical ground, nor conclusively supported by data from experience. Another structural change in the firm has been the growth in size and complexity of modern organizations. The resulting philosophy of decentralized profit and loss responsibility centers which culminated in the 1920s in the doctrine of central profit making with decentralized operational control has led to a wide delegation of decision making power in the firm. Hence, the decision process now consists of many local decisions based on local limited information and is in potential conflict with each other.

Somehow, these add up to consensus decisions a central issue of the firm. This change had however dealt a severe blow not only to the economic concept of profit maximization but also to the validity of micro-economic theory in explaining the Behavior of the firm. A managerial point of view came into being which in a substantial body of writings subjected the micro-economics to thorough criticisms. The result is the conclusion that organizations do not have objective but only the people in them have. Therefore, *the objectives of a firm are in reality a negotiated consensus of objective of the influential participants in the firm.*

Meanwhile, the main reasons while profit maximization has become problematic as the supreme measure of business performance are as follows:

(a)   *Divorce of Ownership from Control:* This is because shareholders are not only concerned with profit maximization. It is not the only criterion by which the appraisal is performed by the company managers. Again, the controllers of business are separated from the shareholders and they have limited awareness of shareholders' goals,

(b)   *The Difficulties of Pursuing Profit Maximization:*. The business environment is now highly complex and uncertain. Yet, the need for long run survival means that certain actions must be taken such as the pursuit of goodwill which will reduce short run profit figure. Certain concern with market share and diversification may be more important than short run profit maximization,

(c)   *Problems of Profit Measurement:* These problems arise perhaps because companies go on continuously (going concern principle) whereas profit must be recorded as to particular period of time. On the day of profit measurement, the company has a whole range of assets and obligations which can be valued in various forms depending on what is going to happen to them in future,

(d)   *Problems of Corporate Social Responsibility* which firms now perform and which are not directly based on profit making, and

(e)   *The need to Minimize Risk and Protect the Autonomy and Security of Techno-structure:* The first requisite for survival by the techno-structure is that it reserves the autonomy on which decision making power depends. This means that it must have secured minimum earnings.

Power passes to the techno-structure when technology and planning require specialized knowledge and group decisions. The power remained secured with the techno-structure as long as earnings are large enough to make accustomed pay to the shareholders and provide supply of savings for re-investment. If earning is less than this level, it will be necessary to appeal to outside suppliers of fund from the capital market. This in turn can ask question and impose condition and hence abridge the autonomy of the techno-structure.

Also, if their costumed dividends are not covered, the shareholders cannot be counted upon to remain silent loyalists. By the most elementary calculation of self-interest, the techno-structure is compelled to put prevention of loss ahead of maximum returns because such a loss can destroy them. If maximization of revenue/returns invite more risk (as it often happens), then the techno-structure should forgo it. The executives of the large corporation do not receive that profit which may result from taking a share while their position in the firm may be jeopardized in the event of a serious loss

9.3. CORPORATE MISSION, VISION, GOALS AND PHILOSOPHY

The concepts of corporate objective cannot by any means be discussed without making adequate reference to the other dimensions such as corporate mission, corporate vision, corporate goals and corporate philosophy. All these are various terms by which performance of modern organizations are measured or assessed. Corporate mission states the definite activities in which the organization as a whole aims at now and in the future. This stipulates what sort of organization it is in now and what it is to become and, by omission, what it is not to do and not to become. In essence, the corporate mission of the firm stipulates the business and the organization and states its basic goals, characteristic, and guiding philosophies. It states the long-term vision of the organization in terms of what it aims or desires.

The mission statement is the beginning or starting point of the strategic management process because it defines the organization character, identifies direction and developmental path. Its aim is to say the context within which intended strategies to be formulated and the criteria against which all strategies are to be evaluated so that the organization can be given a focus and direction. The vision and mission statement of an organization clarify the direction in which the organization wants to move. It describes the future of an organization and provides the guiding philosophy for all the changes needed to make it happen.

For clarification, the basic elements of a mission statement constitute what actually makes up the major components of a modern day organizations mission statements:

(a)   The product or service the company is to offer to its customer,

(b)   Public image such as the information relating to the type of impression the company is attempting to leave with the organization public,

(c)   Company objectives to be achieved; that is, a general   reference to the company objectives will be made   which for most firms include intention to survive   through continuing growth and profitability,

(d)   Technology to be used; the methods and processes by which goods and   services are to be created and delivered to customers,

(e)   Company self-concepts and expressions; this is the company's own views or subjective impression of itself. The company arrives at this self-concept by assessing its   strengths, weaknesses, competition and ability to survive in the   market place, and

(f)   The market; that is, the customers to be served by the company. Who are they?   Where are   they located? And even what are their needs?

In other words, the corporate mission statement of a company consists of some essential parts such as:

(a)   The guiding principles that define the code of conduct that tells employee how to behave,

(b)   A statement of the organization corporate goals that is its principal business aims   or mission as regards the position if aims to achieve in its chosen business,

(c)   A statement of its corporate philosophy; that is, the key beliefs and values of the   company,

(d)   A definition of ratios of the major stakeholders in the business, and

(e)   A definition of the organization business or purpose, that is, a statement of the   principal activities of the organization

On the other hand, corporate goals of modern enterprises relate to what an organization is trying to achieve. They   assign focus and direction to the corporate mission statement and guide strategy formulation. Corporate goals can be categories into two levels, namely; primary and secondary goals. The overriding goal of most economic companies today is to maximize the wealth of stockholders. It involves the increasing long-term returns to stockholders from their shares held in the company. The best way of maximizing the wealth of the stockholders, however, is to pursue strategies that would maximize its own returns on investment (ROT).

In fact, return on investment represents the most objective indicator of corporate efficiency and an overzealous pursuit of short-term returns on investment management practices. Where short un profit maximization or return, on investment is pursued as the ultimate goals, management applies tight cost controllers, cutting expenditures that are considered to be non essential for the moment. Thus, research and development, new capital investments, innovative activity, social responsibility actions and marketing expenditure are undertaken in order to decrease current expenditure and increase current returns on investment.

However, these at times produce some negative effects including lack of innovation, bad public image, under investment, decline in profit growth, poor market awareness; the net effect of this is that long-term profitability and survival may be seriously compromised and endangered since the focus is usually on short run and current profit maximization, which tends to stand sending on research and development and growth related activities.

In modern management, however, to protect against short run Behavior, contemporary managers in organizations should also engage in some secondary goals in addition to the primary goal of high returns on investment. The aim of this is to achieve a balance between short-term and long-term considerations. Secondary goals are established in the following using innovation, productivity, physical and financial resources, market share, manager performance and development, worker performance and attitude, and social responsibility as as indicators or measures of corporate performance.

9.4   SOCIAL RESPONSIBILITIES

As the concept of business responsibility applies to individuals in an organization, so it is to various organizations in an economy. Each organization in a community has to cater for the environment in which it operates. The degree of responsiveness of an organization to the demands of its environment tells a lot on how successful the organization can be. However, the concept which deals with the contributions of an enterprise to its environment is widely referred to in modern management as *corporate social responsibility*

Social responsibility has been defined as a basic obligation or debt of an organization to ensure that its activities, decisions and operations meet the needs and interests of the groups, public, customers, shareholders, employees and government that constitute what is known as the larger society in order to ensure its continuity and survival. It could be argued that in the modern society, private and public organizations have begun to be more accountable to a greater number of constituencies than ever before.

For instance, the notions of the stakeholders have become to be drawn much wider than before. Social responsibility, once decreed as being irrelevant in the early 1950s and 60s in Britain is now at the forefront of organizational relationships. Of course, there are firms that take this concept lightly; there are others who espouse such notions, but are seen to be lacking in the final points when under scrutiny. Again, it is often argued that business organizations in particular will always be responsible only to themselves as you will be seeing later in our discussion of various schools of thought on the issue. We now see in a number of settings that a lack of social responsibility can often be very costly for the firm.

However, the classification of managerial and business Behaviors in term of a hierarchy from purely economic to that of an ethical philanthropy gives us a good guide to help judge firm Behaviors around. Meanwhile, corporate social responsibility pertains to the idea that organizations have obligations to the society beyond their obligation to the owners and also beyond those prescribed by the *law of contract*. The concept of social responsibilities of business assumes that it is the duty of organizations to serve the larger society. That is, it should participate in, and be responsive to, improving the quality of life in the society by adoption of the highest standard of ethical, just and fair conduct. The question then arises as to what role the private and public sectors organizations should play in the society as a whole for specific social groups.

There are three schools of thought on corporate social responsibilities: that is, *the economic, legal and civil schools of thought*. The conceptual leader of the economic school of social responsibilities was *Milton Friedman*, and he opined that there should be *one* and *only one* social responsibility of business organizations; that is, to use their resources and engage in activities designed to increase their profit so long they stay within the *rules of the game*. He was of the opinion that managers should ignore societal functions because such functions could not increase the profit of their company.

Closely related to the economic view is the legal perspective of corporate social responsibilities of the enterprise. It has always been held that a company's sacred duty is a consonance of activities which aims at generating profits whether directly or otherwise for the shareholders. This view goes back to the period of relatively small companies because as for the larger companies, since the beginning of the 19th century, they are supposed not only to achieve private profits but also to provide profits and to provide desirable services to the community.

However, in the case of the small scale companies, the profit motive has always being of paramount importance as was expressed in the case of *Hutton Vs West Cork Company (1983)* where speaking of a company which was about to wind-up, paying compensation to its directors and executives were all rejected. It was held that *directors can only spend the company's money for the purposes which are reasonably incidental to the furtherance of the company's memorandum of association*. The court noted in that case that a company is only to pursue activities which are for the benefits of its members; that is, the shareholders.

A company, for this purpose was defined in the case of *Greenhalgh Vs Adern Cinemas Ltd.* to mean, not a company as a commercial entity distinct from its incorporators but the incorporators as a body. Also in the case of *Parke Vs Daily News Ltd*, a similar comment was made about a company which was about to make a redundancy payment (free gifts) to some transferred employees into another company and was about winding-up. After the completion of the transfer, a general meeting of the company from which the transfer was made was called and it was held in a resolution that *to apply a sum of money in compensating some employees for loss of employment was not legal*. Therefore, a resolution for compensation was invalid although it should be noted that in this case, the company was no longer a going concern but was about to be wound-up.

In the case of a company that was a going concern, such as the case of *Re-Lee Brelmen*, the court was called upon to consider the legality of a deed of convenience entered into by a going concern in which a total sum of 500 pounds was to be granted as pension per annum to the widow of a deceased Managing Director, it was held that *despite the fact that the pension was for the benefit of the widow, since it was not for the benefit of the company, it was ultra vires the company.* Most of the authorities in this area of the company affairs (social responsibilities) appear to state in general terms that:

(a)   The company's funds cannot be applied in making *ex-gration* payments,

(b)   The court will enquire into the motives outweighing any gratuitous payment and the objective such payments intend to achieve,

(c)   The courts may uphold the validity of a gratuitous payment if it has established that;

    (i)   The transaction is reasonably incidental to the carrying out of the company's objects on matters auxiliary to such objects (i.e. those that are closely related but subordinates)

    (ii)   That the action (transaction) is *bona fide* (in good faith)

    (iii)   If it is for the benefit and for the promotion of the prosperity of the company, and

(d)   The duty of providing the validity of such payment or transaction lies in those ascertained to be the beneficiaries.

Perhaps, only a few cases may pass this stringent test. In *Hampson Vs Patient Candle Company Limited,* it was held, *inter-alia,* that *"The Company might lawfully pay some gratuities to their servants because that kind of liberal dealing with servants remove the restrictions between master and servant and at the end might provide for higher productivity.* The issue often discussed with this topic is that *"Charity has no place in the boardroom".* There is a kind of charitable dealings which is for the interest of the company. Such dealings might be a good transaction to boost the profitability of the company such as transactions to and from the company by the provisions of social facilities which directly or otherwise provide more profit to the company.

In the case of *Evans Vs Brunner Bonds Company Limited, a resolution that the directors were authorized to distribute to universities or other institutions in the U.K. for the furtherance of specific research, a total of 100,000 Pound Starlings for educational and scientific research from the reserve account was held to be valid even though the court could not exactly establish how it was going to be for the benefits of the company.* Hence, it can be concluded that even where the doctrine of *ultra vires* has been watered down, it still retains considerable significance when it comes to the rights to engage in non-profitable activities like charitable contributions or donations. The American courts have however been bolder with respect to charitable contributions.

In the case of *A. P. Smith Vs Parlow*, A company made a gift to Princedom University. A Plaintiff as a shareholder questioned the validity of that gift, such an object not being in the memorandum of the company. *It was held that it was lawful exercise if the company implied an incidental power under a common law.* Such jurisdictions have since specifically changed their laws to allow for donations to charity, For instance, the new *South Wale Companies Act provides that the powers of a company shall include powers to make donations for patriotic or charitable purpose.*

Again, the *Michigan laws* allow corporate contributions to social welfare especially where the *ultra vires* doctrine has been expanded to include corporate donations from the accounts which are not authorized by the memorandum of association, and this would appear to legalize corporate donations to clarity. Meanwhile, *the third argument of this school of thought is that social matters are the concern of the government. It is irresponsible and outside the manager's or business executive's job to get involved in activities which do not concern them, which are political or charity in nature.* This school finally opined that if a business company attempts to solve social problems, it would expose itself to criticisms, blackmailing and vandalism from various interest groups with negative consequences on its ability to perform its primary economic responsibilities.

However, the civic (non-economic social responsibilities) school sees the role of modern enterprises in the society as being extending beyond the parochial motive for commercial profit. It sees modern organizations as a means of social values and forces for improving the community and general welfare. The school, pioneered by *Oliver Sheldon* agrees that private companies especially the larger ones should incorporate normative patterns and values of society into their mission and operational objectives, and should help to prevent pollution, to build hospitals and schools, solve problems such as unemployment, inadequate social amenities, etc.

The pioneers and other advocates of this school believe that by assuming a wide range of non-economic responsibility for improving the quality of life, an organization will retain its legitimacy and social acceptance in its domain. These will help to achieve its primary objectives and to avoid undue intervention and imposition of harsh external control on their internal operations by the government or some other powerful public groups. *Therefore, it is important to state that while organizations must strive to achieve their economic objectives, they cannot afford to remain passive or ignorant of their social responsibilities.*

9.5   SOCIAL RESPONSIBILITIES AND ETHICS

The drive towards good, effective and productive management in an organization has from the down of any social system, being the concern for development. However, it must be noted that accompanied with any form of management is the need for moral enlistment. If ethically bankrupt, it would consequently influence its goals and objective. This is evidently clear in the present Nigeria corporate strategic management practice.

Members of organizations in Nigeria as in any other place usually carry out different roles at the work place and also at home. At works, the workers may experience critical dilemmas; they may even disagree with some of them, because of doubt and suspicions about how to proceed, or because of clashes in culture and values. Some workers may be influenced more than others by principles or a sense of duty. Their view may either be influenced by religious or moral beliefs. On the other hand, some workers may have noticed how values, differs between sates, communities and even countries. For example, one society may ban the production and consumption of alcohol whereas another may permit the public use of such substances. These individuals may think that an act is right if it is approved by the social group to which a person belongs and wrong if it is not, and that otherwise moral belief should be regarded as the private concern of each individual.

According to *Donaldson (1989)*, organizational ethics can be defined as *the systemic study of moral (ethical) matters pertaining to business, industry or related activities, institution or practice and beliefs.* The use of organizational ethics is due to the changing nature of employment, as a result of the rapid spread of technology and the impact of various socio–economic and political factors on the structure, size and function of private and public sector organizations. In a business environment, successful organization implies the well–coordinated efforts of two or more persons. These persons enhance each other's activities by the addition of their supplement similarities on their complementary difference.

Persons working together in an organization are often sufficient, powerful, productive and rewarding. But organizations then also sometime produce frustration, oppression and death. Therefore the strategic form of organizational Behaviors is better understanding and management of the people at work. For illustration, the following two tables are taken from *Carroll (1999)* and state the social responsibility positions for firms in terms of ethical and philanthropic as well as economic components.

Table 3: Ethical and Philanthropic Components of Corporate Social Responsibility

Ethical Component (Responsibilities)	Philanthropic Components (Responsibilities)
It is important to perform in a manner.	It is important to perform in a manner consistent with the exceptions of societal philanthropic and mores and ethical norms and Charitable expectations of society.
It is important to recognize and respect new or evolving ethi-cal/norms adopted by society	It is important to assist the fine and performing arts
It is important to prevent ethical norms from being compromised in order to achieve corporate goals.	It is important to allow managers and employees participate in voluntary and charitable activities within their local communities.
It is important that good corporate citizenship be defined as doing what is expected morally or ethically.	It is important to provide assistance to private and public educational institute-ions.
It is important to recognize that corporate integrity and	It is important to assist voluntarily those projects that

| ethical Behavior go beyond mere compliance with laws and regulations. | enhance a community's *equity of life* |

Table 4: Economic and Legal Component of Corporate Social Responsibility

Ethical components (Responsibilities)	Philanthropic (Responsibilities)
It is important to perform in a manner consistent with maximising earnings per share	It is important to perform in a manner consistent with expect-ations of government and law.
It is important to be committed to being as profitable as poss-ible.	It is important to comply with various federal, state, and local regulations
It is important to maintain a strong competitive position	It is important to be a law-abiding corporate citizen.
It is important to maintain a high level of operating effici-ency	It is important that a successful firm be defined as one that fulfils its legal obligations.
It is important that a successful firm be defined as one that is consistently profitable.	It is important to provide goods and services that at least meet minimal legal require-ments.

9.6.MARKETING ETHICS

The social responsibility argument has, according to *Smith (1995)*, moved from the position of buyer beware to that of seller beware; that is, *from caveat emptor to caveat vendor* in the modern industrial organizations. The regulated markets that businesses operate in the modern local and international arena have seen this key shift of focus. Litigation, regulation and consumer monitoring have meant that responsible firms can no longer fall back to the ancient of caveat emptor.

Some observers argue that this change in attitude can be traced to the famous case of the *Ford Pinto* and the campaigning stance taken by *Ralf Nader* to force the United States auto manufacturers to make safer cars. The *Nader* argument for accountability shifted to other sectors where firms were seen as operating sharp practices against the consumer. For example, the campaign against '*big tobacco*' is a continuing one. The acceptance by '*big tobacco*' that their product is harmful has meant very large *payouts* to the United States government in order to avoid certain types of liability.

Smith (1995) gives us a series of statements for us to consider and suggests that marketers often rely on simple *maxims* to evaluate their marketing practices. However, while most of them are useful, they generally lack specific guidance in certain cases. Meanwhile, the following maxims would assist a lot if this can be followed to the letter:
(b)   Do unto others, as you would have them do unto you.
(c)   Would you be embarrassed in front of your family, friends or colleagues if the media published your decision?
(d)   Good ethics is in the long–term interest of the firm.
(e)   Would an objective panel of professional colleagues view my actions as proper?
(f)   When in doubt, don't do it.

The big question that a reasonable manager or administrator asks now is *"What is expected of managers or administrators do in relation to social responsibility?"* The answer to this question is not far fetched, and in fact, it includes the following:

(a) *Assess the power of each group and its Potential:* Managers or those in business must assess the power of each group that constituted the society and its potential threats to organizational objectives and activities, whether it is going to be a threat or an opportunity,

(b) *Monitoring the Environment:* The manager must be at alert by monitoring the activities of the environment and if there is any change, he should quickly respond to it. he should pursue what deem to be the primary goals of the organization, but always with an eye out for constraints imposed by forces in the external environment,

(c) *Managers should not be too rigid or flexible:* When managers go too long without responding, or when they fundamentally disagree with actions demanded by various groups, they risk the possibility of boycotts, picketing, new legislation, proxy contest and strikes,

(d) *Managers or those in Business must be Good Listeners:* Managers must device means of listening to the opinions of the people in their society because this will serve as a source of information to enable opportunities come to the organization, and

(e) *Constant Identification of Society's Need:* Managers must continually get in touch with the society to be able to identify their problems, demands made by the groups in the society and how it can be met by the company without jeopardizing their activities. However, demands made by groups in the society will keep the organization from becoming too selfish and irresponsible actions by these groups, rather than profit or conscience, have often led a firm to pursue socially responsible actions.

9.7   RESPONSIBILITIES TO THE PUBLIC

Business has responsibilities to the public, which many of them have been enshrined in the constitution of the country. Many of these responsibilities have been defined as law; that is, they are legal responsibilities. In Nigeria, it has been defined as law that any company operating in any part of the country should not pollute the environment with their waste product, especially toxic waste. However, in Nigeria, some business people still take the view that the sole function of business is to produce goods and services in order to earn profits. Others adopt the notion that business exists for the betterment of mankind. Between these two extremes, there is a wide range of responsibilities that are accepted by some business people in the country and some of them are as indicated in the following sub-sections.

9.7.1   Improved Standard of Living

The modern business concept is to identify the needs and wants of consumers profitably in order to improve the standard of living of the masses. Also since business is the major source of incomes in many countries especially in Nigeria, the goods and services that business provides set the standard of living of every member of the society since business has a great power to increase or decrease the standard of living in any given economy. A dynamic, existing and expanding business system can make a genuine contribution to the betterment of human life as well as the economic and social development of a country.

9.7.2   Preservation of Natural Resources

Natural resources are free gifts of nature from God which include mineral resources like oil, gold, cement, iron, tree from forests, etc. All these serve as sources of raw materials for our industrial organizations for their continuity in business. Goods cannot be produced without basic raw materials and the supply of many business resources is fixed and cannot be increased especially in a short-run. For example, in Nigeria, all the timber dealers that have been going inside the bush to cut timber for their commercial activities are continuously being warned by the government to plant another one in order to preserve the forest. The timber dealers have the responsibility to plant another one in order to preserve the area. Therefore business has responsibility to use these resources effectively and efficiently, and to create as much wealth with as little waste as possible.

9.7.3   Efficiency in Operations

There must be efficiency in operation of any organization in a country. This will accelerate the economic growth and improve the standard of living of people. The continuous striving for efficiency is a necessary element in the business person's responsibility to himself and to the society, for efficient operation makes more goods and services available at lower cost, than aiding in the conservation of resources.

9.7.4   Preservation of Basic Institution

Business organizations perform their activities in a systematic manner. That is, there is interdependence among business organizations. There are some institutions in the country that formed the nucleus of the economic activities of the nation. Such institutions are government institutions such as Central Bank of Nigeria, Stock Exchange Market, Nigerian Port Authority and the likes. Others are private institutions such as Commercial Banks, Insurance companies, transport firms, and other institutions that are legally established like the judicial system.

Therefore most business organizations accept the need to maintain the basic institutions, which make possible our system of economy. Freedom of our property, freedom of contract and investment liberalism is essential features of our business environment and abuse of these institutions will certainly weaken them and reduce the probability that they will continue unchanged. By accepting the need to exercise his or her rights in a responsible manner, the business organization can contribute substantially to the preservation of these basic institutions.

9.7.5   Community Welfare Program

More and more business organizations in Nigeria are coming to accept the need for a broader conception of business responsibility to the community. For instance, Nigeria Breweries Plc great concern for issue of the environment has been demonstrated through its long year Brewery Environment Protection/Beautification program and through the huge amount of money devoted to design, construction and maintenance of efficient treatment of waste/waste disposal system.

The community welfare programs include a contribution toward the building of a Sickle Cell Center in Nigeria, the establishment of several billions of Naira Education Fund and the construction/refurbishment of facilities in Colleges and Universities. It also includes the purchase of blood bank equipment for various communities, the construction and maintenance of craft Training Workshops in major cities in Nigeria, and the provision of portable entertainment and sometimes educational or cultural programs through radio and television.

An instance of this is the Milo World of Sport on African Independence Television and the Ray Power radio Station in Nigeria sponsored by Nestle Foods Plc. Some companies play an important part in sponsorship of research work and provide fellowships and scholarships for university student not only in Nigeria but also overseas. An example of this is the Guinness Leads University Postgraduate Scholarship being sponsored by Guinness Nigeria Plc.

9.7.6 Safe Guard the Interests of the Others

Business organization must conduct their affairs in such a manner that the rights of others, whether in business or not, are not interfered with more than its necessary for healthy competition especially in a free economy country like Nigeria.

9.9 RESPONSIBILITIES TO STAKEHOLDERS

As individuals have responsibilities to one another as members of a society, so also organizations. Hence, a business undertaking irrespective of its nature and scope has some statutory obligations to its various stakeholders as will be seen in the following subsections:

9.9.1 To Shareholders

Many business organizations in Nigeria as in any other country are owned by millions of shareholders who are very dependent upon the integrity, honesty, and sense of responsibility of management. Business managers must therefore consider the interest of those who have given them their authority and responsibility to work for them as much as possible. Consequently, modern organizations have a lot of responsibilities to their shareholders some of which are the following;

(a) *Protection of Shareholders Investment:* The management basic responsibility is to protect the shareholder's investment and to endeavor to provide a reasonable rate of returns,

(b) *Prompt Payment of Dividends:* The management of any business organization must ensure prompt payment of dividends to their owners, no matter how small as this reinforce their trust and confidences on the caliber of the management entrusted with their equity.

(c) *Establish Cordial Relationship with Shareholders:* There must be cordial relationship between Management and shareholders by establishing sufficient communication with the shareholders to permit them a reasonable judgment of the best interest of the firm in any given management, a better opportunity to explain current policy objectives to the shareholders and to establish better rapport between owners and managers.

(d) *Promote and Protect the Image of the Business:* The shareholders will like to be associated with the company if the name has been in a good record of the public. Therefore, management must strive hard to promote and protect the image of the company among the people.

9.9.2 To the Government

Many business organizations are owned by the government in Nigeria especially before privatization and commercialization program. Notwithstanding, however, they still have certain responsibilities to the government. Both government-owned and privately-owned companies have the following responsibilities to the government in any economy:

(a) *Provision of Financial Support:* One of the businesses' responsibilities to the government especially in Nigeria is to provide the financial support needed to maintain the governmental system. This can be done by paying various forms of taxes and levies imposed by the government on individual companies such as company income tax, import duties, excise duties, special levies, etc.

(b) *Maintenance of Law and Order:* Business organizations must obey the laws and must help develop a system of law, which provides the best possible climate for business enterprises to operate!

(c) *Assist Government in Provision of Social Amenities:* Businesses must try to assist the government in certain areas in order to satisfy the yearnings of the masses by providing certain social amenities such as building of classrooms for schools, construction of roads and bridges, provision of drinkable water, etc.

9.9.3 To Customers

The customer is a member of the general public and shares the benefit of those obligations which organizations accept in its relations with the general public. Business organizations however have a more specific obligations and debts to the customers in terms of corporate social responsibilities among which are:

(a) *Fulfillment of Contractual Obligations:* There is usually a contractual agreement between an organization and its customers. Therefore, a business organization must fulfill its contractual agreement with its customers, whether they are private consumers or otherwise. Any organization which fails to keep its promises will soon finds its market declined.

(b) *Satisfying the Needs and Wants of Consumers:* One of the business concepts is that business organizations should try to identify the needs and wants more effectively and efficiently with the aim of making profit and in order for the business organization to remain in business. The marketers believed that "consumer is the king"

(c) *Provision of Necessary Information to Customers:* It is pertinent for the business organizations to provide necessary information that consumers suppose to know about the company and its various products. Lack of adequate information may cause a great deal of damage for consumers, which may affect the operations of the company. Therefore, business organizations should try to avoid misrepresentation in any of their business activities. For instance, when advertising a product (drug) which is only a pain relief tablets, but in your advert messages, the company should avoid any slogan which may imply that the product can cure malaria and running stomach. This is tantamount to misrepresentation. *Business managers must realize that customers can only* be deceived but once.

9.9.4 To the Employees

The law of employment identifies certain aspects of the business organization's responsibilities to employee, and business certainly has the obligation to accept this minimum responsibility. Unlike the others that formed the society such as public, government, shareholders, customers, etc., business responsibilities to the employees is always immediate, direct and consequential because the employees' life is entwined with his or her employment although it would, probably be impossible to obtain complete agreement among management on the actual responsibilities of a company to its employees.

REVISION QUESTIONS

1.   In your own opinion, what do you think should be the   main motive behind organizational efforts based on your knowledge and experience of the Nigeria industrial environment?

2.   Distinguished management philosophers have sought to remove profit motive from its prominent position as the main objectives of a business undertaking. Discuss your own view of this proposition pointing out reasons for your stance.

3.   While organizations must strive to achieve their economic objectives, they cannot afford to remain passive or ignorant of their social responsibilities. Do you agree? Justify your answer.

4.   What is corporate objective and how can it be determined? Discuss the most recent philosophy of corporate objectives of the modern organizations.

5.   With relevant examples and illustrations where necessary, explain what you understand by corporate mission, corporate vision, and corporate objectives in the contemporary organizations in your country.

6.   Discuss the concept of corporate social responsibility from the economic, civil and legal perspectives. Which of the positions would you support and why?.

7.   What is ethics? Discuss your understanding of the ethical and philosophical components of the corporate social responsibilities of modern organizations. Who are the interest groups in an organization and what are their expectations? Are these expectations being met by the contemporary organizations in your country?

8.	In your own opinion, what are the major
	responsibilities of modern organizations to the
various		publics you may which to identify?

CHAPTER TEN

MANAGING EMPLOYEES AT WORK

Things to Consider:
* * Introduction
* * The Manager's Role
* * Wages Remuneration
* * Trade Unions
* * The Shop Steward
* * Government Participation
* * Personnel Management
* * The Qualities of a Successful Personnel Officer
* * The Office Manager
* * Organizational Change
* * Stores Management

10.1 INTRODUCTION

So far in this book, we have discussed the functions of all managers; their duties and responsibilities, and provided other information of value to managers no matter what departments of the enterprise they work in. Before giving you an introduction to the more specialized work performed by managers working in different departments of a modern organization, we must consider one very important factor which concerns all managers; the men and women with whom a manager works and whom he or she must control and motivate. However, instead of repeatedly using the term *men and women,* we shall use the word *workers* to refer to all those in non-managerial positions.

First it must be appreciated that if there were no workers, there would be no need for managers. Secondly, it must be appreciated that the wellbeing of any undertaking depends to a large extent on the way in which the workers perform their work. If they are contented and work hard and willingly, the organization will benefit. However, if they are dissatisfied and work slowly or badly, and become involved in disputes and strikes, the organization will suffer.

Therefore, every manager, no matter what position he holds, must do his best to ensure that the workers employed by his organization are treated fairly and considerately and that they are encouraged and keen (motivated) to work in the interest of the enterprise. *In fact, the gracious treasure on earth is the human being. If you improve the number and quality of human resource in an organization individually and hence collectively, you would be improving on every other aspect of the organization and consequently their contributions to corporate productivity and profitability*

Today, we constantly hear of industrial disputes, strikes, go-slows, and other actions by workers, and the root causes of these are a lack of knowledge and lack of interest by workers. To understand how these problems have arisen we must look back to the early days of industry. The original system of industry was the family system under which peasant farmers and their families, in addition to tilling the land, all helped to carry out simple manufactures at home, like cloth-making and metal work. The next stage in the evolution of modern industry was the domestic system, merchants supplied the raw materials and the members of the family worked at home and were paid each piece of work they completed.

At a time, it was realized that some people were better at one part of a job whilst others were better at other parts. The merchants then introduced *specialization* and the work to be done was divided into parts and each expert worker performed his task on the work and then passed it on to another worker, and so on. Under the family and domestic systems, the family was the basic economic unit; all its members worked together for the common good of the family, and the whole family benefited from the effort. The merchants who paid well got most trade and the best work, whilst those who paid badly got few workers, that is, those who established a good employer and employee relationship prospered.

Gradually, over the years, small businesses grew up, normally in charge of a master, and often with a number of members of the same family working for the same master. The master knew each person working in the business, and so the family system still remained to some extent. This made for good working relations and the workers retained their pride in their work and a feeling of responsibility.

However, the use of steam power, and later electricity, changed this in two main ways. Factory premise and the machinery they required cost a great deal of money, and few merchants could raise the capital needed on their own. They had to go to banks and other financial institutions, and later the capital market, in order to borrow money, and those who lent the money had an interest in the business and the factory owners had to account for their actions to their financial backers. In most cases, the financial brokers had no contact with, or interest in, the workers. They were interested only in the profits which they could gain from the money they had lent. Also, the workers could no longer work at home or in family groups for the same master.

The situation today is that many of the small businesses have grown into medium sized businesses and eventually into very large industrial empires. Many organizations manufacturing the same items have joined together (merged) to form larger and more economically sized unit. The result is that the relationships between workers and masters have changed greatly. The "master" is now often a body of shareholders (which may number many hundreds) and these are represented by the Board of

Directors with whom the workers rarely come into contact. The worker performs his work simply for his wage, and his little knowledge of the importance of his efforts, and this in turn leads to lack of interest and sense of purpose.

This is especially the case in a large factory where a worker specializes on one job only, a job which is a small part of the whole, and does the same work all day long. He gets bored and does not even see how his day's work has contributed to the whole manufactured article. An example of this is the case of the man whose job it is to fix the wheels on to motor cars. Of course, he gets tired and bored and loses the feeling of pride in his work.

Of course, there are still many small businesses left, but it is with the larger ones that we are most concerned here. In most of the larger businesses, there is a feeling of resentment against the management as a whole; the workers feel that they are being exploited by the "bosses". In a modern society, this feeling is, in most cases, quite unfounded, and is caused by a lack of understanding by workers of the problems of management. However, in some cases, the problems have been caused by bad management practices. Some businesses have tried to remedy the situation, whilst others have ignored it. We shall now consider what can be done in the course of the rest of this chapter.

10.2   THE MANAGER'S ROLE

It is the duty of every manager to promote the best possible employer/employee relationship within his own department or section in particular and, where possible, within the business as a whole. To do this, he needs to possess certain personal qualities. We have dealt with many of these in Chapter One already but it is worth repeating some of them here. First, he must show interest in his subordinates as individuals, and be prepared to assist them where possible. He must not be cold and aloof as this may cause the workers to feel remote from him and thereby lose interest in the affairs of the enterprise.

He must be fair in his treatment, and avoid *"favoritism"*, which is bound to result in resentment. He must have the ability to see another's point of view and to treat people with opposing ideas kindly and courteously. He must be able to keep calm and be able to control his temper, and he must not panic. He must always be able to retain his sense of judgment. Above all, he must always remember that his subordinates are human beings too with their own characters, feelings and emotions. If he wants to get the best out of them for the benefit of the business (and in his own interests too, as an efficient section or department will reflect favorably on him and enhance his prospects for promotion), he must set them good examples, treat them fairly, respect them, and instill in them a sense of pride in their work. A manager who treats his subordinates as mere *"production units"* cannot hope to get the best out of them and expect loyalty or assistance in difficult times.

10.3   WAGES REMUNERATION

This is probably the most important single cause of labor unrest and lack of goodwill in business today. The wages policy of a business is usually laid down by the Board of Directors, and the policy can directly affect the relationship between the manager and his subordinates, although he may have no say in the policy laid down. The manager must, however, be able to appreciate the points of view of both the Board and the workers in relation to remuneration.

To the Board, wages and salaries are just two of the expenses which must be incurred in running the business, and like every other expense must be kept within reasonable level if the business is to be able to run at a profit. The Board therefore has a two fold problem in deciding on wages policy. Firstly, the value of wages paid must be kept at level which will not adversely affect the financial resources of the business and its profitability (problems which are not often appreciated by the workers) whilst at the same time paying wages which will satisfy the workers.

Striking the correct balance between the two extremes is often a very difficult task. On the one hand, if the level of wages paid is too high, the business may incur losses which may even mean that it has to cease operations. On the other hand if the level of wages paid is too low, there will be dissatisfaction amongst the workers, resulting in strikes and other industrial actions which will lose the business production and sales and again reduce profit. Remuneration can be defined as *"recompense for services rendered"* and should be based on the principle of a *"fair wage for a fair day's work"*. It must be accepted that the worker should receive earnings sufficient enough to maintain the standard of living to which he and his family have become accustomed, and modern thinking is that workers should participate in the prosperity of a business.

However, the problems in modern business cannot be over-simplified. There are some businesses which endeavor to maximize returns for the minimum cost. At the same time there are many workers whose only aim is to obtain the maximum wage for the minimum work performed. It is therefore, often very difficult to reconcile these two attitudes, both of which may be in the long run, detrimental to both parties. Meanwhile, it is not within the scope of this book to delve deeply into the complexities of equitable wages remuneration, particularly as policies (some laid down by the governments of countries) vary considerably .We can only attempt to acquaint the reader with the problems which exist, and advice that he studies carefully those existing current literature in the business in which he is employed (looking at both points of view) and does his best to understand them, and not to aggravate the situation.

10.4   TRADE UNIONS

In recent years, Trade Unions have become powerful and influential in many countries. One of the main aims of a Trade Union is to negotiate with employers on behalf of its members, and to obtain the best wages and other benefits for them. In many cases, responsible and experienced Union take into consideration, when making their demands, the problems of businesses and their financial resources. However, there is no doubt that in numerous cases, excessive Union demands have seriously affected businesses, and in some cases have forced them to cease operations. It is not our intention to deal with the pros and cons of powerful Unions and the advantages and disadvantages of them to employers and workers here, because relations between different Unions and different Industries vary greatly, both within a particular country and in different countries.

The system by which a Union negotiates for its members is called *collective bargaining*. A collective bargain can be reached through an, individual's business negotiation with its workers, but it is more usual today for one large business, or a group of similar businesses, to negotiate collectively with the Union representing the workers in that business or businesses. It must however be appreciated that the situation may often be complicated by the fact that the workers in a given business or industry may not all belong to the same Union, so that separate negotiations may have to be carried out with a number of different Union, each of which represents only one section of the work force; unfortunately it often happens that Unions cannot agree on a common policy or approach, which may lead to disruptions through no fault of the employer.

During collective bargaining, each party (employer and Union) will have in mind a wage which is acceptable to it, and also a level which it will refuse to accept. If a satisfactory compromise cannot be agreed or be reached, the situation becomes more serious, and industrial action of different kinds such as strikes may result, until one side gives way or until an independent body (often government appointed) is called in to mediate and arbitrate. Students are advised to read carefully the accounts of negotiations between employers and Unions.

In the cases of successful outcomes, they should try to pin-point the reasons why agreement was reached. In cases where agreement has not been reached, they should follow the consequences which is nothing but industrial action, arbitration, conciliation, and the eventual outcome. In this way they will learn much about modern employer/Union relationships and negotiating methods which will stand them in good stead should they ever be in positions which require decision making and negotiating.

10.5   THE SHOP STEWARD

The shop steward is the workers' representative in the workshop. He represents the Trade Union and if the company is a "closed shop" (that is, a case where every worker must belong to the Union), he can bring the workers out to a lighten strike without reference to the union itself. A tactless remark by a Foreman, a lack of smile by the Manager, a works change to improve efficiency, any small departure from the normal way of Behavior or practice might be sufficient to cause the shop steward to shout: "*Down tools, Comrades*", and a possible production worth millions of Naira could be lost.

10.6 GOVERNMENT PARTICIPATION

In the past, many governments especially in Nigeria has supplied large sums of money to save some important businesses from closing down or reducing their production. This action was taken partly to avoid disasters of importance to the economy of the country, or of great use to the country in time of war, for example, shipbuilders, airplane and motor-car manufacturers and steal works. In return for supplying the money, the government usually took shares in the businesses and secured influence in their managements. In some parts of the world, notably in Africa, Asia and South America, some governments have taken over some businesses completely and have appointed their own directors and managers. This is called *"Nationalization"* as it happens in Nigeria in the 1970s, and compensation to some extent had been given to the original owners, shareholders and managers of the businesses concerned.

There are differing views as to whether government participation and control have had a beneficial effect upon production and profit in some economies especially in developing countries like Nigeria. Government managers may or may not be so efficient if they have no share in profits but are paid fixed salaries, no matter how great. Some workers may prefer their businesses to be publicly owned, but they may not necessarily work harder on that account, especially if their foremen and supervisors are not affected in their pockets by greater production. What is certain is that, in Nigeria, those organizations which have government influence or control are no freer than are private businesses from labor problems and other difficulties.

In some European countries Trade Unions have become so strong that they have persuaded a number of organizations to introduce two important advances for workers. These are retirement on full pay (or equivalent) at the age of 60 instead of the usual 65, and co-opting workers to the Boards of Directors. It is claimed that these advances have been successful; that is, they have resulted in increased production by workers generally, and in a more harmonious and strike-free atmosphere in these organizations.

Many developing countries such as Togo in West Africa, however, cannot afford the luxury of experiment and trial and error, and the trade unions in such countries have been put under government control to a greater or lesser degree. Whilst the government ensures by law that the workers have good pay, conditions, pensions on retirement and other social benefits, the trade unions on their part have agreed to government control and, in some cases, to ban strikes and other forms of industrial action. No doubt, in such cases, joint committees of government officials and trade union officers exist to make decisions on the most important matters which affect workers wages inflation, working hours and conditions, retirement, pension, and so on.

Relationships between government and trade unions vary considerably from country to country, and as a future management expert you should make yourself familiar with the relationship which exists between the government of your own country and the trade unions. You should also make yourself familiar with any government regulations in force in your country with regard to workers: minimum rates of pay, social security benefits, etc., bearing in mind that changes in such regulations occur from time to time.

10.7 PERSONNEL MANAGEMENT

The existence of a personnel manager or personnel officer in any organization is a good example of the assignment of responsibility. The responsibilities for dealing with the personnel (staff or human resource) in certain defined matters are transferred to the personnel or human resource manager by the Board of Directors, Managing

Director or General Manager, on the one hand, and by the departmental managers or departmental heads on the other.

The Managing Director or General Manager of a large company like the U. A. C., Kingsway, Lever Brothers, etc, has ultimate responsibility for all departments; production, sales, stock control, offices, finance, accounts, etc. For each department, the board appoints a head or manager. The manager of each department has staffs that carry out their work under his orders. So the departmental managers have direct and close contact with their clerical or technical employees, as the case may be. Every departmental manager has enough to do; train his staff in the specific jobs they have to perform and to control them and ensure efficient work in both quality and quantity.

He has no time, in most cases, to interview applicants for employment, to test them for ability, education, experience, etc., to engage them on particular terms and conditions, to keep records of their service, to arrange promotion, welfare, medical assistance, holidays, pensions, etc., and to deal with complaints, disputes and the numerous human problems which may arise from time to time. This is where the Personnel Manager comes in; he is appointed to deal with all those matters which we have just mentioned and to relieve the General Manager and a half-dozen or more Departmental Managers of staff burdens which are not directly concerned with promotion and its associated services.

The Personnel Manager has to maintain close contact with the Departmental Managers, because he has to be told their staff requirements from time to time, in addition to other matters relating to their staffs. At the same time, the Personnel Manager must be in contact with his General Manager who, as the representative of the Board of Directors, lay down staff policy; hours of work, rates of pay, bonuses, incentives, holidays, pensions, etc. The personnel Manager, who may have a staff to assist him, accepts responsibility for carrying out the personnel policies of the company.

10.8. THE QUALITIES OF A SUCCESSFUL PERSONNEL OFFICER

It is not everyone who can carry out the work of a Personnel Officer; the post demands qualities of a special kind. A Personnel Officer has to hold discussions with people in all standards in life: the illiterate and uncouth cleaner or watchman, the skilled and proud technician, the stubborn man in a grievance, the truculent Shop Steward, the aggressive and authoritarian Foreman or Supervisor and not least the Departmental Manager himself. To work with this great variety of people, he must show tact and understandings, he must in his talk descend to the level of the uncouth and rise to the height of the educated; he must suit his speech and choose his words to attain his main objective; that is, the maintenance of a smooth-working, happy, efficient staff. To each man he must by implication say: 'You are right, but.....' and make him happy whilst agreeing to a compromise.

The Personnel Manager is delegated to recruit and engage staff for all departments of the company, so he must have some understanding, if not a complete knowledge, of the work of all departments. For those technical departments, like Finance, for example, he will no doubt consult the Financial Controller or Chief Accountant, who will assist him in preparing a Job Description and in interviewing likely applicants. A *Job Description* or *Specification* is a detailed list of the abilities which a particular post requires. The job of a *Leger Clerk*, for instance, demands a certain standard of education and a fair knowledge of Bookkeeping: the post of Chemist requires a different kind prepared in advance, with the aid of the relevant Departmental Managers, job descriptions for every one of the many different kind of jobs carried out throughout the Company.

When a Vacancy or Vacancies arise, the Personnel Manager is relied upon to fill the posts without delay. A foresighted Personnel Officer will have books containing several prospective applicants with the required qualifications, whom he can invite for an interview. If he has no qualified applicants available, he must have ready sources of supply on which he can call immediately; such sources might be private *Employment Agencies, Government Offices, Trade Unions, or Technical Associations,* and so on. If such contacts fail to produce the right personnel, he has, on the alternative but to advertise.

The newspaper, magazine, trade journal, television, or other medium which the Personnel Manager will depend on is a function of the kind of the post which he has to fill. In any case, his advertisement must be prominent, must give a brief but clear job description and must state attractive terms, conditions and promotion prospects. A clear job description ensures that the Manager will not waste time dealing with useless applications; attractive terms should ensure that a reasonable number of applications will be received.

Assuming that a number of people have applied in writing, the Personnel Manage or his staff must examine the letters and decide which applicants appear to be most suitable for the post. He then calls them for an interview which he personally, together with the appropriate Departmental Head, conducts. He must have ready in advance a list of the questions which he has to put to the applicants. It is important that the questions be framed in such a way that the applicant is compelled to give a full answer and not just *Yes* or *No.* In this way, it should be possible for the Personnel Manager to judge better the character and history and abilities of the applicant. It is important at the interview to put the applicant at his ease right from the start; unless he is comfortable and confident he may mislead the interviewers and give the impression of unsuitability for the post.

When all the called applicants have been interviewed, one at a time and told that they will be notified of the choice as soon as possible, the Personnel Manager and Departmental Head consult together and come to a decision. The successful applicant is then notified in writing and the letter of appointment lays down clearly and without ambiguity the following main items:

(a)   The Duties of the Post,

(b)   The Salary, terms, conditions, etc,

(c)   The Prospects of promotion,

(d)   Holidays,

(e)   The Pension schemes, if any, and

(f)   Any other special matters relevant to the post, such as a statement as to whom the applicant will be responsible, welfare facilities, social activities, etc.

These days, with the powers of Trade Unions being what they are, it may happen that for the particular post in question, the relevant Union representative will have to give his approval. If such is the case, that approval must be sought before the applicant is notified of his success.

The Personnel Department does not need to train a new employee in the specific tasks he will actually carry out. That is done by the departmental Head, a foremen or supervisor. In cases where the new employee needs general training or education before he can be trained for his actual work, the personnel manager has his system or organization ready, he will himself conduct the required tuition, or arrange for the employee to receive it at a school or technical college at certain convenient times. The Personnel Department is usually responsible for seeing that certain facilities, which keep the staff happy and contented and which assist them in working well, are maintained and are operated smoothly. These are a Canteen for cheap meals, social, recreational and sports organizations, medial services, safety measures in the works and elsewhere, adequate Lighting, Heating, Ventilation, Water Closets, Tea intervals, etc.

Although the normal stages of promotion are notified to new employees on engagement, it often happens that a worker who proves to be exceptionally good is recommended by his Departmental Head for a more senior and better-paid post. The Personnel Manager is then consulted and, after another interview, puts the recommended promotion into effect. It also happens on occasions that, owing to illness or retirement, an attractive post become vacant. In such a case, the Departmental Head and Personnel Manager must consult and decide whether to promote an existing member of the staff, or to carry out the procedure for the engagement of a new person from an external source.

It is very rare these days for an employee to be dismissed and such cases are confined to *"gross misconduct"*. Nowadays, the decision as to dismissal, and of making staff redundant, can be made only in consultation and agreement with the relevant Trade Union. The Personnel Manager and Departmental Head usually approach the Union representative jointly. The personnel Manager no doubt has the greater say on behalf of the Management, and needs to use his powers of persuasion and knowledge of human nature to full, to succeed without having to pay too high a compensation, and without risking a "walk-out" of a whole section of staff.

The conditions for age of retirement (usually 65 for men and 60 for women) and for company pension, are notified to employees on engagement and of course they are kept informed of changes during the course of their employment by negotiations between the Management and the Union concerned. The Personnel Manager is, of course, usually one of the company representatives in all negotiations regarding members of the staff. It sometimes happens that a company needs to reduce its staff, by agreed retirement before the normal retirement age, owing to the introduction of labor-saving equipment, or different methods, or change of products. In such cases, the Union must be consulted and an agreement reached regarding compensation or transfer of staff to other branches.

The task of keeping records of each member of the staff is solely the concern of the Personnel Department. The record are entered at regular intervals and show date of engagement, commencing salary, increases in salary, holidays, absences, promotions, illnesses, Behavior, and any other matters relevant to the history and progress of each employee. The staffs of the Personnel Department are not allowed to deal with the records of staff senior to them: these are usually kept by the Personnel Manager. The records of the Personnel Manager himself and of Department Heads and Senior Executives are or should be kept in the confidential files of the General Manager.

From the foregoing, it is clear that although some duties relating to staff are solely in the hands of the Personnel Department (for example, Staff Records and Social Amenities), other relationships are also the concern of the Heads of the various departments. For instance, the Personnel Manager may engage junior and general employees like Messengers, Cleaners and Watchmen without reference to other Heads, but where professional and technical staff like Accountants, Draughtsman, Welders and other skilled people is concerned, he must engage them in consultation with the appropriate Heads.

Also, it must be remembered that the Heads of Departments like Offices, Finance, Factory, and so on are in closer contact with their staff than the Personnel Manager and they know more about their conduct, workmanship and other matters. Thus, when the problems of Training, Promotion, Retirement and Dismissal arise, the Head of the relevant department is the first to know the situation and to advise or consult the Personnel Manager. More important still is the matter of the feeling or atmosphere in a department, say in the factory, or assembly room, where manual workers sometimes start with a grievance, real or imaginary. It is the Head of the Department, together with his Assistants, Foremen and Supervisor, who are in continual contact with the staff, who can do most to create a happy environment or "work climate" and keep the staff contented and motivated. The existence of a Personnel Department, therefore, does not relieve the Departmental Managers and their assistants from the responsibility of maintaining a satisfactory situation in their own spheres.

The Personnel Manager's job is not a happy one, in spite of rules, regulations, established policies and agreed methods, consultation and negotiations, it still happens that workers suddenly "*down tools*" and stage a "*walk-out*". The Personnel Manager is frequently reminded that he is not dealing with inanimate materials, wood and iron and machines, but with human beings with human weaknesses, frustrations, jealousies, boredom, grievances, personal and individual incompatibilities and, above all, the politics of right and left.

To keep a staff contented and motivated, to maintain reasonable production without interruption, demands the wisdom of a *Suliman* and the patience on the Job. The Personnel Manager is pulled in two opposite directions; the Board and Shareholders on one side and the workers and Shop Stewards on the other. If he is too firm with the staff, he risks "*industrial action*" leading to loss of production and loss of profits: if he is too weak and gives way to the staff, he again risks loss of profits.

A new headache for the Personnel Manager is women. Today, in Nigeria, Britain and most of Europe, equality of the sexes in pay and position has the force of law. He can expect that the proportion of female to male staff will continue to grow. How should he act when confronted by tearful women, complaining about each other, complaining about their work, complaining about the men with whom they work side by side? No doubt, in such cases, the shop Stewards will leave the Personnel Manager to find his own solutions, or suffer.

Then there is the matter of race, color and religion balances. With the best will in the world for racial harmony, dispute between colleagues do arise and if the mention of race is raised in the midst of other abuse, who must be called upon to be judge and to pass sentence? None, but the poor Personnel Manager! The work is demanding, but rewarding for those with the right qualities, temperament and training.

10.9   THE OFFICE MANAGER

In small businesses, the owner may be able to manage several or all departments and the time he devotes to office work may be small compared with the time he spends in the workshop or salesroom or on buying raw materials. In fact, it may be only in odd hours or after working hours that he is able to sit down, file his correspondence, answer letters, pay bills, check his income and make entries in his account book. To the small businessman, the office is the *Cinderella* of his world, a necessary evil to be endured but not to be pampered but encouraged.

In a large business, however, the very opposite prevails; the office is a very important department and may even be divided into several sections such as Correspondence, Finance, Accounts, Wages, Buying and Selling, Records and Statistics, and so on. The Manager of such an office, to be able to train, check, supervise and control his varied staff efficiently, and ensure prompt, and proper attention to the business of the office, must have a wealth of managerial qualifications, as you will now see

10.9.1 Composure

He must be composed. He must himself be a capable correspondent, able to write and to train staff to write letters which are brief and to the point, polite but decisive, calculate to achieve their objectives, to reduce expenses and increase incomes and in general to enhance the reputation of his company for business-like efficiency and promptness in attention to orders, complaints, and the variety of letters which come its way. His English, or other Language of his country, must be correct in spelling, grammar and composition. It often happens that the only contact he will have with a valued customer is by correspondence and the customer will judge his Company by the kind of letters he receives from it. A recent survey of office Executives (Managers and senior assistants) showed weaknesses in the spelling of such commonly used words as *Separate, Maintenance, Briefly,* etc. the Office Manager therefore has the responsibility of maintaining the Company's good "image" through his letters,

10.9.2 Fair Knowledge of Business and much of staff

The Office Manager, although not directly concerned with the production and sales sides of the business, needs to know only a little about his company's products; what they are, how they are made, where and how they are sold, and so on. He must, on the other hand, know much about the work of the staff of his office, so that he can train them, check their work and generally control the quality and quantity of their output. This means that he must understand the typewriter and the typists and perhaps have an idea of speed and accuracy of computer operation.

He must know quite a lot about Finance and especially Banking, Checks, Receipts, Invoices, etc. He must have a good knowledge of Accounting and have the ability to check entries in the accounts books and check Bank Statements. He must know something of elementary Mathematics and Statistics to be able to prepare and analysis the records of the company's daily and seasonal activities, records of income and expenditure, records of advertising results and costs, Stock records, customer's records, and so on.

10.9.3 Knowledge of Office Equipment

The efficient Manager of an office will keep acquainted with all kinds of office equipment and machinery and ensure that any new invention is brought to his notice, especially if it is claimed to increase the speed and efficiency of office work and to reduce its labor requirement. The commonest and most important equipment will include electric typewriters, Dictaphones, stationary and rotating filling systems, postal franking machines, an internal communicating system, calculators, accounting machines, a letter opening machine, perhaps a shredder, a duplicating machine, a photo-copying machine and many others.

10.9.4 Organizing Ability

The Office Manager must be a capable organizer to ensure that his office is not dependent on the presence of one or more individuals in key positions. He must see that several persons are able and trained to do the work of others, so that in cases of illness or holidays, there will always be people available for every kind of duty. In this respect, he must not forget himself and from time to time, he must delegate a variety of his own duties to members of his staff whom he finds most promising.

Of course, to be successful in his duties and responsibilities, he must be cooperative with the heads of other departments, who may often have to call upon him for correspondence, records and statistics which affect their own work. His filling system must permit the finding of such requirements without delay. It would be a poor Office Manager indeed who had to tell the Sales Manager, for example, that he would have to wait a day or two before he could give him an analysis of the sales of the previous year.

10.9 THE OFFICE MANAGER AND ORGANIZATIONAL CHANGE

The foregoing are the special qualities necessary for success as an Office Manager and they are additional to the general qualities of any kind of Manager, which were described in Chapter One of this book. Office Manager must be adaptable and prepared to change his organization and working system, like filling for example, in accordance with the availability of more advanced equipment and machinery and especially with the growth or expansion of the business.

As far as possible, all kinds of office work are best carried out by the Office Manager controlling a set of rooms adjoining each other and communicating in such a way that people who have frequent contact (like Correspondent and Typist) do not have to waste time and effort in walking far to meet. An office Organized in these lines is ideal, but cannot always be achieved. It is a centralized office and is only practicable when it is situated in close proximity to the other departments of the business, like the factory, storerooms, and designers' rooms, and so on. Big businesses, like Motor Car manufacturers, for example, have buildings and grounds which are spread over a wide area. There is the Draughtsmanship building, the Tool-makers workshop, the Assembly shops, the Paint shop, the Testing yard, and so on.

All of these need somebody to maintain records and or the *"paper work"* as it is called. They cannot all descend on this one centralized office to obtain a permit to draw a pot of paint, or a tool from the parts stores, or to notify the office of material used, and so on. The necessity arises, therefore, for the office work to be split into sections and to be situated in various parts of the business area; this splitting into sections is called decentralization.

Of course, even in a decentralized office organization, there must be a Main Office, where the records entered and kept by the subsidiary small offices, are unified, controlled and analyzed. The overall office Manager will have his own room in the Main Office and will have appointed Assistant managers or Supervisors to control the subsidiary offices on his behalf. This is one aspect of the delegation of responsibility which we discussed earlier in this book.

The subsidiary offices will not be a copy of the Main Office on a small scale, they will not require sections like Finance, Accounts, Statistics, etc. They will be somewhat different from each other in kind of work and will merely carry out the paper work required by the department or workshop to which they are attached. The Draughtsmanship rooms may include a small office to keep records of current and present designs of cars and parts, have a Copying Machine and perhaps be staffed by a Clerk and Typist. The parts Storerooms may also need a Clerk and a Typist to keep records of articles in store and of items received and handed out daily.

It often occurs, when decentralization is necessary, that sections like Finance, Accounts, Sales, etc, are completely separated from the Main Office. In such cases, the separated sections are put in the charge of a head like the Financial Controller, the Chief Accountant, the Sales Managers, and so on. Not all these heads of sections will be responsible to the Office Manager. Some, like the Financial Controller, the Chief Accountant and the Sales Manager may be directly responsible to the general Manager or Managing Director of the Company, or even to the Company secretary.

Different businesses are organized on different lines and it does not follow that two businesses, making or dealing in the same kinds of goods, will have the same kind of organization, the same structure or even administration. The Main Office, in charge of the Office Manager who may be directly responsible to the General Manager or Secretary, will usually still hold the records of the results and the analyzes of the various sections and sub-offices. The Main Office will still, as a rule, be equipped with the furniture and machines to carry out the bulk of the work and will be staffed comprehensively. It is however useful here to have a brief description of the most important equipment and machines available to a modern office carrying out a large volume of work to know that they exist and to realize how far the modern office has developed from the old fashioned rooms where the only visible equipment comprised Manual Typewriters, Cabinets, Shelves and a Telephone.

The first of these equipments is the T*ypewriters.* The electronic Typewriter is in common use today. Its advantages are that the typist needs to exert little pressure on the keys and can work faster and the pressure is sure to be even and avoids variation in depth of blackness of the typed words. Improvements in this typewriter include one in which the kind of type can be varied so that bold types and italic types can be introduced in between the other types in a letter. Another development is the machine which automatically arranges the lines to be equal in length, so that the right hand margins are even, just as you see in   printed material, like a newspaper.

Next is the *Dictating Machine.* With this machine, the correspondent, clerk or whoever else would formerly dictate directly to a shorthand-typist, can now speak into a microphone and his message is recorded on a tape. The typist can then in her own room type the message by listening to it being played back through her ear-phone. The dictator and typist may never see or meet each other. The dictator can start, stop, play back and erase at any moment during his dictating to the machines. The typist cal also start, stop and play back at will when listening and typing. However, she must be able to spell correctly the words she hears.

There is also what is called *Calculating Machine*. There is now wide use a great variety of these machines from the Electric pocket C Calculator to the Office Computer. The most common machines to-day are the electrically operated Desk Adding machine, and the Desk Calculator which performs all four Arithmetical processes addition, subtraction, multiplication and division. It is rare to-day to see clerks poring over a list of figures to be added up. On the other hand, the dependence of clerks on calculating machines renders them liable to forgetting the basic multiplication tables, much to their disadvantage when buying and selling in shops and markets. One can see cashier in large shops adding five tens, on a cash Register, instead of simply registering the number 50.

Again, there are the *Franking Machines*. Machines for affixing approved impressions instead of Postage Stamps on envelopes have been in use for many years. The most modern improvements include a machine which can stamp and stack envelopes faster than the eye can follow them; it is, of course, electrically operated. This is followed by the *Letter Opening Machines*. The simplest of these machines is the one which merely cuts a shred off one side of the envelope. The speed attained depends on the speed with which the operator can feed and take back the envelopes, one at a time, from the guarded cutter. The cutter revolves inside a casing and operates electrically.

Again, most offices today have *Duplicating Machines and Copiers*. Manual Duplicators of various kinds have been in use for many years. Today, electrically operated *Duplicating Machines* are quite common and have reached an advanced stage having overcome many of the disadvantages of their forerunners. Photocopying machines, used instead of Duplicators when only a few copies of a document or drawing are required, use several different methods, such as the ordinary Photographic, the Heat Transfer and the Electrostatic processes.

Next, we have the *Accounting Machines.* There are now of great variety and can carry out some quite complex functions, such as invoicing, Cash Book work, Accounts entering, Pay-roll preparing, Expenditure analyzing Statistical work, Stock controlling, etc. These machines are electrically operated and look like advanced typewriters with a keyboard for figures as well as letters. Finally, there are the *Filing Systems.* There are now very many systems available to suit all kinds of businesses. *Flat Card* systems are popular for records or note which does not include actual correspondence; the card can be kept vertically in a small cabinet, or festered together horizontally so that the edges of the entire Card are visible and accessible.

Where correspondence is included, the most popular system is to keep the correspondence filed alphabetically in *Arch Lever Files.* These files can be kept standing vertically in a cabinet (if not required continuously) or kept on a circular rotating stand close to the clerk who requires them for constant use.

10.10 STORES MANAGEMENT

The stores and stocks of business, large or small, comprise so great a proportion of the capital of the business that very often the success or failure of the business depends on the efficiency of the stores Manager. The chief kinds of articles which a business holds in store are: *Raw Materials* (like the wood of different kinds and sizes of a furniture factor and the cloth, bindings and other materials required), *Tools and Machines* (like the farmers, chisels, saws and the cutting and sewing machines of the furniture factory), and *Finished Goods* (like the beds cabinets, tables and chairs made by the furniture factory).

It is the responsibility of the Stores Manager to ensure the following:

(a)   That the *Raw Materials* in stock must always be available and sufficient to carry out the orders for finished goods,

(b)   That the *Tools and Machines* must always be available and in good condition for the workers' use, and

(c)   That the *Finished Goods* must correspond to the quantity of raw materials supplied to the workers who made the goods.

To carry out these responsibilities, the Stores Manager must have an organization and a system which he can control and which include the following:

(a)   *The Stock-rooms* for the three different kinds of articles must be located in positions which are most convenient for the staff who need access to them; for example, *Raw Materials* should be kept near to the workers and *Machinery* should be in the factory itself. *Finished Goods* should be near the last of work and close to the front which they can be dispatched to customers,

(b)   Conditions in the Stock-rooms should be such that the stored articles are free from the hazards of fire, damage, theft, etc, and can be conveniently handled and recorded, and

(c)   The records of stock should be maintained correctly and constantly so that they may show the quantity of each article remaining in the store at any moment, show for each article a low level figure at which more stock must be ordered, and show when any article becomes obsolete or otherwise useless and should be removed or replaced and also indicate when the quantity of an article in stock is more than required and ties up too much of the capital of the business.

The Stores Manager can never relax for a moment in his control of the stores. At any moment, the company can decide to make a *"spot check"* of one or more of his stock and send auditors or other experts to count the articles in stock and see whether the quantities agree with those shown in the stock records, without warning the Stores Manager in advance. A spot check should not be confused with *Annual Stocktaking,* whereby at the end of the company's financial year, a physical counting of stock is made. In this case, the Stores Manager knows the date of counting in advance and can prepare for it. It is the counted stock which is recorded in the company's books and in the final accounts to estimate the profit or loss of the company in the financial year.

The value of the items recorded is the cost price and not the selling price. If the counted stock is less in quantity than that shown in the daily stores records, it must be assumed that damage and/or carelessness have occurred and the responsibility for finding an acceptable explanation rests with the Stores Manager. Laxity on his part can involve the company in losses, but efficiency can ensure that the planned and forecast production and profit are achieved.

REVISION QUESTIONS

1.   Who is a manager and what does he do in his organization? What are his personal qualities that qualify him to be a manager?

2.   Write short, but self-explanatory, note on the following:
    (a)   Trade union,
    (b)   Shop Steward,
    (c)   Government participation in business,
    (d)   Qualities of successful personnel manager,
    (e)   Office Manager

BIBLIOGRAPHY

Bird B.(1989),"*Enterpreneurial behaviour*", *Scott Foresman & Co ,April,*.

Breck, E. F. L (1965): *The Principles and Practice of Management,* Longmans, Green.

Breck, E. F. L. (1967); Management: *Its Nature and Significanc,* Pitman

Chandler Jr. A. D, (1962). Strategy and Structure, Cambridge, Mass: M.I.I Press, p. 13.

Churchman, C. W. (1968): Challenge to Reason, New York McGraw-Hill.

David Ewing (Ed.) (1964). Long Range Planning for Management. New-York. Harper & Row pp. 3-5.

Clueck, W.F. (1976), Business Policy. Strategy Formation and Management Action 2nd Ed. McGraw-Hill Inc. USA p. 3

Ernest Dale (1965): *Management: Theory and Practice,* McGraw-Hill.

George Bull (ed) (1969): *The Director's Handbook.* McGraw-Hill Publishing Limited, Britain.

Hanika F. de` P. (1965): *A Guide New Thinking in Management for Managers.* An Administration staff College publication, Hutchinson.

Hopper Frederick (1961): *Management survey.* Pitman.

Howsard, R. A. (1988): Decision Analysis, Practice and Promise" *Journal of Management Science,* vol. 34, No 6 pp. 679-695.

Gulick, L. (1937): Notes on the Theory of Organization, in *Papers in the Science of Administration, Institute of Public Administration.*

Nielsen, P.B (1994), Danmarks Statistik & Erhvervsfremme Styrelsen: Nye virksomheder

Olayemi Akinwumi (2005,) <u>Nigerian Culture and Society:</u> ", Women Entrepreneurs in Nigeria". *Africa Update Newsletter Oct 19, 2005*

Omolaja M. A. , Obikoya J. O., Ashiru A. T., Alalade A. B. and Ganiyu,I. A. (2001): *Mangement of Small Scale Enterprises,* _CESAP, Olabisi Onabanjo   University, Ago- Iwoye, Nigeria.

Omolaja, M. A. (1999): "A Comparative Analysis of Public and Private Enterprises in Nigeria", in Justice A Sokefun (ed.): *Management and Legal Policies: Issues in Public and Private Enterprises* (Chapter One), MICAP Publishers, Ijebu-ode, Nigeria.

Omolaja, M. A. (1999): "Trade Unionism: *The Nigerian Perspective* (Chapter Nineteen) in *Organizational Behavior: Socio-Psychological Perspectives"* in   Balogun,S.K and Obasan, K.A (Eds:), CESAP, Olabisi Onabanjo University, Ago-Iwoye, Nigeria, Pages

Omolaja M. A. (2000): "Nigerian Business Environment", in Obikoya,J.O,and Asiru A.T (Eds.) *Introduction to Business, (*Chapter Two), CESAP, Olabisi Onabanjo University, Ago-Iwoye, Nigeria, Pages

Omolaja, M. A.(2000): "Problems and Future of Nigerian Business Enterprises"   in Obikoya,J.O, and Asiru A.T. (Eds.) *Introduction to Business,* (Chapter   Thirteen), CESAP, Olabisi Onabanjo University, Ago-Iwoye, Nigeria.

Omolaja, M. A. (2000): "Management Practice in Today's Environment" in Obikoya, J. O and Adebanjo T. A. (Eds.), *Elements of Management,*(Chapter Two), CESAP, Olabisi Onabanjo University, Ago-Iwoye, Nigeria, Pages.

Omolaja, M. A. (2000): "Motivation: Theories and Practice" in Obikoya, J.O, and Adebanjo T.A. (Eds.) *Element of Management*

(Chapter Seven), CESAP, Olabisi Onabanjo University Ago-Iwoye Nigeria.

Omolaja M. A. (2001): "Human Resources Training and Development" in Obikoya,J.O, Edun Taiwo, Aluko Olusola and Omolaja Muhammed A.(Eds:), *Human Resources Management and Industrial Relations*, CESAP, Olabisi Onabanjo University, Ago-Iwoye, Nigeria.

Omolaja M. A. (2001): "Human Resources Management and Industrial Relations Functions in Modern Organizations" in Obikoya,J.O, Edun Taiwo, Aluko Olusola and Omolaja Muhammed A.(Eds:) *Human Resources Management and Industrial Relations*, CESAP, Olabisi Onabanjo University, Ago-Iwoye, Nigeria, Pages.

Omolaja, M. A and Olusola Aluko (2001): "Managing Interpersonal Relationship in Organizations: An Introduction to Human Resources Management and Industrial Relations ", in Obikoya,J.O, Edun Taiwo, Aluko Olusola and Omolaja Muhammed A (Eds:), *Human Resources Management and Industrial Relations*, CESAP, Olabisi Onabanjo University, Ago-Iwoye, Nigeria.

Omolaja, M. A, Obikoya J.O, Edun Taiwo, and Aluko Olusola. (Eds.) (2001): Human Resources Management and Industrial Relations in Nigeria, CESAP, Olabisi Onabanjo University, Ago-Iwoye, Nigeria.

Ade Oyedijo (1995): *Principles of Management,* Paramount Books Limited, Ibadan.

Ross, J.E. (1976):*Modern Management and Information System,* Reston publishing, Reston.

Wikinson E. and Poster R.S. (1963): *Management Principles and Practice,* First Edition, Dommigton Press, Great Britain.

Miner, John B. (1974). *The Human Constraint: The Coming Shortage of Managerial Talent.* Rock Vile M. D.: The Bureau of National Affairs Inc.

Munford, K. A. (1974). "Management Development With or Without the Boss". *Personnel Journal.* Vol. 52, No. 2 Feb. 1976.

Stonner, J. A and Freeman R.E. (1995): *Managements.* New

Koontz, H. O`Donnel, C. & Weihrich, H. (1980). *Management* 7th ed. McGraw-Hill.

Payne, B. (1963). Planning for Company Growth. New-York McGraw-Hill Book Co. p. 7.

Radovic Markovic M.(1994) ,Entrepreneurship"   ,Faculty of Management ,BK, Belgrade, ,p.p.189 ,

Radovic Markovic M.(1995),"Guide for Successful

Business",, UMS, Belgrade, pp. 212

Radovic Markovic M.(1998), The Design of Successful

entrepreneur's Personality", UMS, 1998. ,Belgrade ,p.p.135

Radovic Markovic M.(2005),"Women and Small

Business – from   an Idea to its Realization", "Poslovni Biro", Belgrade pp,164.

Radovic Markovic M. (2006),"Entrepreneurship –

Theoretical and Practical Guide on all aspects for starting Successful Small Business",.Link group ,Belgrade, pp 306

Radovic Markovic M.(2006),"Self-employment–home

Business",Space, Belgrade,205pp.186.

Ralph C. Davies (1951), The Fundamentals of Top Management, New-York. Harper & Brothers p. 179.

.Ray, Malcolm (2005,. *Business in Africa Online* "Africa's courageous women entrepreneurs" Oct. 19,

Scott, B. (1965). *Planning for Company Growth.* New-York. American Management Association, p. 21.

Steiner, A. Geoge (1969). *Top Management Planning* Macmillan Publishing Co. Inc. 3rd Av. N. 1, p. 6.

Turn Bum and Stelker G. M. (1961): *Production Planning and inventory Control.* McGraw-Hill New York.

Thierauf, R. J. Klekamp. R. C, Geeding D. W, (1977). *Management Principles and Practices.* John Wiley & Sons New-York.

Willis E. Forsyth, "Strategic Planning in the '70's" *Financial Executive.* October 1973, p. 97.

Donnelly, J. H. (JR), Gibsori, J.L. and Ivancerich, J.M. (1995): Fundamental of Management. Boston, Richard D. Irwin, Inc; p. 220.

Kinard, J. (1988) Management Lexington, D. C. Health and company, p. 292.

Knight, K. (ed) (1977) Matrix Management: A Cross-Functional Approach to Organization: Gower. Pp. 114-115.

Mullins, L.J. (1999). Management and Organizational Behavior, London, Financial times Pitman Publishing, K93.

Oyedijo, A. (1995). Principles of Management. "Ibadan, Paramount Books Limited, p. 8.

Robbins, S.P. (1996) Organizational Behavior: Concepts, Controversies, New Jersy, Prentice-Hall, Seventh Edition p. 5.

Rue, L. W. and Byars, L.L. (1992) Management: Skills and Application Boston, Richard D. Irwin, Inc, p. 248.

Schein, E. H. (1988) Organization Psychology, New Jersey: Prentice-Hall, Third Edition p. 292.

Bass, T. (1959). The effect of the situation factors and leadership style on leader Behaviors. *Organizational Behavior and Human Performance,* 29, 368-377.

French, J. R. and Raven, B. (1960). "The Bases of Social Powe" in *Group Dynamics,* Cartwright and A. F. Zander, (Evanston, 111: Row, Peterson, pp. 607-623).

Fiedler, F. E. (1951). A method of objective qualification of certain counter transference attitude. *Journal of clinical psychology,* 7.101/-107.

Greene, C. W. (1975). The reciprocal nature of influence between leader and subordinate journal of Applied Psychology, 60/187-193. House, R. J. (1977), Path-goal theory of leadership, journal of contemporary Business, 3/81-98;

Katzand Kahn (1978). *Social psychology of Organization:* (Wile). Korman, A. K. (1966). *Consideration, Initiating Structure and Organization Criteria-A Review",* Personnel/Psychology. Winter, pp. 349-361.

Kootz and O'Donnel (1959). Management: International Students Edition (McGraw-Hill Book Co. Singapore).

McGrawgor (1960). The Human Side of Enterprise New York, McGraw-Hill,

Stodgily, R, M. (1948). Personnel Factors Associated with leadership: A Survey of Literature; *Journal of Applied Psychology,* pp. 35-71.

Szllagy, A.D. and Enlancce, M. J., (1981). *Organizational Behavior and Performance* 2nd ed. Scotf Foreman & Co Glenview, Illinois.

Tannenbaum & Schmidt (1958). How to choose a leader pattern. *Harvard Business Review.*

Bennet, R. 91981): *Managing Personnel and Performance* (London: Business Books).

Cofer, C. N. *et. al.*(1964): *Motivation: Theory and Research* (New-York: John Wiley & Sons) page 684-691.

Cole, G. A. (1986): *Management Theory and Practice.* English Language Books Society/DP publications, pages 48-64.

Chung, K. H. (1977): *Motivational Theories and Practices.* (Columbus: Grid publishing Company)

Dale Yoder (1963): *Personnel Management and Industrial Relations* (Pitman, 5th ed.).

Davis, K. (1977): *Human Behavior at Work* (New Delhi Tata: McGraw-Hill Inc).

Douglas McGregor (1960): The Human Side of Enterprise (McGraw-Hill Inc).

French, W. L. (1978): *The Personnel Management Process* (Boston: Haughton Mifflin Co.)

Herzberg, F, *el. al* (1959): *Motivation to Work* (New York: John Wiley). Hicks, H. G. *et. al.,* (1975): *Organizations: Theory and Behavior.* (Tokyo McGraw-Hill Kogakusha) pages 290-293.

Hunneyager and Heckman (1962): Hum,an Relations in Management (Edward Arnold, 2nd ed).

Iven's M. and Broadway, F. (ed) (1966): *Case Studies in Human Relations: Productivity and Organization* (Business Publications). John Marsh (1957): *People at work Essays and Commentaries* (The Industrial Society).

Kinard, J. (1988): *Management* (Lexington D. C. Hesalth and Co.), page 269.

Lester, R. A. (1966): *Manpower Planning in a Free Society* (Princeton University Press).

Maslow, A. H. (1943): Theory of Human Motivation, *Psychological Review.* Vol. 50, pages 370-396,

Michael, S. R. *et. al.* (1973):*Organizational Management: Concept and Practice* (New York: Intext Educational Publishes).

Obikoya, J. O. (1996): *Essentials of Personnel Management.* Pious Debo Press, Ijebu-Ode, Nigeria

Oyedijo, Ade (1995): *Principles of Management*. Paramount Books Limited, Ibadan, pages 207-234.

Pigors and Myers (1965): Personnel Administration: *A Point of View and a Method* (McGraw-Hill, 5th ed.)

Sanzotta, D. (1977): *Motivational Theories and Applications for Managers* (New York: AMACOM)

Scott, Clothier and Prigel (1961): *Personnel Management* (McGraw-Hill, 6th ed.).

Weithrich H. and Koontz H. (1993): *Management: A Global Perspective*. 10th ed. McGraw-Hill International editions.

F. E. X. Dance (1970): "The 'Concept' of Communication". *Journal of Communication* 20, No, 2, pp. 201-210.

Andrew J. Dubria (1997): *Essentials of Management*. International Thomson publishes, p. 290.

Michael Argyle (1990): *Body Communications* 2e (Madison, CT; International Universities Press, 1990).

Alan Zaremba (1989): "Working with the organization Oral Grapevine", personnel (March 1989), pp. 34.

John. B. Bush and Alan. L. Frohman (1991), "Communication in a Network"' Organizational Dynamics (Autumn 1991) pp. 23-26.

Adeyemo A. & Deji Popoola (1981): "Workers" Participation in Management in Nigeria. Personnel Management Journal July-Sept. (PERMAN).

Argyris, Chris (1957): Personality and Organization, (New York: Harper and Brothers) p. 187-991.

Brantely K. Watson, (1974): "The Maturing of Multiple Management", Management Review, p. 7.

Cavey, H. H. (1937): Consultative Supervision" Nations Business p. 44 Clark R. O. et al (1972): "Workers Participation in Management in Britain, London, Heinemann Educational Books.

David B. Ekpenyong (1992): "Worker Participation in Decision Making: A Means Towards Radical Economic Development in Nigeria Journal, July/Sept.

Fred G. Lesieur (1958) ed., *The Scanlon Plan,* Net York: John Wiley & Sons.

McCormick Charles (1938): Multiple Management (New York: Harper and Brothers).

Obikoya J. O. (1996): Essential of Personnel Management Ijebu-Ode, Pius Debo (Nig) Press.

Paine, Thomas H. (1974): "Flexible Compensation Can Work/"Financial and Executive, February pp. 56-66.

Raymond E. Miles, (1971): "Participative Management: Quality vs Quality", California Management Review Summer pp. 48-5,

Reed, M. powell and john L. "Participative Management: A Panacea?" Schalcter (1971): Academy of Management Journal p. 165-73.

Robert K. Goodman, J. H. "What Employees think of the Scanlon Wakeley, and R. H. Ruh, (1972) Plan", Personnel, September-October, p. 28.

Robert A. Ruh J. Keneth White and Robert R. Wood, (1975): "Job Involvement, Values, Personal Background, Participation in Decision Making and Job Attitudes: Academy of Management Journal p: 300-312.

Schregle J. (1976): "Workers Participation-in Decisions within Undertakings "International Labour Review, Geneva ILO, jan-Feb.

Strauss, G. & Rosenstein, E. (1970): "Workers" Participation: A Critical Review" Industrial Relation Journal, February 9.

Tannebaum A. S *et al* (1974): *Hierarchy in Organizations: An International Comparison,* San Francisco, Jossey-Bias Publishing Company.

Thierauf, R. J. R. C. Klekemp and D. W. Geeding (1977): *Management Principle and Practice* (New York: John Wiley & Sons).

Vaughn Blankenship and Raymond E. Miles, 91968): "Organizational Structure and Managerial Decision Behavior" Administrative Science Quarterly, June, pp. 106-20.

Vroom, V. H. (1964): *Work and Motivation* (New York: John Wiley & Sons). R 226.

Vroom V. H. (1960); *Some Personality Determinants of the Effects of Participation* (Englenwood Cliff, N. J. Prentice-Hall).

Walker K. (1990): "Industrial Democracy" The Times Management

Bursk, E. and Chapman, J. (1965): *New Decision-Making Tools for Managers* (New York, mentor Books).

Carison, Dick (1982): *Modern Management: Principles and Practice* (London Macmillan Press).

Druker, P. F. (1977): *Management: Tasks, Responsibilities, Practices* (London: Pan Books), pp. 400-411.

Grass, M. (ed.) (1974): *Control of Working Capital,* (London) Grower Press).

Heinz Weihrich and Harold Koontz (1993): *Management: A Global Perspective.* McGraw-Hill, Hightstown) pp. 578-595.

Kenneth, C. L and Jane P. L. (1991): *Management Information Systems,* (New York: Macmillan Publishing Co).

Kinard, J. (1988): *Management* (Lexington: D. C. Health and Company), p. 97.

Omolaja, M. A. (1999): *Information Systems in Organizations: Apparitional Approach* (Campus Publications, Abeokuta), pp. 79-100.

Oyedijo Ade (1995): *Principles of Management* (Paramonut Books ltd., Ibadan), pp. 180-203.

Peter, Lorange *et al* (1986): *Strategic Control* (St. Paul, Minn: West Publishing Co.), p. xvii.

Reinhart, L. H. *et al* (1981): *The Practice of Planning* (New York: Van Nostrand einhold), p. 5.

Robber, N. *et al.* (1984): Management Control Systems, 5m ed. (Homewood, 111: Richard D. Irwin).

Rue, L. W. and R. W. Fulmer (1973): *The Practice and Profitability of Long Range Planning* (Oxford, Ohio: The Planning Executive Institute).

Wilsons, R.M.S. (1979): *Management Control and Marketing Planning* (London: Heineman educational publishers), p. 101.

Barthol M. Kathryn and David C. Marlin (1994), *Management* 2nd ed. (New York: McGraw-Hill Inc).

Cole G. A (1995), *Management: Theory and Practice* (London: DP publications ltd). Pp. 397.

Marion Harper, Jr. (1961), "A New Profession to Aid Management", *Journal of Marketing,* p. 1. in Kotler P. and G. Armstrong 91987), *Marketing; An Introduction* (USA: Prentice-Hill, Inc). p. 88.

Weihrich Heniz and Harold Koontz (1994), *Management: A Global Perspective* (USA, McGraw-Hill, Inc).

VDM publishing house ltd.

Scientific Publishing House

offers

free of charge publication

of current academic research papers, Bachelor´s Theses, Master's Theses, Dissertations or Scientific Monographs

If you have written a thesis which satisfies high content as well as formal demands, and you are interested in a remunerated publication of your work, please send an e-mail with some initial information about yourself and your work to *info@vdm-publishing-house.com.*

Our editorial office will get in touch with you shortly.

VDM Publishing House Ltd.
Meldrum Court 17.
Beau Bassin
Mauritius
www.vdm-publishing-house.com

Made in the USA
Las Vegas, NV
24 September 2021